For Larry, Debby and Fern
Lots of love & Kisses
Aunt Faun.

Ask Mom & Dad for Vol II

SELECTED WRITINGS OF
ARTHUR T. VANDERBILT

VOLUME I

A DOCKET CLASSIC

SELECTED WRITINGS OF
ARTHUR T. VANDERBILT

Speeches, Lectures, and Other Writings of the late Arthur T. Vanderbilt, Chief Justice of the Supreme Court of New Jersey, with an Essay on Vanderbilt by the late Charles E. Clark, Chief Judge of the United States Court of Appeals, Second Circuit

Selected, Edited and Introduced
with Biographical Data

By

FANNIE J. KLEIN AND JOEL S. LEE

OCEANA PUBLICATIONS, INC.
DOBBS FERRY, NEW YORK
1965

PRINTED IN U.S.A. ALPERT PRESS, INC.

ACKNOWLEDGMENTS

Gratitude is expressed to RUSSELL D. NILES, Chancellor of New York University, and to MIGUEL DE CAPRILES, Dean of New York University School of Law, for their encouragement and support.

A bibliography of Vanderbilt's writings compiled in 1957 by the HONORABLE PHILBRICK McCOY, Judge of the Superior Court, Los Angeles County, and long a worker with CHIEF JUSTICE VANDERBILT in the struggle for judicial administration improvement, was of great service.

Acknowledgment, with thanks, is made to the following for permission to reprint in this volume the materials which have previously appeared in their publications:

American Bar Association
American Bar Foundation
Washington and Lee University
New York University School of Law
New York University Law Review
New York University Press
Yale Law Journal
Alfred A. Knopf, Publisher
University of Nebraska Press
New York Times

——— o ———

Estate of Arthur T. Vanderbilt

TABLE OF CONTENTS

	PAGE
Acknowledgments	v
Preface	ix
Citation Bestowed by the Fellows of the American Bar Foundation	xi
American Judicature Society—Golden Anniversary Award	xii
Chronology of Arthur T. Vanderbilt	xiii
Arthur T. Vanderbilt by the Honorable Charles E. Clark	xvii

THE LEGAL PROFESSION

PROFESSIONAL RESPONSIBILITY	3
The Five Functions of the Lawyer: Service to Clients and the Public	4
ADVOCACY	7
The Six Factors in the Work of the Advocate	7
Opening a Case, Summation	14
Arguing an Appeal	25
Notes	50

MODERNIZATION OF THE LAW

ADMINISTRATIVE LAW	53
Legislative Background of the Federal Administrative Procedure Act	54
PROCEDURE	66
The Importance of Procedure in the Work of the Practicing Lawyer and in the Study of Law	67
The Place of the Federal Rules of Civil and Criminal Procedure in the Movement for Judicial Reform	80

TABLE OF CONTENTS

PAGE

The Major Problems of Procedure.................................... 93

CRIMINAL LAW AND PROCEDURE................................. 96

The New Federal Criminal Rules 98

Foreword, *Organized Crime and Law Enforcement*............ 102

An Experiment in the Trial of Indigent Criminal Cases.... 111

SUBSTANTIVE LAW 114

The Growth of Substantive Law 115

Fox v. *Snow* 138

CONSTITUTIONAL LAW 152

Judicial Deference as a Grave Cause of Constitutional
Imbalance 153

Tudor v. *Board of Education* 158

COMPARATIVE LAW 178

Reconciliation of the Civil Law and the Common Law...... 179

Notes 189

CITIZENSHIP, POLITICS, AND PUBLIC SERVICE

Better Minds for Better Politics 204

CLASSIFIED BIBLIOGRAPHY 213

MEMORIALS AND OTHER BIOGRAPHICAL
MATERIALS 224

HONORARY DEGREES AND AWARDS 226

INDEX 227

PREFACE

To the everlasting honor of those who were acquainted with his life's work, Arthur T. Vanderbilt, even during his lifetime, was adjudged by them to be a great legal personality. At a memorial convocation at Vanderbilt Hall, New York University, in October, 1957, former American Bar Association President Charles S. Rhyne said:

> "Occasionally there lives a man who walks as other men walk, who talks as other men talk but who is endowed with such an indomitable spirit, such a dynamic heart and such a tremendous capacity for leadership and creative productivity that he is not as other men. To know Chief Justice Vanderbilt was to see this combination in a perfect blend. His supreme monument will always be built by the stories of his own accomplishment."

As a lawyer, scholar, educator, leader of the bar, statesman, and judge, he was in the forefront of a continuous struggle to shape the law and the legal system to meet the urgent requirements of a complex industrial society.

A representative selection from his voluminous writings is presented in two volumes. A full bibliography is offered in Volume One to those who would read more. All of the materials are of interest to students of law, of government, of public administration and of the social sciences, in and out of school. The items in Volume One were selected, if such a distinction can be made, for the attention of law students and students of advocacy.

Although the original edition of both volumes is clothbound, a paperback edition of Volume One is issued to make it more readily available to law students.

The late Chief Judge Clark's essay, included in Volume One because it describes procedural advances, is focused on Vanderbilt's role in the development of the science of judicial administration. Many of Vanderbilt's writings on judicial administration appear in Volume Two, which will be of particular interest to prelegal and legal educators, lawyers and judges.

An introduction to each topic includes biographical information and background material. A chronology of Vanderbilt's life is contained in Volume One.

Legal opinions are not usually regarded as Selected Writings. However, a few have been chosen for reprinting as illustrative of Vanderbilt's judicial thought. A list of cases, classified by subject, in which he wrote opinions appears in Volume Two.

As much as any man of his time, Vanderbilt exemplified the Athenian ideal of the citizen dedicated to the welfare of his society. If any reader of these volumes receives inspiration from Vanderbilt's written words, our purpose will have been served.

FANNIE J. KLEIN.
JOEL S. LEE.

THE FELLOWS OF THE
AMERICAN BAR FOUNDATION

The Fellows of the American Bar Foundation take pride in presenting this certificate to ARTHUR T. VANDERBILT in recognition of his noteworthy research in law and government. Trial Lawyer, Corporation Lawyer, Counsellor, Scholar, Educator, Bar Organization Leader, Author, Statesman, Trial Judge, and Appellate Justice — he stands as the only living American who has achieved conspicuous national success in all branches of the legal profession. As Dean of the Law School of New York University, he discovered that, beyond the teaching of law as it is, there is a creative function in legal education — the building up of a philosophy and jurisprudence and an informed opinion to which lawyers, lawmakers and judges may look for guidance and inspiration. He conceived and brought into being a great Law Center — the first of its kind — for serious research which delves into the past with a large and free outlook making it tributary to the service of the present and future. Realizing that many judicial systems are archaic and that the problems of procedural law are as serious as those of the substantive, he gave up his practice ten years ago to accept appointment as Chief Justice of the Supreme Court of New Jersey in order that he might take the lead in creating for his native state a judicial system which could serve as a model throughout the land. Now approaching seventy and nearing the end of the judicial interlude of his magnificent career, but looking forward to many years of still further fruitful living, he has the universal affection and respect of the legal profession and the people of this country.

Chicago, February 16, 1957.

(s) WILLIAM T. GOSSETT,
Secretary of the Fellows.

(s) E. SMYTHE GAMBRELL,
Chairman of the Fellows.

The American Judicature Society

Presents its

Golden Anniversary Award

honoring the late

Arthur T. Vanderbilt

in recognition of services in promoting

The Efficient Administration of Justice

Leader as president of the American Judicature Society to Promote the Efficient Administration of Justice,

Innovator as founder, president and guiding spirit of the Institute of Judicial Administration,

Pioneer as chief justice of the first modern and efficient state court system in America,

Proponent of Minimum Standards of Judicial Administration as president of the American Bar Association,

Statesman, author, lawyer, teacher, administrator, judge and citizen seeking efficient and effective administration of justice under law in the courts of his nation,

The American Judicature Society to promote the Efficient Administration of Justice

founded July 18, 1913, by

Woodbridge N. Ferris   James Parker Hall

Herbert Harley

Edward W. Hinton, Frederick Bruce Johnstone, Albert M. Kales
Frederick W. Lehmann, Nathan William MacChesney
Roscoe Pound, Harry Olson, John B. Winslow

John H. Wigmore

ARTHUR T. VANDERBILT CHRONOLOGY

July 7, 1888   Born, Newark, New Jersey.

1904   Graduated from Newark High School.
Editor, *The Acropolis*; President, Senior Class; Member Debating Society.

1910   A.B., Wesleyan University (Middletown, Connecticut).
Phi Beta Kappa; Editor, The Argus; Manager, Debating Team; Manager, Football Team; President, College Student Body; Member, Gamma Phi Chapter of Delta Kappa Epsilon. The President of the University said of him, "The most unusual and gifted undergraduate I have known in all my experience."

1912   M.A., Wesleyan University.

1913   LL.B., Columbia University School of Law. Admitted to New Jersey State Bar. Teacher, Newark Central Evening High School.

Sept. 12, 1914   Married to Florence Althen; five children; three daughters, twin sons.

1914—1948   Instructor, New York University School of Law, 1914-1918; Professor, 1918-1943; Dean and Professor of Law, 1943-1948. While Dean, instituted drive for building funds; New York University Law Center completed 1951, named Vanderbilt Hall in his honor. Subjects: contracts, equity, administrative law, insurance, trusts, judicial administration, procedure.

1919—1947   President, Essex County Republican League; Chairman Clean Government. Delegate to Republican National Convention, 1936, 1940, 1944.

1922—1948   Counsel, Essex County, New Jersey.

1926—1927   New Jersey's Counsel for the Port of New York Authority.

1930—1940   Chairman, New Jersey Judicial Council. Largely through his efforts, New Jersey courts were reorganized by constitutional revision in 1947.

1932—1934   Member, General Counsel, American Bar Association.

1933—1934	First Chairman, Section of Insurance, American Bar Association.
1933—1937	Chairman, National Conference of Judicial Councils. His leadership in the improvement of the administration of justice received national recognition in his election to this office for four successive years.
1934—1935	Member, Executive Committee, American Bar Association.
1934—1937	Vice-President and Member of Board of Trustees of New Jersey State Bar Association.
1934—1957	Trustee, Wesleyan University.
1935—1937	Member, Board of Governors, American Bar Association.
1937—1938	President, American Bar Association. During his presidency a vigorous program for improvement in the administration of justice was initiated. With Judge John J. Parker as chairman, the Section of Judicial Administration devoted the year to study in order to suggest reforms and formulate standards in many areas of the administration of justice. The seven committee reports filed in 1938 and Vanderbilt's *Minimum Standards of Judicial Administration,* published in 1949, have served to stimulate the efforts of the states to measure up to the standards suggested by these committees.
1937—1957	Chairman, Executive Committee, National Conference of Judicial Councils.
1938—1939	Chairman, U.S. Attorney General's Commission to Confer with Committee of Senior Circuit Judges Appointed by Chief Justice Hughes to draft bill for Administrative Office of the United States Courts. This office was established by legislation in 1939.
1938—1940	Third President, American Judicature Society, succeeding Charles Evans Hughes and Newton D. Baker.
1938—1956	Chairman, National Committee on Traffic Law Enforcement. Impetus he gave culminated in adoption, in 1951, of *Traffic Law Enforcement and the Sixteen Resolutions of the Chief Justices and the Governors* by the Conference of Chief Justices and approved by the Governors' Conference.
1939—1941	Member, Attorney General's Committee on Administrative Procedure. Administrative Procedure Act was passed in 1946.

1941—1942   Member, New Jersey State Constitutional Revision Commission. New Constitution ratified 1947.

1941—1944   Chairman, Advisory Committee appointed by the United States Supreme Court to draft rules of procedure in criminal cases in the Federal District Courts. Work of this Committee resulted in adoption of Federal Rules of Criminal Procedure, effective in 1944.

1942   Inaugurated Annual Survey of American Law, published by New York University Law School.

1942—1945   Special Assistant to the Attorney General of New Jersey to defend validity of referendum on constitutional revision.

1944   While Dean of New York University School of Law he wrote his *Report on Prelegal Education.* Approved by the American Bar Association, it was adopted by the Association of American Colleges in 1945 with the recommendation that it be sent to every member college president, filed with the registrar and called to the attention of the curriculum committee in each institution.

1945—1957   Member, President's Highway Safety Conference.

1946—1947   Chairman, Board of Trustees, Wesleyan University.

1946—1947   Chairman, War Department's Advisory Committee on Military Justice. The work of this committee resulted in substantial amendments to the Articles of War and laid groundwork for Uniform Military Code in 1950.

1947—1948   Director of American Bar Association's Survey of the Legal Profession.

Nov. 3, 1947   Sworn in as Judge of Circuit Court of New Jersey, prerequisite to his appointment as Chief Justice of the Supreme Court of New Jersey.

1947—1957   Inaugurated Citizenship Clearing House (now National Center for Education in Politics) in 1947; Chairman, 1947-1957.

1947   Established Inter-American Law Institute at New York University School of Law under which a one year program of study on comparative law is offered to well-trained lawyers from Central and South America.

1948—1957   Member, Council of New York University, President of Law Center Foundation. The Chancellor of New York

University said of him, "The greatest thing that ever happened to New York University."

1948—1957	Trustee, Rutgers University.
Sept. 15, 1948	Formally undertook duties of first Chief Justice of the Supreme Court of New Jersey under the constitutional revision of 1947.
Sept. 15, 1951	Dedication of Vanderbilt Hall, New York University School of Law.
1951	Elihu Root-Samuel J. Tilden Scholarships initiated. A result of Vanderbilt's planning, these scholarships are awarded annually to 20 young men who give promise of becoming outstanding lawyers in the American tradition.
1952—1957	Established Institute of Judicial Administration at New York University School of Law. He was its president from 1952 until his death in 1957. The Institute has become nationally and internationally known for its services to the improvement of the administration of justice.
1953—1954	Chairman, Conference of Chief Justices.
1953	Institute of Comparative Law, established, under which a program similar to that of the Inter-American Law Institute is offered to lawyers from other countries.
June 16, 1957	Died, Short Hills, New Jersey.

ARTHUR T. VANDERBILT

By the Honorable CHARLES E. CLARK

Arthur T. Vanderbilt was a many-sided person who enhanced all aspects of the law and found time to be an unusual public citizen as well. So many and so varied were the aspects of life he touched that it is indeed difficult to think of another career at the American Bar equally well rounded. Thus he was a pre-eminent trial lawyer, a commanding political leader, the president of the lawyers' greatest professional organization as well as of other reform societies or groups, a continuous and successful missionary for law reform, a writer and scholar of note, a law professor for many years, a law dean leading his school to new progress of instruction and research, and finally, until his untimely death, the chief justice of the highest court of his state. Throughout all these activities he preserved a lively interest in matters of public concern, notably university education and scholarship, serving as trustee of his alma mater, Wesleyan, and actively engaged in the affairs of New York and Rutgers Universities and the Phi Beta Kappa Society. It is not my present purpose in this brief Foreword to recount or evaluate all these manifold activities; indeed, I fear it would be presumptuous for me to make the attempt. Rather I shall stress that activity which is sure to have a lasting effect upon the courts and which I am confident will always be associated with his name. I refer to his leadership in the field of judicial administration, where he actually first defined the need and the method of action, then wrote the basic provisions in the state constitution and laws, and finally accepted responsibility for execution of the policy as chief justice. Various among us have participated in one or possibly two of such movements; I know of no one else who has been active, and even more, has been leader, in all.

What is the science and the art of judicial administration which so engrossed both his mind and his heart? For this we have his own definition, since he was an articulate person and this was his favorite subject. Probably his most considered statement is in his last series of lectures, those at the University of Cincinnati in 1957, just a few months before his death, on *Improving the Administration of Justice — Two Decades of Development*. The kernel is found in the second lecture, entitled *The Application of Sound Business Principles to Judicial Administration*. Thus he says pointedly:

> "The most surprising paradox in the whole field of judicial administration is the contrast between the high degree of efficiency in the administration of most large business corporations, many of them with lawyers as chief executives, and the almost complete lack of administrative efficiency in most judicial systems. The courts of this country have become notorious for their reluctance to accept and put into effect even the most basic and simple principles of business administration. Up until twenty years ago virtually no effort had been made to introduce sound principles of business management into the area of judicial administration. As Chief Justice Taft so aptly expressed it in a speech before the American Bar Association in 1921, 'each judge paddled his own canoe' under a 'go-as-you-please system.'" [Pp. 49, 50.]

He then defines and explains in some detail what he considers to be the five essentials for the effective and efficient administration of a judicial system: "a simple integrated court structure, a Supreme Court laying down policy by rule, a Chief Justice as the executive head, an Administrative Office to provide staff assistance, and Assignment Judges to translate policy into action at the local level." [P. 80.] This, then, is the system he secured for New Jersey and administered as chief justice for the last eight years and a half of his life.

The analogy of the application of sound business principles to judicial administration undoubtedly appealed to the advocate in Vanderbilt, and it has persuasive force. Yet it is far from exact. A business executive has a singleness of purpose and a power of execution which makes his task in many ways simpler than that of a judicial administrator. As he himself says, "the time-honored concept that a judge must be completely free and independent in his

xviii

judicial determinations" has resulted in the "invalid assumption" that a judge must be independent in matters of administration as well. Nevertheless the independence of the judiciary is an ideal which has to be cherished. It is the cornerstone of our judicial process. However, it is not amount of output, but rather quality which is the test of a good court. The weight of traditional methods, with often a procedure which has come down from the past, also constrains against efficiency. With the pull of diverse objectives, the increased burdens of heavy calendars, the clash of independent personalities, it requires a truly dynamic personality to command the respect and demonstrate the vigor for effective administration of the courts. Unfortunately, this skill does not appear a natural one for a lawyer or a judge, and our methods of choice of judicial administrators, based on legal prominence, political acumen, or even age and seniority, are not those to emphasize administrative capacity. Even with a good basic plan, there is much remaining to be done to achieve the human effectiveness in executing the plan. Here, also, Vanderbilt was unusual; his control of the New Jersey court system during his term was a demonstration of an orderly efficiency which surmounted even the problems of individual personality among the judges.

I have been intrigued to think how Vanderbilt became so interested, both as teacher and judge, in the adjective side of the law; and I have no doubt but that it was his early career as an effective trial lawyer and advocate. There is no question that much of substantive law teaching is away from the hurly-burly of the trial courts. To one who comes to teaching from the courts, the bulk of the traditional curriculum seems bookish and academic. So a practitioner turned scholar longs to bring the courtroom to the schoolroom. Further, he has a sense of futility lest the major problems of actually getting court work done are being bypassed. Hence it is significant that Vanderbilt continually preached the need of procedure courses in the schools; his address to the Association of American Law Schools, in 1943, on *Procedure as the Core of Undergraduate Law Study* is typical. Having urged this view in various addresses particularly aimed at law professors, he prepared his own original *Cases and Materials on Modern Procedure and Judicial Administration* (1952), which opens with a notable essay: *The Importance of Procedure in the Work of the Practising Lawyer and in the Study of Law.* As reflecting his personal and original approach, this volume, unlike any other, combines a study of both civil and criminal procedure; indeed, it is built around the Federal Rules of both Civil Procedure and of Criminal Procedure, the latter particularly owing much to him as chairman of the Supreme Court's Advisory Committee which drafted them. This undoubtedly is the ripe product and the final distillation of his long teaching experience.

Meanwhile he had developed and perfected his ideas of judicial administration which I have spoken of above. When he was president of the American Bar Association in 1938, the Federal Rules of Civil Procedure had just been adopted. As president, he opened the first American Bar Association Institute on the rules held in connection with the Association meeting at Cleveland, Ohio, in July, 1938, and he wrote the Foreword to the published proceedings which have since been accepted by the Supreme Court as authoritative interpretations of the new procedure (*Mississippi Publishing Co.* v. *Murphree,* 326 U.S. 438). At that same meeting, under his inspiration and the chairmanship of Chief Judge John J. Parker—a kindred reforming spirit—the Section of Judicial Administration and the House of Delegates of the American Bar Association approved the notable series of reports prepared by distinguished specialists which state the ideals of judicial administration in all pertinent legal fields. Again Vanderbilt wrote the Foreword for what has since become a bible for the Association and for legal reformers generally. The Association has reprinted the series several times and they form the cornerstone for the later full and complete statement of principles and practice in the states found in the now classic "Minimum Standards of Judicial Administration," edited, of course, by Arthur T. Vanderbilt, and published in 1949. This still remains the measuring rod by which reformers throughout America may test how far or how little their local jurisdiction has progressed in the ways of court reorganization and reform. This, then, is the rich background against which Vanderbilt's constructive work in New Jersey is set.

Success even in New Jersey did not come at once and in full bloom. The first attempt at constitutional revision in the form of a new judiciary article went back to a system as proposed and detailed by Vanderbilt as first chairman of the New Jersey Judicial Council in 1930-32. Then he and a small group worked against political opposition and legislative discouragement to build public support and demand for improvement. Meanwhile, Congress had enacted, in 1939, the law creating the Administrative Office of the United States Courts, with Vanderbilt as a chief supporter of the new legislation in his capacity as chairman of the Attorney General's Committee to Cooperate with the Committee of Senior Circuit Judges. But the first draft of a model state constitution was defeated at the polls in 1944. A constitutional convention revitalized the proposal in 1947 and the new constitution was ratified that year by overwhelming vote, the opposition of notorious politicians then proving a boon after the campaign of enlightenment. Vanderbilt was appointed a circuit judge to be eligible for promotion and then, in late 1948, Chief Justice to be, as the constitution provided, the administrative head of all the courts of the state now united in one court structure.

Under the Chief Justice's leadership, the new Supreme Court moved swiftly to assume its responsibility. Rules of civil, criminal and appellate procedure were quickly drafted, studied and promulgated before the effective date of the new court system. An administrative office was organized and an administrative director appointed, who immediately went to work to collect the necessary statistical information as to the judges' workload and the state of judicial progress. Pretrial procedures were put into effect and traffic law enforcement was improved and made effective. Nine assignment judges were named for key points in the system to keep the court workload properly organized and cared for. A representative judicial conference was organized to maintain continuous study of the court load. Immediately, the new system showed amazing results in meeting the backlog and since then the yearly reports of the Administrative Director show that this level of efficiency has been maintained.

A key device in the system is the required weekly reports from each trial judge. This was indeed an innovation, if not an encroachment, on the supposed prerogatives of notably independent officials.

The judicial reaction is noted by a then colleague, now an Associate Justice of the Supreme Court of the United States. In his memorial address on October 3, 1957, Justice William J. Brennan, Jr. said with respect to the "Vanderbilt Legacy":

> "Never one to indulge notions he was convinced were misguided, he grasped the nettle on his first day as Chief Justice. He announced rules of administration controlling the day-to-day work of the judges which, it is an understatement to say, produced initial consternation in judicial ranks. The rules prescribed fixed court hours and court days throughout the state to be observed by all judges by their actual presence on the bench throughout the hours prescribed. Conduct of judicial business in chambers was expressly forbidden. Judges were required to file weekly a report detailing the matters attended to during the prescribed court hours and noting any matters wherein decision was reserved. The noting of reserved matters was required so that the Chief Justice might keep a watchful eye on the time taken by the judges to dispose of such matters.
>
> "The great contribution of Arthur T. Vanderbilt is that he provided the positive proof that the cause of justice need not suffer from delays, technicalities or the evils of maneuver and surprise." 6 N.Y.U. Law Center Bull. 7 (Fall, 1957)

In many ways, the weekly report was the cornerstone of his system of court control. It was much more than a showing of individual judicial productivity. It enabled the Chief Justice to have continuously at hand an accurate picture of the entire system so that he could spot places of congestion and delay and supply the necessary remedies. This he did quickly and efficiently by the dispatch of judicial personnel to places of need and the temporary relief of judges who needed time to complete their adjudications. I remember an occasion when he was describing to me the practical working of the system and had pointed out that each judge was required to make his explicit and full report weekly, on Monday, to the Administrative Director of the previous week's court activities, that the Director collated the information and made his report on Tuesday and that it lay on the Chief Justice's desk for action at quarter of eight on Wednesday. With an attempt to be facetious, I asked him "Why quarter of eight?" And the answer was surely complete; "Because that's when I need it." So I found that he came in to his Newark office from his suburban home at Short Hills to start work every morning at that hour—surely unusual for most judges. Indeed, when his last illness set in, he was on his way to his office to attend to these tasks.

In this inadequate sketch of a very full life, much perforce has been omitted. But I cannot close without reference to an action by the great Chief Justice looking to the future which may, in the long run, furnish the outstanding star in his crown. I refer to his founding in 1952 of the Institute of Judicial Administration that is a permanent non-profit corporation chartered under the laws of New York of over 600 leading lawyers, judges and laymen charged with the task of a continuing study—originally on a national, and now on an international basis—of the problems of court organization, administration and procedure with the purpose of developing an art as well as a science of judicial administration. So long as he lived, Chief Justice Vanderbilt was its president, and it has already become the outstanding center for correlating all source material and research publications in its unique field. It has already developed a series of advisory and consultative studies where its advice has been sought here and abroad in problems in original or improved court organization. A broadened field of opportunities open before it continuously. It was uniquely designed to carry on the faith and perpetuate the ideals of the most notable law reformer of an era.

October 27, 1963.

CHARLES E. CLARK.

The
Legal
Profession

Professional Responsibility
Advocacy

Arthur T. Vanderbilt was born in Newark, New Jersey, in 1888. His branch of the Vanderbilt family, according to Professor W. Barton Leach, had but a tenuous connection with the piratical Commodore Vanderbilt who was noted for his Machiavellian comment "What do I care about the law? I got the power, ain't I?" Educated in the public schools, Vanderbilt worked his way through Wesleyan University in Middletown, Connecticut, receiving a Bachelor of Arts degree in 1910 and a Master of Arts degree in 1912. In 1913, he was awarded a Bachelor of Laws degree from Columbia University Law School, and was admitted to the New Jersey Bar the same year.

Vanderbilt soon became a leader of the bar of his state. For thirty-five years he enjoyed an active general practice appearing in important cases not only in his native state but in other states, in the federal courts, in the Supreme Court of the United States and in the Canadian courts. His skill as an appellate advocate is illustrated by his record in the New Jersey Court of Errors and Appeals, at that time the highest court. During the period 1928-1932, he argued 21 cases in that tribunal, winning them all.

He counted among his clients banks, insurance companies, and industrial corporations, but at the same time he represented those whose civil liberties were threatened and served as counsel to other lawyers in problems involving many fields of law. When he became Chief Justice of New Jersey in 1948, he had achieved a reputation as one of the nation's leading advocates. His lectures at Washington and Lee University constitute a distillation of his wide experience in the field of advocacy.

The Five Functions of a Lawyer was a lecture delivered by him to the American Law Student Association on August 24, 1953. Thirty-four years of teaching and his contact with practicing lawyers impelled him, in his introductory remarks, to comment on the failure of many lawyers to attain full growth because they never glimpse what is rightly expected of them.

"For them, alas, their responsibilities begin and end with serving their clients and for them the law is only

3

a set of mechanical rules which they attempt to manipulate for the interests of their clients."

Such a lawyer, he thought, would never enjoy the "durable satisfactions" that come with a well-rounded and complete life in the law. A recurring theme in Vanderbilt's writings is the lack of a sense of public responsibility on the part of the bar. He has often described how wide was the intellectual background of the lawyer of one hundred and fifty years ago and how deep the interest in the political struggles and constitutional problems of those times.

It is hoped that the extract from **The Five Functions of a Lawyer** will impel a reading of the full address. **The Six Factors in the Work of an Advocate** are from his Washington and Lee lectures, **Forensic Persuasion.**

THE FIVE FUNCTIONS OF THE LAWYER *

1. First of all, a truly great lawyer is a wise counselor to all manner of men in the varied crises of their lives when they most need disinterested advice. Effective counseling necessarily involves a thoroughgoing knowledge of the principles of the law not merely as they appear in the books but as they actually operate in action. In equal measure counseling calls for a wide and deep knowledge of human nature and of modern society. Most difficult of all, truly great counseling calls for an ability to forecast the trends of the law.

---

* The Five Functions of the Lawyer: Service to Clients and the Public, 40 A.B.A.J. 31-34 (1954), 23 Utah, B. Bull. 173-181 (1953).

Very often what the client really wants to know is not what the law is today but what it will be at the time the problem under discussion is likely to come up for adjudication in the courts. This is what Mr. Justice Holmes had in mind when he said, "Prophecies of what the courts will do in fact, and nothing more pretentious, are what I mean by the law." This may not have seemed pretentious to Holmes, but what profession demands greater skill in meeting its obvious requirements?

2. Next the great lawyer is a skilled advocate, trained in the art of prosecuting and defending the legal rights of men both in the trial courts and on appeal. Unless a lawyer has had experience as an advocate, it is difficult to see how he can be a thoroughly competent counselor, for he will not be able to evaluate his client's cause in terms of the realities of the courtroom. It is in the courtroom that the law is applied to concrete facts in specific cases, and it is the advocates who, with the judges, in the last analysis set the course of the law.

Advocacy is the most intensive work a lawyer is called on to do. It was not until I was fifty that I began to understand that the decision in every great case is likely to be written with the lifeblood of some lawyer. Advocacy is not a gift of the gods. In its trial as well as in its appellate aspects it involves several distinct arts, each of which must be studied and mastered. No law school in the country, so far as I know, pays much attention to them. Indeed, it seems to be blithely assumed with disastrous results that every student coming to law school is a born Webster or Choate. Clearly somewhere in the course of his professional training our complete lawyer must learn the arts of advocacy.

3. The third task of the great lawyer is to do his part individually and as a member of the organized bar to improve his profession, the courts, and the law. As President Theodore Roosevelt aptly put it, "Every man owes some of his time to the upbuilding of the profession to which he belongs." Indeed, this obligation is one of the great things which distinguishes a profession from a business. The soundness and the necessity of President Roosevelt's admonition insofar as it relates to the legal

profession cannot be doubted. The advances in natural science and technology are so startling and the velocity of change in business and in social life are so great that the law along with the other social sciences, and even human life itself, is in grave danger of being extinguished by new gods of its own invention if it does not awake from its lethargy. A few law professors have pondered long and hard on these problems, but the law schools by and large have done nothing about the matter beyond an occasional unpopular and generally ineffective course in legal ethics.

4. In a free society every lawyer has a fourth responsibility, that of acting as an intelligent, unselfish leader of public opinion— I accent the qualities "intelligent" and "unselfish"—within his own particular sphere of influence. In our complicated age sound public opinion is more indispensable than it ever was; without it even courageous leadership may fail. Did not President Franklin D. Roosevelt warn us as early as October, 1937, over four years before Pearl Harbor, in his Japanese quarantine speech in Chicago, of the dangers ahead? And did not the newspapers of both parties throughout the country condemn his speech as warmongering? And did not Charles Lindbergh in February, 1939, over six months before the outbreak of World War II in Europe, warn the English that he had actually seen 30,000 war planes in Germany? And did not the English practically drive him from the country for telling them, for merely telling them, a fact that was of supreme importance to their individual welfare and to their survival as a nation?

How different might history have been and our life today, if only one American lawyer in each city had written a letter to his paper or made a speech supporting the President or if an English barrister in each community in his country had reminded his contemporaries that Lindbergh was undoubtedly an expert on airplanes and that he could certainly count to 30,000? No individual class in our society is better able to render real service in the molding of public opinion.

5. Finally, every great lawyer must be prepared, not necessarily to seek public office, but to answer the call for public service when it comes. The attorney whose professional thoughts begin

and end with his own private clients is a pitiable mockery of what a great lawyer really is. Training for public service is a lifelong career. There is no sadder sight in the legal profession than that of a lawyer who has long dreamed of unselfish public service but who has been so engrossed in serving private clients that when the call does come to him for a public career he has so lost contact with the spirit and problems of the day that his efforts in the public interest prove abortive. What should have been a crown of laurel frequently turns out to be one of thorns.

These five—counseling, advocacy, improving his profession, the courts and the law, leadership in molding public opinion and the unselfish holding of public office—are the essential functions of the great lawyer. Education in these five functions of the lawyer is partly the province of the college, partly the duty of the law school, but in large measure it is the responsibility of the individual lawyer not only while in law school but throughout his working years. This is practicing law in the grand manner—the only way it is worth practicing.

THE SIX FACTORS IN THE WORK OF THE ADVOCATE *

Before proceeding to discuss in some detail the various types of forensic persuasion to which I have alluded, it will be helpful to enumerate and then to comment briefly on the six factors that are involved in the work of the advocate. As I proceed you may find it interesting to take a personal inventory of your own stock in hand by way of preparation for becoming an advocate.

1. The capacity for grasping all the facts of a case in all of their interrelations and implications quickly and comprehensively.

---

* Forensic Persuasion. Vol. I John Randolph Tucker Memorial Lectures 39-92. (Washington and Lee University, 1952). The Six Factors in the Work of an Advocate appears in 7 Wash. and Lee L. Rev. 123-30 (1950). The lectures have been rearranged in logical sequence and the footnotes have been renumbered.

2. A thorough understanding of the fundamental principles and rules of law and the ability to apply them to the facts of a case.

3. Knowledge of human nature in all of its manifestations and an ability to get along with people generally.

4. A comprehension of the economic, political, social and intellectual environment of modern litigation—for cases are never tried in a vacuum.

5. The ability to reason concerning the facts, the law, the personalities involved in litigation, and the environment of a case in such a way as to solve the pending problem in the most satisfactory way possible.

6. The art of expressing one's self clearly and cogently, orally and in writing.

The temptation is strong to delve into a thoroughgoing analysis of the part that each of these factors plays in a lawyer's life, but I must content myself with a brief comment on each.

1. Every experienced advocate will tell you that *mastering the facts* of a case is the most difficult part of his work. There are likely to be as many different versions of the facts of a case as there are witnesses and parties in interest, and it is by no means improbable that these versions may change materially— and quite without any intentional dishonesty, such is the frailty of human memory—from the time the witnesses are first interviewed to the day of trial. It is the lawyer's duty to know as many of these different versions of the facts as he possibly can before he comes to court, both from interviewing his own witnesses and through a pretrial examination of his adversary's witnesses, and to anticipate in his imagination those hostile versions of the facts that for one reason or another he is unable to ascertain in advance of trial. This effort to obtain a comprehensive grasp of the facts of a case from his client's point of view and to anticipate his adversary's case is seldom a routine matter; it often calls for a high degree of constructive imagination in which a knowledge of human nature that is at once broad and

deep is required. This diversity of view as to the facts means that he must maintain a tentative attitude toward the facts of the case that are disclosed to him, realizing full well that at the trial he will learn things that he has never dreamed of before. By knowing or anticipating the story of each witness he will often be able to explain away seeming contradictions and thus to point up the truth. On crucial items at least he should be able to repeat the testimony of the witness in their own words, and on the argument of an appeal he should also be able to tell where every statement of fact appears in the record and to refer to it quickly. Such skill rarely comes by grace; one's faculties for organizing and remembering facts must be assiduously cultivated. Fortunately, it is his privilege —nay, his duty—to forget the facts of a case as soon as it is over, for otherwise the advocate's mind would become an intellectual junk yard.

Though the lawyer must know all of the facts of his case and everybody's version of them, it is essential that he should not harbor the notion that he is bound to tell either the trial court or the appellate tribunal all that he knows. Indeed, there could be no surer way of losing a case. Knowing all of the facts, he must skillfully confine his presentation to those which are most cogent and persuasive. His power of selection, of arrangement and of emphasis will be the measure of his genius. He will do well to remember the force that inures in the concrete intance in contrast to vague generalities and he will never forget the wisdom of Macaulay's dictum in painting a picture to either jurors or judges: "Logicians may argue about abstractions, but the mass of men must have images."

Not infrequently in complicated cases counsel will be called upon almost overnight to learn about an entire art or industry with which he may previously have been totally unfamiliar. Thus, years ago I was called upon to defend some insurance companies that were being sued for the loss of certain paintings which the plaintiff described as the works of certain old Italian and Dutch masters. The defense was that they were not the old masters they were represented to be, but fraudulent reproductions. The preparation and trial of the case called for a thorough knowledge of the paintings of the Italian and Dutch artists in question, of the characteristics and techniques of each of them, of the kind of canvas on which each worked, and the chemistry of the pigments each used, in contrast with the canvas and pigments disclosed by the charred remains of the pictures that had been insured. My investigation required not only much study of books but conferences with experts on art, on canvas, and on pigments, matters on which I was blissfully ignorant before being called into the case. Every experienced trial lawyer has scores of such experiences.

2. Little need be said to this audience about the second element in the advocate's work, because the acquisition of a thorough understanding of the fundamental *principles and rules of the law* is one of the chief aims of every law student. To understand the law, however, in its proper perspective to the other factors in the lawyer's work we would do well to remember that in contrast to the facts of a case, which are generally specific and concrete, the rules of law always are abstract and they deal with the relations between persons or between person and things. It is therefore most important to form the habit of noting to one's self, throughout every step of a case and in dealing with every one of the many versions of the facts, the rules of law that apply thereto. The advocate will, of course, be interested not only in the controlling rules of substantive law and the principles underlying them, but also in the rules of pleading by which issues are presented in the court, and of evidence by which they are proved there. This process of applying the law, substantive and procedural, to the facts of the case is the converse of the process that the student is accustomed to use in the study of cases, but it will give him no difficulty if he has done his law school work thoroughly.

3. The third element in every law suit, and quite as important as the facts and the law, is the advocate's *knowledge of human nature* and an ability to get along with people. I am referring not only to the lawyer's client and his witnesses, but also to his adversary and his client and his witnesses, and the judge, the

jury and everyone with whom he has to deal in the conduct of the suit. Each of them is a unique personality. Their variety is infinite. A single mistake in drawing a jury may cost the plaintiff his case, while at the same time a deft choice may mean victory for a defendant. "The proper study of mankind," says Pope, "is man." And for no one is this more true than for the trial lawyer. He must learn to judge character as much by a man's voice and his manner as by what he sees in his face and what he says. It is a difficult art but a fascinating one. The prospective advocate may learn much through observation, more through conversation, but most from daily contact with people. He should school himself to make his study of human nature a lifelong habit. He may learn much through the study of the world's great literature, notably the Bible and Shakespeare, that he will not be able to discover elsewhere.

4. Next the advocate must know the economic, political, social and intellectual environment of his case and the *trends of the times*. He must know whether he is working with or against what Dicey has well called "the assumptions of the age":

> There exists at any given time a body of beliefs, convictions, sentiments, accepted principles or firmly rooted prejudices, which, taken together, make up the public opinion of a particular era, or what may be called the reigning or predominant current of opinion . . . . It may be added that the whole body of beliefs existing in any given age may generally be traced to certain fundamental assumptions, which at the time, whether they be actually true or false, are believed by the mass of the world to be true with such confidence that they hardly appear to bear the character of assumptions.[1]

All this calls for a knowledge of the social sciences in the broadest sense of the term as well as of the humanities and for insight in forecasting the trends of the future. As a profession we have been slow to recognize this responsibility. Indeed, I suspect that even you may think I am speaking not as a practical man of the law but as an erstwhile educator in urging on you desirable but not essential attainments. The matter is so vital that I cannot permit any doubt of your responsibility for preparation in this field to linger in your minds. I summon to my aid two of the greatest corporation lawyers in the country. Says Edward F. Johnson, General Counsel of the Standard Oil Company of New Jersey:

> Unless the lawyer is keenly sensitive to such [social] trends, advice acted upon today is likely to fail to meet the test of judicial scrutiny years later. . . . To statute and decision has been added a new legal dimension—the dominant public interest. A lawyer's advice based upon a two-dimensional study of the law is likely to result in as great a distortion of reality and to be as flat as a two-dimensional painting without depth or perspective. A sound lawyer—sober, hard-headed and realistic craftsman that he is—pays heed to every relevant fact, whether or not that fact is to his liking.[2]

Hear also William T. Gossett, General Counsel of the Ford Motor Company:

> The lawyer representing business today, if he is to live up to the challenge of his new responsibilities, ... will be alive to the social, economic and political implications of the time; he will avoid a narrow, shortsighted approach to his client's problems; he will act with due regard for the social responsibilities of the enterprise; he will have the courage to advise against a business program or device which, although legally defensible, is in conflict with the basic principles of ethics. Failing this, he not only will be ignoring his obligations to society, he will be doing a disservice to his client, who may find himself in the position of winning a legal battle but losing a social war.[3]

5. The fifth factor in a lawyer's work is the *ability to reason* concerning the facts, the law, the personalities involved in litigation and the environment of the case in such a way as to solve a controversy in the most satisfactory way possible. There is little need to talk to law students about this, for the great educational achievement of our modern law schools has been in training their students to think as lawyers think. It is the necessity of reasoning about concrete facts, abstract law, complicated personalities, and the complex social scene that calls for such a variety of traits in the trial lawyer and that in turn makes his work so absorbing. While the lawyer thinks both inductively and deductively in prep-

aration for trial and the courtroom, it is important to observe here that in forensic persuasion he uses largely the deductive approach.

6. Finally, the advocate must be able to *express himself* in words. He must master the use of words or they will be likely to master him. He must cultivate the arts of both written and spoken expression until their use becomes second nature to him. I do not have in mind any tricks such as sometimes masquerade under the guise of semantics. Many a case is won or lost according to the skill of counsel in translating his points into language that may be grasped by his particular audience. After he has completed his study of the facts, the law, the people of a case, and the environment, after he has exhausted his powers of reasoning, he will still have the problem of making himself so clearly and forcibly understood as to be able to persuade his hearers. They must feel—and he must be able to make them feel—that he is uttering realities and not mere words. Self-expression is, indeed, a lifelong adventure.

The law student will note that with the exception of the second factor in the advocate's work, an understanding of the law, and of the fifth, the art of legal reasoning, all of the elements that enter into his work are attributes one would expect to find in any educated and enlightened good citizen. They are not narrowly professional. The more the student has learned and the more he has trained his faculties in each of these fields, the easier will be his initiation in the arts of advocacy.

All advocacy involves conflict and calls for the will to win, But the conflicts of advocacy proceed under very definite rules, the first of which is that the contestants must be gentlemen. They must have character. This means that they have certain standards of conduct, of manners, and of expression that are so habitually theirs that they do not have to stop in an emergency to argue with themselves as to whether or not they should conform to them. They are free to concentrate on the task at hand. The prospective advocate may learn much from a study of the functions of the several steps in forensic persuasion and of the different kinds of tribunals he will be called upon to address, so that here, too, in his hour of testing he will not have to stop, when his mind should be on the merits of his case, to debate with himself the intricate questions of trial or appellate tactics. He will have learned the basic rules of the contest in which he is engaged. Nothing, of course, will take the place of actual experience in developing his own skill, but a study of the problems inherent in the various phases of advocacy and of the experience of others may save him from making a multitude of unnecessary mistakes. The advocate must also learn that hard work is his daily lot. As Lord Chancellor Eldon graphically put it: "I know of no rule to give them but that they must make up their mind to live like hermits and work like horses." But the reward is great. To quote Judge Cardozo, "What we give forth in effort comes back to us in character. The alchemy is inevitable." Character, capacity for hard work, the will to win and a study of the methods of the advocate round out the requirements in preparation for the art of advocacy.

OPENING A CASE

The opening of a case to a judge or to a judge and jury is a matter of great importance to the outcome of the litigation. The opening is the picture which you present to the court or jury to give them a preview of your case before they listen to the evidence. What they get out of the evidence you will introduce will depend in large measure on the skill with which you have prepared them for it through the picture of your case. Your opening will set the pitch and the tempo of your part of the trial. Making an opening, therefore, is no mere matter of form but constitutes an art of very real importance.

Openings are of two kinds, one to a judge sitting alone and passing on both the law and the facts, the other to a judge and a jury with the judge as the arbiter of the law and the jury as the trier of the facts. In opening a case to a judge sitting alone it is important to know whether he has read the pleadings, whether there has been a pretrial conference at which the issues in the case have been simplified by him for purposes of trial, and whether he has read your trial brief. If he has, he is likely to suggest that you waive an opening, but if you can open the case without, of course, going against his instructions, it is highly advisable to do so; first, because many judges get things through the ear better than they do through the eye; second, because even if he has read the pleadings, the pretrial conference order and the trial briefs, there is a definite advantage in being able to summarize them at the outset of the trial; and finally, because it will be helpful to your client and your witnesses if they can see your entire case in perspective before they testify. One way or another, it is as essential that the judge have a preview of the facts as it is for the jury. In opening to a judge it is permissible and often desirable to state the issues of law as well as the issues of fact to be tried so that he will have the entire situation before him. In opening to a jury, however, counsel will rarely have occasion to deal with problems of law for those are for the court, but he will ordinarily confine his attention to a presentation of the facts of the controversy.

Trial judges differ from each other quite as much as appellate judges do, and jurors are infinite in their variety. The advocate's problem is, therefore, one of adapting his tactics in the particular case to the characteristics of the tribunal he is addressing. However much the judges and jurors may differ, there are certain general principles concerning an opening that have as much force as if they were written law. Start by identifying the parties and their respective counsel. In the ordinary case the opening should be brief and simple. It should be a statement of what you expect to prove. Generally it is a mistake to go into detail or to narrate what you expect each witness to tell. Your audience will get lost in details, and besides your witnesses may not say what you expect them to say on the stand. Stick to essentials. Emphasize the elements of liability and the ingredients of your claim for damages. While explaining your case to the judge or jury give them the drama of the litigation and endeavor to arouse their interest in your side, without, of course, any direct appeal.

Let the facts tell the story. It is always wise to understand what one hopes to prove. The jurors have a way of remembering what counsel said he was going to demonstrate, and if he fails to do so they are likely to hold it against him and his client. It is far better to let the judge and the jury discover for themselves interesting things in your case, once you have aroused their interest and sympathy, rather than to endeavor to tell them everything. What they discover for themselves they are most likely to remember, when they come to decide the case.

Summarize and suggest evidence, therefore, rather than recount it at length. Do not, however, make the jury guess what your proof is going to be. Above all things, be sure that you tell the jury enough to make out a prima facie case, otherwise you may be in danger of having your adversary move for a nonsuit on your opening and succeed on his motion. Ordinarily the best way to present the facts of a case is in chronological order. Strive for continuity. In any event, it is important that the judge and the jury see that you have a plan and order about your presentation. Nothing so wearies a tribunal as to have to skip backward and forward in their case. Nothing could be more likely to cause them to lose faith in you and your cause.

There are few cases in which there is not some fact or some witness that counsel wishes he could get along without, but which, nevertheless, is there and must be recognized. It is better to be frank with the jury about these matters, though, of course, without overemphasizing them. If you must rely on a witness with a shady past or a criminal record, mention it casually, minimize it if you will, but do not let it come later in the case as a surprise. If there is a letter that should not have been written but which cannot be ignored, mention it and tell the jury that you will explain it and how. On the other hand, an opening is no place for an argument. That is the function of your summation. Not only should counsel not argue in his opening, but he should avoid any statement that can call for proper objection from his adversary. Nothing will so wreck an opening as legitimate interruption by opposing counsel. Do not, therefore, refer in your opening to evidence that you know will be held inadmissible later on in the trial, because counsel will much surely object, break the thread of your opening and give you a bad start with the jury.

Either side may waive an opening but it is never advisable to do so. It creates a bad impression. The jurors will think either that you have something that you don't want to tell them, that you prefer to play poker until the evidence is all in, or that you think the case is not important enough to explain to them. In any event, they will feel cheated and they will not like it.

Always take notes of your adversary's opening so that you can quote in your summation anything that he says in his opening he will prove but fails to. It is not that you will not remember what he said in his opening, but it always impresses the jury for you to appear to have his exact words on crucial points available in written form.

The opening should not be a humdrum affair. It should create a sense of expectation on the part of the jury. Everything that I have said about style and delivery and obstructions in the argument of an appeal applies with equal, if not even greater force in a trial court. Don't read anything to the jury if you can avoid it. Paraphrase a document rather than read it. Don't let anything get between you and the jury except, if you need it, your one-page outline of your opening. Do not rant or rail either in an opening or a summation. Let your language be simple, your manner direct. Max Steuer, who was one of the greatest jury lawyers of his day, habitually spoke so softly to the jury that very often the judge and opposing counsel had to ask him to raise his voice so that they could hear what was going on between him and the jury. This method may not give you a great reputation as a jury orator, but if you are as interested as your client presumably is in the verdict I commend it to you. Mr. Steuer was so careful of the effect of little things on the jury that he never carried a leather briefcase for fear that the jury would get a wrong notion of him. He kept all his papers in a simple large filing envelope—a detail, if you please, but it points up what I have been saying about not letting anything get between you and your jurors. Mr. Steuer never let anyone sit at the counsel table with him and he was happy when opposed by a half a dozen lawyers. He would play David, they Goliath. Do not pound the rail of the jury box. The story is told of a trial lawyer who was so annoyed at his adversary doing so that he told the judge his adversary reminded him of something he had omitted to do in his address to the jury. He asked for permission to take care of it. He advanced to the jury box and thumped the jury rail three resounding whacks and then sat down. The jury got the point; his adversary's speech had been demolished. Finally, do not lecture the jury. Treat them with the same respect that you would treat an appellate court. Indicate that you have confidence in their honesty, their intelligence and their practicality. Then sit down.

SUMMATION

Summations, like openings, are of two sorts. A summation to a judge sitting alone is quite different from a summation to a jury and very much like the argument of an appeal with the exception that it is before a single judge instead of a bench of judges, and also that the judge has just heard the evidence and it is fresh in his mind as it has developed during the trial. With these exceptions taken into account, everything that has been said about the argument of an appeal would apply with equal force to a summation before a trial judge. The facts are to be marshalled in orderly fashion from your client's point of view and the rules of law applicable thereto should be presented as clearly and cogently as possible. In dealing with the facts and likewise with the law counsel should make proper us of what he has learned is going on in the judge's mind from the judge's remarks and his attitude as the trial progressed. Counsel has had a preview of the judge's mind which should help him in deciding both what to say and what not to say. There is, of course, the chance that the judge may change his mind in the final moments of the trial, but the chances are against it. Any questions from the bench during the course of the summation should be quickly, tersely and frankly answered. They are entitled to a weight that does not attach to the questions of any one appellate judge; they are obstructions in the path of your victory; and quite literally they must be disposed of before counsel may safely proceed. If a one-page summary of one's argument is helpful on appeal, it is doubly helpful in summation before a trial judge in organizing one's thoughts on the facts and on the law. Simplicity and clarity are quite as important as in any argument before a jury.

Quite as much as with a jury, no result is ever impossible in summation to a judge. Let me give an illustration from my own experience. One afternoon as I was returning from an argument in our Supreme Court I found a client waiting for me at the railroad station. He was the head of a large tool manufacturing concern and at the time we were in the midst of World War I. He told me that one of his most important foremen ha[d] been arrested the day before, charged with driving his automobile while intoxicated and that he was going on trial before a local justice of the peace that evening. I suggested that we interview the foreman, but my friend said that would be useless, that he not only had been happily drunk but he had driven his car several times up over the sidewalk for the sheer joy of frightening people, though he had not injured anyone. I inquired about the judge and my client told me that he was a retired school teacher, a man of probity, very strict and fond of reading "The Lives of the Chief Justices," to whom, it was suspected, he saw some slight resemblance in himself. The offense carried with it a minimum mandatory jail sentence of thirty days. The prospect was not alluring, especially as the foreman had picked out a Sunday morning right after the close of church services when people were on their way home from divine worship to try his sidewalk jumping. And the foreman had a name that was decidedly Teutonic.

The justice of the peace usually held court in his kitchen, but in this instance the audience was so large that he had a table brought into his garden and set up there. I shall not attempt to tell you how many witnesses testified to the foreman's antics. Fortunately, none of them seemed to bear him any ill will. His previous conduct had been exemplary. They all commented on his character and his good nature. There was little evidence I could offer beyond his record of hard work for long hours seven days a week for many months in the war effort and the fact that he had three sons at the front. With the evidence all in, the justice asked me if I had anything to say, with the accent significantly on the word "anything." Without stressing my words too much I said that I had no intention of attempting a jury speech which I knew in the circumstances and with his reputation would be unavailing, but I did want to point out some significant facts. First of all, the charge was driving an automobile while intoxicated. True, several witnesses had testified that the defendant was drunk, very drunk, in fact, but not disagreeable and malicious, just happy and carefree, but he had been a good family man with a fine record up to the time of the present charge, and his services were much more needed in the factory superintending the production of war tools than they were in the county jail repenting his folly. Once more I managed to bring in the word 'intoxication' in the complaint in contrast with the word 'drunk' in the testimony, but I made no effort to press the distinction. I noticed however, a glint in the judge's eye, whether friendly or not I could not fathom, as I continued with my general remarks on the state of affairs in the factory, in the world at large and with families divided, the flower of youth doing their duty all over the globe. The foreman's two daughters fell to weeping silently and before long most of the women in the audience were teary eyed and more than one grown man was busy blowing his nose. I reminded the judge of his hard responsibility and wished that I could suggest some way out of the dilemma, but I realized that he was sworn to do his duty and I was no man to dissuade him, but where there's a will there's a way and the world was tumbling all about us. When I concluded, the judge went into his kitchen and came out with a copy of the Revised Statutes, which he opened ostentatiously. He read the section that the defendant had offended. He reviewed the evidence, I must say, with great effect to the accompaniment of tears from the feminine part of his audience. He commented on the danger to the public resulting from the defendant's conduct. He spoke, too, of the great strain that the defendant had been under and the service that he had been rendering his country as well as of the courage of his sons. He then referred again to the statute book and called attention to the fact that the charge was driving while intoxicated and he then laid great stress on the fact that while the many witnesses had testified that the defendant was drunk, not a single one had testified that he was intoxicated. Therefore he had no choice but to acquit the defendant, but in doing so he warned him that the next time he was drunk someone would possibly be found who would testify that he was intoxicated. I bowed in due respect to the judge's wisdom as he received the thanks of the defendant, his wife, his daughters and his friends, who seemed all of a sudden to make up the entire audience. Nobody doubted that in the circumstances justice had been done, whatever might be said of the judge's canons of statutory construction.

One of the most troublesome aspects of summation to a single judge is met when he becomes interested in reading a pleading or a trial brief or a judicial decision during the course of your argument or when he is interrupted by one of the court officers with some message. If the interruption promises to be a short one, counsel had better continue as if nothing had occurred. If the interruption continues, there is nothing to do but to take the risk of offending the judge by stopping short in your speech until you have regained his attention. Quite different is the judicial habit of shutting one's eyes. This does not always portend slumber. I recall visiting in the Court of Appeals of the Province of Ontario not so long ago and seeing a judge with his eyes shut and his head curled up on his left shoulder and his arms folded. I wrote a note to my guide and asked who the little brown bear was who seemed to be hibernating on right end. A note written in reply told me the little brown bear was Mr. Justice Middleton but that he was not hibernating, as I should see presently. Within three or four minutes he unfolded his arms, opened his eyes and asked counsel if he was acquainted with such and such a case. Counsel confessed that he was not and then the judge suggested that they take a look at it. Presently counsel was admitting that the case was in point and seemed to state him out of court, whereupon the judge kindly said that he should not feel too bad because unfortunately the case had not been properly digested or indexed and so counsel should not be expected to know about it.

A fine summation to a jury is a dramatic event. Mr. Justice Holmes has painted the type; speaking of George Shattuck he said:

> He was a great man with the jury in every way. His addresses carried everything before him like a victorious cavalry charge, sometimes, it seemed to me, sweeping the judge along with the rest in the rout.[4]

The facts will necessarily predominate. Ordinarily the law will be given to the jury by the court, or in some jurisdictions has been given to the jury before counsel starts his address. It is the facts, then, that demand the advocate's attention. Not only the facts but all of the reasonable inferences and deductions and conclusions which may be drawn from them are counsel's province. The effective organization of one's material, clarity, force and sincerity are the paramount considerations. Make the most of the opening minutes of your address to the jurors, for then they are most attentive and most receptive. Next in importance to the opening of your speech is the conclusion, provided, of course, you haven't lost their attention in the meantime. If you see the attention of the jury flagging and you can't revive it, get to the end of your remarks no matter how much more allotted time you may have.

Do not go outside of the record in your summation, for otherwise opposing counsel will have just cause to interrupt you and your address will be spoiled. Organize the facts and present them succinctly. Generally the chronological order is best. Make only such deductions and inferences from the testimony as will appeal to the intelligence of the jury. If you are far-fetched in your reasoning, you will be sure to draw down on your head the ridicule of your adversary. Be reasonable. In many instances the inferences that may be drawn from the testimony are far more important than the testimony itself. I recall a case where the plaintiff and several of his employees did not take the stand, though they could have given evidence to rebut much of the defendant's proof. The defendant's counsel in summation took about ten minutes to summarize his defense, and then spent the rest of the time telling the jury what the plaintiff and his employees could have proved had they been on the stand and then taunted the plaintiff's attorney to tell why he did not put them on the stand. The plaintiff's attorney saw that he had to explain his failure to do so and used up all his time in doing so and never got around to summarizing his own case, with the inevitable result that he lost the verdict.

Regardless of what the technical rules of law may be, every argument to the jury to be effective must appeal to the jury's concept of essential fairness and justice. Juries are rarely interested in technicalities. Ordinarily the fewer points the jury is called upon to deal with in the summation, the better. It is likely to be fatal if one scatters one's fire in too many directions on a multitude of points. On the other hand, although it is unwise to develop too many points in a summation, it is well to remember that there are twelve different minds on the jury and it is better to appeal to more than one type by more than one different argument. Take a middle ground. Develop a few of your strongest points. And in the course of developing your strongest points you must at the same time make sure to point out the weaknesses of the defendant's side. An advocate must be able to say with Montague Williams: "I am by trade a reader of faces and minds," and if you find that you are losing the interest of the jurors on one front you should seek at once to arouse it on another. To have control of your case you should have an outline of your summation either in mind or on a single page, just as the advocate does on the argument of an appeal. If you can find a telling slogan or catch phrase that the jury may leave the courtroom remembering, so much the better. Don't read to the jury any

more than you can avoid. There may be men who can read well
to a jury, but I have never heard one. There is one exception:
when you come to the crucial parts of the case very real advantage may be had in quoting briefly from your notes of counsel's
opening or a vital line from a witness's testimony, but not too
much, of course; just a word or two to show that your opponent
has misstated or overstated his case in his opening, just a line
or two from the testimony to show exactly what it was that an
all-important witness had to say may well prove decisive. On the
other hand, never memorize a summation. The course of events
at the trial may force you to change your plan of attack or of
defense and with a memorized speech this is indeed difficult.
The odds are all in favor of a man with a good clear outline from
which he can vary as necessity demands. All your effort should
be devoted to persuading the jury that the facts and the law are
on your side and that justice and honesty will prevail if their
verdict is in your favor; otherwise they are not likely to decide
for your client, however eloquent you may be.

Though one may never thank a judge for listening, it is permissible and generally advisable to thank the jury, not obsequi-
ously but courteously and briefly, for their attention. In appropriate cases one will do well to impress the jury with the importance of their power. Put the burden of the decision on the jurors'
souls. Speaking of a case where Marshall Hall did just this for
twenty minutes without touching upon a single fact of the case,
Solicitor General Melville said: "After twenty minutes of dispas-
sionate and pulverizing rhetoric the jury were in a state of
pulp."[5] It is no wonder, then, that one of their number was
physically overcome and actually fainted. Such appeals must, of
course, be reserved for cases of grave importance or they would
seem ridiculous, but the thought of the importance of the jury's
function should never be out of counsel's mind in any case, however restrained his effort may be in the circumstances of the case.

In dealing with adverse witnesses who clearly have not told
the truth, it is generally better to treat them as if they had made
a mistake rather than as if they were deliberate perjurers. The
sympathy of the jury is apt to be with the witness rather than
with the advocate who has exposed him. It is only in those cases

where the perjury is beyond the shadow of a doubt that it is safe to attempt to destroy the witness and not merely his testimony. It is equally important not to indulge in far-fetched inferences from the testimony or in any kind of extravagant claims. If you represent the defendant, your opponent coming after you will surely explode your rhetoric. Even if you are speaking last, remember that the jury thinks better of any argument that is reasonable and that is clear. Above all jurors insist on sincerity —they are likely to favor the man who seems to subordinate himself to his cause and who is giving it everything within his power. Such a man is likely to win the confidence of the jury without being in the least familiar with them. Courtesy, clearness, common sense, fairness, moral earnestness, should mark the progress of a summation to its conclusion. As long as human nature is what it is, true eloquence springing from the mind and the heart of the speaker will be a factor to be reckoned with in any courtroom and at no time more than in summation. One final word: young lawyers are much concerned over their nervousness in public address and especially in summations. They should know that every speaker worth listening to is nervous, nervous about his equipment, his preparation, his audience, the hundred and one things that may go wrong. It may interest you to know that as great a speaker as Woodrow Wilson never made an address without his knees shaking for five or ten minutes. This sensitivity to an audience is one of the marks of the great speaker. A speaker who lacks this quality cannot hold an audience. The remedy is the understanding of the conditions of the particular address you are called upon to deliver, thorough preparation and experience. You must learn to make your nervousness work for you. . . .

ARGUING AN APPEAL: (1) SUBSTANCE

The argument of an appeal is the climax of a case. All the long and wearisome work of interviewing clients and witnesses, of gathering facts, of assembling the law, of drafting the pleadings, of attending to the various pretrial proceedings, the preparation of the trial briefs, the trial itself, possibly the argument of a rule to show cause why a new trial should not be granted, the preparation of the appellate briefs and of the entirely separate and distinct notes for the oral argument: all of these are to be distilled into an argument of a half an hour. It is the most concentrated and yet the most exhilarating work that the advocate is called upon to do. The trial court has had the advantage of hearing the opening and the summation of counsel, the presentation of evidence, the cross-examination of witness, the arguments on the admission of evidence, and perhaps a motion for a nonsuit or a directed verdict. The trial court absorbs the content of a case bit by bit. The appellate tribunal, however, will know nothing of the facts, none too much of the law, and none of the background of your case save as it gleans them from the cold pages of the printed briefs or absorbs them from counsel at the oral argument. You face a select audience that is experienced, professionally critical but not unfriendly, and keenly interested in knowing the facts and applying the law to them and more or less prepared for the occasion. The challenge is great; the entire outcome of the case, victory or defeat, will be influenced by the effectiveness of your oral argument.

There are several different methods of argument on appeal, and a brief discussion of the several kinds will throw light on the entire process. In the English appellate courts, for example, the briefs are only two or three pages long, they merely show how the case came up and list the points to be argued, but without written argument or citation of cases. The argument is entirely oral and there is no time limit except as the judges think the subject has been exhausted. Therefore the judges do not hesitate to interrupt counsel as frequently as they need to, to get the facts and to express their views on the law, and counsel do not object to such interruptions. Indeed, they welcome them because they show what the judges are thinking and give counsel an opportunity to meet the views of the judge. Some years ago I heard Sir William Jowitt, now Lord Chancellor, take three days to present the facts of a very complicated appeal from India. Everything about the man, his diction, his manners, proclaimed him the master of the situation. Speaking entirely without notes, only once and then upon a very minor matter, did he have to correct a statement of fact on a suggestion from his solicitor. His tone, while conversational and reserved, left no doubt as to the intensity of his effort and of his will to win. Each question asked him by the court, instead of constituting a setback, seemed to be used by him to advance his presentation. He gave one the impression of a swimmer who enjoyed breasting the waves and who had the knack of surmounting them. This method of argument takes much longer than we are accustomed to, but it produces decisions that are very obviously the joint work of court and counsel. A series of cases in which I was interested some years ago, each of which involved the same questions of law, took six days in the Supreme Court of Canada, eight in the Supreme Court of Jamaica, and the same amount of time in the Supreme Court of Nassau, and in the Privy Council the appellant, who alone was called on, took five days. The same issues were argued, and I think equally thoroughly, in a half day in the United States Court of Appeals for the Fourth Circuit with the aid of elaborate briefs which the court had studied before the argument. The English system does have the advantage that counsel are always quite sure how the case will be decided before the argument is over, and generally on what point. In the case that I have referred to as having been argued by Sir William Jowitt, I asked the registrar of the Privy Council when the case would be decided. He told me that the judges would confer on the matter at the conclusion of the argument, which was on Friday afternoon, someone would write the opinion over the weekend, the judges would confer about it Monday morning and I should be able to read it in the London Times, Tuesday morning — and there it was on Tuesday morning.

In the early days of the United States Supreme Court arguments were equally long. *McCulloch v. Maryland* took six days, and the *Girard Will* case ten days. Unlike the English practice, questions were rarely asked by the judges. Though the time for argument was gradually lessened as the work of the Court increased, the attitude of the Court toward counsel did not change. President Nicholas Murray Butler of Columbia University used to tell of his journeying to Washington at the turn of the century for the sheer delight of listening to "models of legal reasoning," as he termed the argument of counsel. There are still courts in which the justices rarely ask questions. Chief Justice Marvin B. Rosenberry of Wisconsin delights to tell of one such court, which was visited on a hot summer afternoon by a farmer and his young son. As counsel droned on, a fly lit on the exposed brow of one of the justices and he waved it away. The fly persisted and the justice repeated his movement, whereupon the farmer's boy nudged his father and exclaimed quite excitedly, "Look, Dad, one of them is alive!"

In more recent years questions from the bench have frequently run away with the arguments in the Supreme Court of the United States. Indeed, Justice, then Professor, Frankfurter stated fifteen years ago:

> ... the extent to which argument has become a Socratic dialogue between Court and counsel would startle the shades of Marshall and Taney even as they would have hampered the eloquence of Clay and Webster.[6]

One experience I had in which I answered thirty-two questions from a single justice in the course of an hour's argument leads me to question the soundness of the reference to Socrates, but of this more later. My discomfiture in the case I have mentioned reminds me of the story that is told in Seattle of a longshoreman who struggled to become a lawyer and finally attained his ambition of arguing a case before the United States Supreme Court. He was no sooner under way with his argument than he was beset with a question from the justice on the right end of the bench and another from the justice on the left end. Complaining to the Chief Justice, he said that he had worked out his argument carefully, that he could get through it in an hour if he were left alone, and therefore he pleaded with the Chief Justice to control his end men. Chief Justice Taft smilingly said that such would be the order of the day—and it was.

There are many appellate courts in which the appeals are assigned for the writing of decisions to the various justices in rotation in advance of hearing argument. Human nature being what it is, it inevitably follows that the judges who are not charged with the writing of an opinion in a particular case are not likely to take as great an interest in the case as they would if they thought they might be called on at the court conference to write the opinion. Judges in one great court have been known even to slip out for a cup of tea when a case was on in which they would not be primarily responsible for the opinion. This system, of course, is all wrong, but where it exists, counsel will do well to use all his ingenuity to ascertain who is the judge who has been assigned to write the opinion in his case. Sometimes the judge may be detected by his asking more questions than any of the others do. Generally his law secretary will be in evidence in the courtroom, busy taking notes. In such cases counsel will, of course, give the opinion writer more than usual attention while not seeming to neglect the rest of the bench. Where this practice of "one-judge opinions" prevails, the bar should exert its influence to end it. Such opinions are inevitably inferior to those in which the entire court really participates.

An increasing number of courts follow the example of the United States Court of Apeals for the Fourth Circuit in reading the briefs in advance of argument. In my court not only do we read the briefs and as much of the record as may be necessary in advance, but each of us prepares a typewritten summary of the points raised on the appeal and of our tentative views with respect thereto. We even go one step further, we tell counsel at the outset of the argument the points in their briefs that we are most interested in hearing argued, but we leave it entirely to them to use their time as they see fit. The great advantage of reading the briefs first is that if there is anything in the briefs that is not clear, the judges have a chance to ask counsel about it when he reaches the point in his argument, whereas if briefs were not read until a later date that question must necessarily go unasked. There can be no doubt that any argument will be much more effective if the judges have read the briefs in advance, for in these days so great is the volume of decisions that no judge can be expected to, or does in fact, know all of the decisions of his own state. If the judges come to the oral argument fortified by a study of the briefs, the statements of counsel both as to the facts and the law have a force and a meaning they otherwise would lack. Counsel, too, have the satisfaction of knowing their briefs have been seriously studied at a time when the study will do the most good.

But whatever method of argument may be pursued in any given jurisdiction, there are four essential matters that need concern the advocate: (1) the statement of the question or questions to be argued, (2) the statement of facts, (3) the argument of law and (4) the relation between counsel and the court, *i.e.*, between the speaker and his audience. The same four elements must be considered in preparing a brief, but the written brief, save in the rarest instances, cannot hope to move its readers. It achieves its objective if it convinces. The aim of the oral argument, however, is to persuade. The human presence and particularly the human voice can convey meanings, can produce reactions, both favorable and unfavorable, far beyond the power of the printed page. More often than most counsel imagine the oral argument may change a judge's mind, no matter how carefully he may have studied the briefs in advance. There are several reasons for this: first, ideas are developed in the clash of oral argument that never appear on the printed pages of the brief; second, many judges by reason of their years of courtroom experience get more through the ear than they do through the eye; finally, the oral argument inevitably tends to develop far better than can any brief the case as a whole in a way that delights the mind of a judge who has an instinct for order and system.

I propose to deal first with the content of the oral argument and then with the style of its presentation and finally wtih a variety of obstructions that often impede or defeat counsel's purpose as an advocate. But in starting I must at least indicate that though oral argument has its roots in the printed brief and counsel may refer to it frequently, the oral argument is as different from a written brief as a love song is from a novel; and I am assuming that at your age you know the characteristics of each

of the latter without any need for definition or illustration
on my part. Counsel should never read from his brief except
perhaps the shortest of quotations from the most pertinent authorities. His argument should be delivered seemingly extemporaneously, preferably with nothing intervening between the court and
himself except a one-page outline of his argument which he should
keep before him so as to be sure not to skip any important point
due to any interruptions from the bench. Next to reading from the
printed brief itself there is nothing worse than reading *ad infinitum* from a sheaf of longhand notes which give evidence of having
been prepared late the night before the argument or even on
the train on the way to court. For the court the decision of an
appeal is the most important type of judicial business. The judges
realize they are making law. If they are worth their salt, they are
putting all they have in experience, in time, in energy and judgment into their work. They may never tell you so, but they cannot help but resent anything that it, or that seems to them to be,
casual about your preparation for your part of the judicial function. But more of this also later.

In most jurisdictions a succinct statement of the question or
questions to be argued is the first element of a brief. This is to
aid the court in reading the statement of facts that follows intelligently in the light of the issues. Yet many counsel vitiate this
requirement by obscure and verbose statements of the questions
to be argued. Why they do so is an unsolved problem of abnormal
legal psychology. Even the judges who do not read the briefs
in advance of argument are likely to glance first at the opinion
of the court below and then at the statement of the questions
in each brief while counsel is warming up. If the appellant's
headings are not enlightening but the respondent's are, whose
point of view, I ask you, is likely to be uppermost in the minds
of these judges as they listen to the argument? In those jurisdictions where the judges do study the briefs in advance of the oral
argument, many counsel seem to think that the court reads the
appellant's brief through before turning to the respondent's.
This assumes that the judges look on the briefs as literary efforts
to be digested in their entirety, but ordinarily they do not have
that point of view. They will read first of all the appellant's

statement of the questions to be argued and then the respondent's. They do this because they want to see whether counsel agree on the issues and if they disagree, in what respects.

After comparing the statements of the questions to be argued the judges wil next read the appellant's statement of facts, following that by a study of the respondent's statement of facts to see how far the parties agree on the facts and wherein they differ. If necessary the judges will look up in the record the points of difference to which they are referred to by appropriate citation of pages and lines in the brief. And may a kind fate help the lawyer who neglects to cite the appropriate spots in the record to justify his statement of facts and vainly expects the court to analyze the whole record for him in a hunt for something that it was clearly his duty to point out to the court. Worse yet is it for counsel to give an incorrect citation, either by design or mistake. But the most unpardonable offense of all is to cite a page and line of a record for a statement of fact made in the brief when no such fact appears on the cited page—when all that counsel really intended to do, or at least so he assures you at the oral argument, was to draw an inference from something that appears on the cited page without telling you that he is indulging in inference or from what he is drawing the inference. Words of inference or reasoning are plentiful in the English language, and it is unforgiveable for counsel to draw inferences in his statement of facts without saying affirmatively that he is so doing and without telling the court from what facts he is drawing them. If counsel do not agree in their statement of the questions to be argued, the court's task in reading the statements of fact is more difficult than it would have been had they agreed, but still the judges can read each statement of fact with the differing views in mind as to the questions to be argued.

Next the court will read the appellant's argument of law one point at a time, then the respondent's response thereto, then the appellant's reply, and come to a tentative opinion on each point. If counsel understood how briefs are read—indeed, if they understood the only intelligent way in which they can be read—the briefs and the oral argument would be far different from what many of them now are. It is surprising, too, how often even the most thoroughgoing study of the briefs fails to reveal some controlling point that will be developed for the first time on oral argument, driving the court back to a rereading of the brief after the oral argument and before the court conference at which a discussion of the case will take place.

In the written briefs the statements of the issues to be argued, as we have seen, comes first, but this is not necessarily so in the oral argument. If counsel are in agreement as to the questions to be argued, as is generally the case, a preliminary statement by the appellant of the questions will give point and direction to the subsequent statement of the essential facts. If, however, counsel have not agreed in their briefs on the questions to be submitted to the court for decision, counsel will do well ordinarily to state his facts first and then to pose the questions before plunging into his arguments of the law which he contends are raised by the facts. The ideal opening for an oral argument is the plain statement in a single sentence or two of how the case came to the court, its jurisdiction over the case, and what the question or questions are to be argued.

The greatest art in the argument of an appeal lies in the statement of the facts of the case. Counsel should know every fact in all of its ramification and be able to turn to it in the record without fumbling. Heaven forbid, however, that he should attempt in the statement of facts to tell all that he knows of what he should know! He must be able to extract from the record the relatively few facts that are significant and controlling, and to state them in language and in a manner that will capture the attention of the court. It was said of William Murray, better known as Lord Mansfield, the greatest of the English judges, that when he finished the statement of facts in a case, it seemed quite unnecessary to argue the law. Generally the facts should be summarized in chronological order. Always remember that the court does not know the facts of a case—indeed, the court is not interested in the facts except for the ephemeral purpose of deciding the case—and no effort should be spared to make sure that it has the correct view of them. Counsel will search far without

finding any better example of how to present the facts of a case
than may be found in some of the great opinions of Chief Justice
Hughes, who both at the bar and on the bench had the rare gift
of marshaling his facts so that they seemed to be marching to
martial music at his direction. A study of his opinions will reveal
a scarceness of adjectives and adverbs the vitality of his verbs,
and his precision in the use of prepositions and conjunctions.

Not only must counsel know every fact, all of its implications,
and where to find it in the record, not only must he be able to
state the pertinent facts succinctly and attractively, but he must
never under any circumstances misstate a fact. And if an adversary
should ever accuse him of misstating a fact, he must go to all
lengths in meeting and demolishing the challenge. I had this
happen to me once and I spent all but five minutes of my allotted
time in answering the charge, citing page and line of the testimony. I then condensed a half-hour's argument of the law into
five minutes and won my case, but I should have preferred to
have lost the case than to have had the court think I had misrepresented intentionally or innocently any fact of the case or
any rule of law. Sometimes the challenge may be facetious. I
remember a case in which I was representing Roger N. Baldwin,
long the distinguished head of the American Civil Liberties Union,
in an appeal to our former Court of Errors and Appeals on a charge
of unlawful assembly. He had been convicted and his conviction
had been sustained in our Supreme Court. The outlook was grim.
I described how a company of silk strikers marched out from their
headquarters to the City Hall Plaza in Paterson, two by two, led
by two beautiful girls carrying American flags, for the purpose
of reading the American Constitution there. One of the justices,
who had an eye for beauty, asked me where in the record it was
stated that the girls were beautiful. I told him with an air of
studied inocence that I had assumed the court would take
judicial notice of the fact that any girl carrying an American
flag was *ipso facto* beautiful. "Quite so, quite so," he murmured.
Subsequently he wrote an opinion that has become an outstanding landmark in this country on unlawful assembly. I also remember going to see Chief Justice Gummere of the New Jersey

Supreme Court on a pressing matter one summer and apologizing for interrupting him. He told me he was glad of the interruption because he had spent most of the day in the boresome work of checking item for item every statement of fact in the brief of a prominent lawyer because he didn't want to be unfair to the man's client, but he couldn't accept any statement this lawyer made without verification. All the while this particular lawyer fancied he was getting along famously with the court, though at a loss to understand his more than occasional reverses.

The statement of the questions to be argued and the presentation of the facts, important though they are, are merely introductory to the argument of the law. The argument of the law of a case is the climax of an appeal. Every appellant must face up to the fact that he has failed below either through the fault of the trial judge, the jury or himself. He has the laboring oar and he has to row upstream, and he should frankly recognize it by the earnestness of his manner, albeit restrained by courtroom decorum. The respondent, on the other hand, is in a different position, at least until the appellant has had his day in court. He has won his prize below and he is merely seeking to save it.

How best can counsel argue the law of a case on the appeal? Not, as I have already said, by reading the brief, nor by quoting at great length from innumerable cases, however pertinent. Rather will he dwell on the controlling rules of law and the principles underlying these rules. In discussing any decisions cited in his brief he should summarize the facts and state the holdings concisely, giving references to the pertinent pages of his brief, but he should not quote from them, save for short, pertinent excerpts. He will also give the court the benefit of the learning of the great writers on the subject under discussion and of the Restatement of the Law when it is available, but again without lengthy quotations. His argument at its best will move forward with logical precision and the successive steps in the development of his thesis will never be lost in a maze of citations and quotations. While developing his own case affirmatively, he will step by step be answering his adversary's contentions. His reasoning will always be as inseparable from the facts of his case as are the two sides of a coin. He will know a great deal more about the law of his case than he possibly can hope to tell the court in the limited time allowed for his argument. He will be as prepared to answer all questions that may be put to him on the law as he is on the facts. Particularly will he know all of the facts of each of the cases cited, not only in his own brief but also in his adversary's. Nothing can be more embarrassing to counsel than to have to admit he does not know the facts of a case he has cited in his brief.

Counsel should hesitate to rest his case on mere technicalities, however strongly embedded they may be in earlier decisions. He should never feel safe unless he can and does demonstrate the reasonableness and the utility of the rule he is advocating. More and more it is becoming important to tie the law of the case to its social environment and to show its relations to the assumptions of the age in which we live, and counsel should be prepared to do this in telling phrase that will serve to drive home the justice of his case.

Be brief, then, in your argument. Argue rather than quote. Stick to the facts of your case. Tie your argument to the great underlying principles of the law. Do not neglect to demonstrate the utility of the law you are advocating. And remember that even at its best listening to an argument is arduous work. Lord Denman was speaking out of a lifetime of experience when he said: "Remember also to put forward your best points first, for the weak ones are very liable to prejudice the good ones if they take the lead. It would be better advice to say never bring them forward at all, because they are useless."[7]

What has been said about the posing of the questions to be argued, the statement of the facts of the case, and the argument of law may have created the impression that the oral argument is simply a distillation of what appears in the brief. Nothing could be further from the truth, as becomes apparent when one adds to the picture the presence of opposing counsel and of the judges on the bench. Professor George Herbert Palmer in his little masterpiece, *Self-Cultivation in English,* adjures us to " 'Remember the other person, . . . every utterance really concerns two. Its aim is social. Its object is communication." The advocate will do well to always keep the judges in mind in arguing his appeal. It is their minds he is aiming to move, and yet he knows that there is nothing that would so quickly defeat his cause as the slightest attempt to prejudice their minds or to gloss over any of the pertinent facts of a case or to ignore any of the earlier opinions of the court, however unfavorable they may be. Indeed, he owes the duty to the court as a matter of ethics to disclose to the court any decisions adverse to his position of which opposing counsel is apparently ignorant and yet which the court should consider in deciding the case. Some lawyers flatter themselves on their ability to appeal to what they, off the record, term the "whimseys" of the judges. I have seen this done more than once to an individual judge, nauseating though it is. That a judge permits his leg to be so pulled is presumptive proof of approaching judicial senility. I have never, however, witnessed a successful consummation of the maneuver in an appellate court, for the simple reason that such an appeal to one judge would inevitably offend everyone else on the bench.

It is much more to the point to reflect on what is going on in the minds of the judges. This you can readily do by putting yourself in the judge's place and giving thought to how you, if you were a judge, would be affected by this or that alternative presentation of the matter. Yet I dare say that this is a thought that does not by any means occur to every counsel. In thinking of what you would do if you were judge, moreover, you should think not merely of what would be going on in your mind as you sat on the bench, but even more of what effect the argument would have on you in the discussions of the conference room and in the writing of the opinion.

It is not the glitter of the courtroom argument that counts in the ultimate decision of an appeal. When I was a law clerk my preceptor made it possible for me to hear some great arguments. Mr. A, as I shall call him, was a great favorite of mine. He was hearty and full of wit and humor. He was pugnacious and determined. He knew all of the facts and he knew all of the cases and he told the court about them with relish. He was often opposed by Mr. B, who had no flair at all for the rough and

tumble of oral argument, though he very obviously was not
without a sense of humor whether the tide was running with him
or against him.   His delivery was jerky and his favorite gesture
reminded me of nothing so much as a washwoman pushing the
clothes up and down a scrubbing board.   I was all for Mr. A and
after each argument I so reported to my preceptor.   Finally he
had enough of it; he asked me one day if I hadn't followed
through the decisions which had come down after each argument.
Mr. A had lost them all, Mr. B had won; Mr. B's arguments had
substance!

There are, of course, various types of judicial minds.   Some
judges are much given to standing by the existing order even
where others think it has outlived its usefulness; *stare decisis*
means much to them.   Then again there are some judges who
are much more influenced by the letter of a decision than they
are by the reason that underlies it and properly controls it.   Still
other judges realize that the law is forever seeking to escape from
the technical or irrational limitations of its earlier limited experience to a greater usefulness based upon a frank consideration of
things as they actually are.   Then, too, much depends on the
particular field of law under review; every court is more open to
new applications of old principles in certain fields of the law than
in others. Thus, it is generally easier to conform the law to new
situations in the field of commercial transactions than it is in
the law of real property, or in meeting new social conditions
in the administration of criminal justice than in changing the
law of trusts where the rights of beneficiaries are so frequently
involved.   Aside from knowing the type of judicial mind he is
addressing, the more a lawyer knows of the individual judge
the more persuasive his argument is likely to be, not so much
by knowing what to say as what to avoid saying.

Even more fundamental than any of these considerations, and
one that is all too often ignored, is the fact that until the court
has read the briefs or heard the oral argument, it has not the
slightest notion of the questions at issue or of the controlling
facts.   Indeed, we may go further and say that except in the fields
in which the particular judge may have specialized, he is quite

unlikely to know the law even of his own state in complete detail, though he should be expected to have grasped its general outlines and its underlying principles. Hence, the experienced advocate will not hesitate to state the questions at issue forcefully to sketch the controlling facts in such a way that they cannot be misunderstood, or even to state his views of the law with conviction, not in any sense of 'telling the court' but simply by way of imparting to a bench of interested judges the results of his thoroughgoing study of the controlling principles of law. His argument to satisfy every type of judicial mind should run the gamut from particular rules and decisions to the statement of underlying principles and should conclude with a skillful summation of his fundamental propositions of law keyed to the pertinent facts of his case.

There is one difference between the advocate's point of view and the judge's. Unconsciously the advocate seeks the strength to present his cause effectively; the prayer of the appellate judge is for *light*—light and *not heat*. The advocate will do well to remember, too, that the longer the apprenticeship served by a judge at the bar in the trial of cases and the argument of appeals, the more likely he is to be influenced and really moved by what he hears rather than what he reads, a consideration that can only serve to inspire counsel to his best effort in the appellate court. The advocate should keep in mind at all times that judges are not usually bookish fellows who have lost their touch with the actualities of life. In their work on the bench they have to deal practically with everyday problems very much as they did when they were practicing lawyers. Counsel will do well to respect the court's antipathy to contradictions in statements of facts. They irritate the mind of the trained judge out of all proportion to their intrinsic significance. Chief Justice White is reported to have said that if a lawyer stated that an incident occurred in March and a few minutes later mentioned it as happening in May, he felt as if he had been stabbed in the mind. After such an intellectual stabbing, can the appellate judge be expected to give credence to counsel's presentation of the law? Nothing can be more damaging to an argument or to counsel's standing with the court than for him to make a statement which the subsequent examination of the case by the court will show to be untrue. On the contrary, if you have a troublesome fact in your case or if some earlier decision of the court stands in the way of your argument, it is often better to admit it frankly rather than to attempt to conceal it. You may be sure that your adversary will spare no pains to exhibit it as its worst, and frank disclosure of your difficulty *may* enlist the help of the court. Lord Macmillan explained this psychological process with his customary felicity as "the instinct for rescue":

> When you know that your case is confronted with a serious difficulty in the shape of an awkward passage in the evidence or an embarrassing precedent, do not shirk it. Read the awkward passage with all emphasis or quote the authority without flinching, and point out the difficulty which it creates for you. You will almost invariably find that the first instinct of the judge is to assist you by pointing out that the evidence is less damaging to you than you represented or that the precedent is on examination distinguishable. The court is favourably disposed by the absence of all concealment of the difficulty and is attracted by the very statement of the difficulty to address itself to the task of solving or alleviating it. A good man struggling with adversity always makes an appeal to the judicial as well as to every other generous mind! A solution which the judge finds for a problem, too, is always much more valuable to the advocate than one which he himself offers to the Court, for the Court is naturally tenacious of its own discoveries and your opponent who ventures to challenge its solution finds his adversary not in you, but in the Court—a much more serious matter![8]

The most vexing problem in oral argument in the opinion of many lawyers is questioning from the bench. Questioning may be very helpful to counsel by revealing some difficulty a judge is having with the case and enabling counsel to resolve it, when otherwise the doubt would have been carried, unanswered, into the conference room. One of the greatest difficulties that the advocate has to contend with is the judge who is always identifying the instant problem with some other case that he has had years ago, even though the two situations are not in fact at all analogous. I remember hearing the late Chief Justice Crane of the New York Court of Appeals say of one of his colleagues, "If you will grant his assumptions of fact, his conclusions are irresistible." A frank question from the bench will frequently disclose some misconception of law or of fact that can be speedily disposed of to great advantage. On the other hand, if the question is one on which counsel is not prepared and on which he could not reasonably be expected to be prepared, he had better say so frankly and ask leave to supply a supplemental memorandum. It is foolhardy to answer a question on oral argument if one does not know what one is talking about.

There are, however, questions from the bench that are definitely disconcerting and that serve no good purpose. Such, e.g., are the questions that would have never been asked if the judge had read the brief. I gravely doubt the propriety of a judge asking questions without first doing counsel the courtesy of reading his brief, except, of course, under the English system with their skeleton briefs and, even more to the point, no time limits on argument. Next are the questions that admit of no answer. In the Chicago Water Diversion litigation years ago Colonel J. Hamilton Lewis had just finished the argument of his first point and time was running against him. As he was about to plunge into his second point, one of the distinguished jurists remarked, "But, Colonel Lewis, I don't think I quite understand your first point." The Colonel savagely brushed his pink whiskers upward and forward and in his remarkably metallic voice shouted, "Unfortunate, Sir, most unfortunate! My second point is . . . ." Even more subject to criticism is a running debate between counsel and a judge, for the very nature of their positions makes the contest unequal. Finally, there are questions, rare to be sure, where it is obvious that a judge is definitely endeavoring to thwart counsel's argument. Even then it is often better to suffer much rather than to make a retort discourteous. Not all of us have the wit to reply as one distinguished lawyer did a few years ago to a grossly improper question from the bench of the Supreme Court in the United States: "Your Honor, were I to attempt to answer your Honor's question, it would stand for all time as a classic example of the blind leading the blind." Questions from the bench call for as much skill and restraint as the answers from counsel. Rightly used, they can do much to facilitate sound decisions.

At what point should counsel answer a question of a judge? If the question is simple, especially if it is a fact question and can be dealt with readily without interrupting the train of the argument, it should be answered forthwith. Such a disposition of a question creates the best effect. On the other hand, if the inquiry is foreign to the point he is presently arguing and he can answer it better at a later point in his presentation, counsel should frankly say so, and then when he comes to that part of his argument he should expressly tell the judge that he is answering his earlier question. If approached in this way, the answers to questions from the bench can become the most stimulating part of the oral argument, but if counsel reflects any annoyance at being interrupted, either by voice or manner or the content of his reply, he will be doing his case unnecessary harm.

Able counsel has it within his power to curtail questions. Chief Justice Hughes, while at the bar, disliked questions. His biographer, Mr. Merlo Pusey of the Washington Post, has written me that his remedy was:

> . . . to present his case so clearly, so quickly, and so forcefully as to forestall any questions which might arise in the judge's mind before the question could be asked. That seems like a pretty large order, but he seems to have succeeded in many instances. Judge Cardozo told his associates on the Supreme Court that when Hughes appeared before him in New York, he always waited for twenty-four hours to make his decision to avoid being carried away by the force of Mr. Hughes' argument and personality.

Where the court is in the habit of asking questions, the advocate would do well to set aside at least a quarter, maybe more, of his allotted time for answering questions from the bench. Nothing can make counsel feel more harassed in the arguments of an appeal than to have planned a presentation using all of his allotted time only to find that the court is asking a wide variety of questions, with the result that he will either have to omit a part of his argument entirely or abbreviate each and every part of it. Above all the appellant should reserve at least a few minutes of his time for possible rebuttal of his adversary's argument. I have never been able to understand the ineptness of counsel who fail to do this; their helplessness and obvious agony is a pitiable sight to behold. Counsel, moreover, need feel no compulsion to use all his allotted time or to make a rebuttal argument, for rebuttal, like cross-examination, may be very dangerous. To be effective it must always be brief and on a telling point. The greatest advocates rarely exhaust their time. When they are through they sit down, much to the delight of the court and their waiting brethren at the bar. It is a great mistake, as your own John W. Davis has well put it, for counsel to think that he has a contract with the court to take his entire time.

Let me conclude my discussion of the substance of an argument on appeal with a reference to the most important document in the courtroom from the standpoint of the advocate. I refer to the one-page summary of his oral argument which he will have in clear sight on the lectern before him whether he needs to use it or not. It will doubtless have been written and rewritten a dozen times as counsel has worked and reworked each part of his oral argument to eliminate everything that is not essential. The summary is his best safeguard that each part of the oral argument will be treated in due proportion. Counsel will doubtless know it by heart, not from memorizing it but from its continued rewriting and rehearsal. In addition to noting the catchwords of his chief facts and his points of argument, the summary will contain page references to any items he may plan to quote from either the brief or the record. I need hardly add that it will be quite different in purpose from his brief. In its final edition it will be the capstone of his preparation for the oral argument. On the worth of his summary will depend in very large measure the success of his appeal. Its greatest merit is the aid that it furnishes to counsel in readjusting his argument to the exigencies of any situation that develops. With this map of the entire battlefield before him and with his forces and those of his adversary clearly indicated, he can call up his troops in the order that best suits his purpose. Without this means of adaptability many a cause would otherwise be lost in confusion.

ARGUING AN APPEAL: (2) STYLE

I have endeavored to present the chief rules that must govern counsel in planning the content of his oral argument. They arise out of the nature of an appeal and the personalities of the advocate and of the judges, for experienced counsel talks only to the judges on the bench and not for the benefit of the audience, even of newspaper reporters. An acceptance of the inescapable bounds from which he must not stray in his oral argument will do much to relieve the advocate from the tension which inevitably accompanies—and very properly should accompany—his appearance in an appellate court. The more he knows and the more he respects as a matter of conscious choice the boundaries that necessarily restrict the content of his argument, and the more thorough and painstaking his preparation, the greater will be his self-confidence in the courtroom. The success of an oral argument, however, depends to a large extent on the advocate's appearance and bearing, the shades of meaning revealed by a cultivated voice and his style. Intellectual vitality and buoyancy, too, regardless of physical age, is an indispensable quality of great oral argument. Holmes has expressed the thought magnificently in speaking of Sidney Bartlett: "His manner was no less a study than his language. There was in it dramatic intensity of interest which made him seem the youngest man in the room when he spoke." [9]

In the few seconds that it takes after his case is called for the advocate to rise from the counsel table, gather his papers and approach the lectern and utter the magic words, "May it please the Court," he will be giving the court a preview of his entire argument. If he stumbles over his chair as he leaves it, if he bundles his books and his papers, his glasses and his pencil in his arms like a schoolgirl, if he waddles to the scene of action, if he puts on his glasses and then takes them off before he starts to talk, the court will know just about what it is in for. On the other hand, if he walks promptly but unostentatiously to the lectern, places all of the appellant's briefs on the right, the respondent's on the left and the single-page outline of his argument on the middle of the table before him, the court will know before the utterance of a single word that he has an orderly mind and that he knows what he wants to do with it. If he has any papers to present to the court in opening, they likewise will be arranged in orderly fashion and conformable to the practice of the court. Order is an indispensable ingredient of effective argument, and everything the advocate does and says should reflect an orderly mind. Of course, he may fail at first for want of practice, for we are not born courtroom orators any more than we are born swimmers. From Demosthenes and Aristotle to Cicero and Quintilian, practice has been emphasized as the first law of public speaking. Several of the great chief justices of the United States are known to have practiced the delivery of their opinions before reading them in open court. Chief Justice White never felt himself equipped to present a matter for the consideration of the court in conference unless he could recite the facts of the case without referring to any papers. If these great men found practice necessary, what advocate dares to forego similar preparation?

The earlier the young lawyer begins to get used to the sound of his own voice, the better for him. If he learns how to stand; if he knows just how much volume to employ in speaking, for too much voice is quite as bad as too little; if he knows how to pace his delivery, not so slow as to weary the judges, not so fast that his thought does not sink in; if he understands the importance of emphasis, derived not necessarily from raising or lowering his voice or by increasing or decreasing its volume but by means of a simple pause, he will find that he is far less likely to be nervous than if he had to get acquainted with all of these things in the courtroom when his mind should be concentrated on the single task of transferring his argument from his mind to the minds of the judges. Forensic persuasion in an appellate court is a form of public speaking where moral earnestness and sincerity of manner command a high premium and where the slightest exhibition of artifice may destroy an argument no matter how sound its content may be. Gestures, at least planned gestures, would seem to be totally out of place. The advocate must never forget that his audience is likely to be as well versed as he in all of the techniques of delivery and even more sensitive than he may be to any false note. Counsel should learn to stand up straight, balanced on his two feet and to look the court in the eye. Nothing should come between him and the court. His summary should be in type so large that he does not need to be forever putting on and taking off his glasses to read it. One of the great objections to the reading of briefs or excerpts therefrom or of a long argument memorandum is that it interferes with counsel giving his entire attention to the audience that he is seeking to win.

The tone of voice that would be in keeping at a political rally or even in a large deliberative assembly is quite out of place in the appellate courtroom. The orotund quality, the accent of declamation, are as foreign to a good argument as they are to a prayer. We frequently hear it said that the ideal voice for public address is the conversational voice, but the term is likely to mislead, if not, indeed, to be entirely misunderstood. The conversational style of public address that harks back to Wendell Phillips is the ideal he must master. It is never casual or thin or unsustained, but always direct and personal. It requires no little art to talk conversationally using simple language yet with such intensity of purpose and such obvious elevation of thought as to carry with it the conviction that the speaker believes wholeheartedly what he is saying.

Always remember that there are no punctuation marks in an oral argument unless you put them there as you speak. There are no paragraphs in the courtroom unless you make your transition from one line of thought to another stand out as clearly as a pump handle. Avoid the use of such words as "former" and "latter." They are bad enough to encounter on the printed page when you can read back and discover—sometimes—what "former" and "latter" refer to, but you cannot do this when listening to a public address. You should likewise eschew at all hazards attempts at cross-references either forward or backward in your address. The judges just cannot follow you. Each sentence must stand by itself.

Much depends on a good opening. Counsel should plan and replan his first few sentences until he knows them by heart without ever having gone through the conscious process of memorizing them. If he can get his airplane off the ground in the first minute or two, the battle of delivery will be half won. Throughout the entire argument counsel must give the impression of complete intellectual earnestness and drive, while at the same time exercising self-restraint in word and manner. This in turn will reflect itself in the tempo of his delivery. Judge Parry in his *Seven Lamps of Advocacy* gives an interesting example:

> Bethell [later Lord Westbury], for instance, was a master of deliberation, remembering Bacon's maxim that "a slow speech confirmeth the memory, addeth a conceit of wisdom to the hearers." Shorthand writers listened eagerly to his speeches, fearing to miss a sentence that would ruin their report. Repetitions and unnecessary phrases were banned, and useless words he looked upon as a matter in the wrong place. His voice was clear and musical, and he had a telling wit. Students from the first thronged the court to learn his magic, and judges listened to him with respect. When he was a junior it is said that Sir John Leach, the Master of the Rolls, succumbing to his arguments, said, "Mr. Bethell, you understand the matter as you understand everything else." And that was the real secret of Mr. Bethell's eloquence.[10]

The time will undoubtedly come when his mind will play a trick on the advocate and for a moment he will not have the slightest idea of what he has been saying or what he wants to say next. There is an interesting passage in the *Autobiography* of Andrew D. White, the great president of Cornell University, in which he tells how President Tappan of the University of Michigan advised him as a young professor, when he confessed his trepidation at delivering his first extemporaneous lecture, ". . . never stop dead; keep saying something." The summary of your argument, which is the only paper spread before you on the lectern, will quickly help you out of any such temporary embarrassment. Another difficulty that frequently afflicts public speakers is the embarrassment of getting so snarled up in the involutions of a series of complex and compound clauses that they cannot find a way out of the labyrinth of a sentence they have constructed. This will never disturb an experienced speaker. He will break off when he is lost in the maze of his own words, saying, "In short," and then summarize his thought in a very brief and telling simple sentence. Let me quote Professor Palmer again:

> Of Patrick Henry, the orator who more than any other could craze our Revolutionary fathers, it was said that he was accustomed to throw himself headlong into the middle of a sentence, trusting to God Almighty to get him out. So must we speak. We must not, before beginning a sentence, decide what the end shall be; for if we do, nobody will care to hear that end.[11]

Nor should the speaker be too much disturbed if occasionally he finds himself giving voice to sentences with plural subjects and singular verbs or *vice versa*. The thought is paramount; grammar a mere means to an end.

The speaker will be helped much by a proper attitude toward the court. Too much respect is as bad as too little. Your attitude should be one of restrained decorum. The seats on the bench are, or should be, arranged at such a level that you can look the court in the eye, looking neither up nor down. Counsel will do well to seem to address the entire court, while at the same time keeping his eyes on the center of the bench. Sooner or later you will be attracted instinctively to some one particular judge without anyone knowing that you are addressing him especially, least of all the judge himself. You will find yourself preparing your argument with him in mind and observing the effect of your argument on him. I did this for a quarter of a century, and I doubt that the particular judge ever knew that I had any special interest in him, for he lived in another part of the state and I am sure that I never had a hundred words of conversation with him in his lifetime. But somehow or other he did write a considerable number of the opinions in the cases in which I prevailed.

Listening to oral argument five hours a day is hard work even if you have read the briefs in advance. Accordingly, if you can give the court a fraction of an excuse for a passing smile,

without, of course, seeming to lug your humor in, you will be
doing your cause no harm. But woe betide you if your effort
does not appear spontaneous! Remember, however, that it will
do you no good to become known as a professional humorist.

I have been speaking chiefly of the physical aspects of style
in oral argument, first, because these are matters which seem
most to concern the novice, and, second, because they are matters concerning which there can be no dispute as to the objectives to be sought and little room for argument as to the means
of attaining them. When we turn to style in the sense of diction,
we are dealing with larger considerations. "Style," the rhetori-
cians grandly tell us, "is the man." Whatever may be the truth
of this statement generally, with respect to oral argument style
is, first of all, the subject matter of the argument, next, the judges
to whom it is addressed and, finally, the man who is making the
argument. What might be entirely suitable diction in the appeal
of a conviction for murder would be entirely out of place in the
argument of the constitutionality of a tax structure. There is as
much variety in courts as there is in subject matter. Adaptability
to the subject matter and to the court stands foremost among
the requisites of style. The supreme test of diction in oral argument is whether it pours forth extemporaneously or seemingly so
and whether the advocate creates the impression that he is talking
realities that become lodged in the consciousness of his hearers
rather than mere words or propositions of law for the judges to dis-
sect calmly. Of one thing we may be very sure and that is, although
the advocate may be inspired by his cause and stimulated by the
judges he is addressing, no oral argument can be greater than
the man who is making it. His knowledge of the facts, his comprehension of the law, his grasp of human nature, his understanding of the assumptions of the age, his power of reasoning,
his knowledge of the wellsprings of literature, his skill in the
choice of diction, his moral character, and his passion for justice
set the limits beyond which his oral argument cannot hope to go.

THE LEGAL PROFESSION

The Six Factors in the Work of the Advocate.

[1] Law and Public Opinion in England During the Nineteenth Century 19-20 (1905).

[2] Address in Report, Fiftieth Annual Meeting of the Maryland State Bar Association 190, at 201, 203 (1915).

[3] Address at the Sixth Conference of the Inter-American Bar Association, Edison Institute, Dearborn, Mich., May 24, 1949.

[4] George Otis Shattuck in Speeches 70, at 72 (1913).

[5] Marjoribanks, For the Defence 235 (1929).

[6] Frankfurter and Hart, Business of the Supreme Court at the October Term, 1934, 49 Harv. L. Rev. 68, 107 (1935).

[7] Parry, The Seven Lamps of Advocacy 78 (1924).

[8] Some Observations on the Art of Advocacy in Law and Other Things 200, at 203-204 (1937). Cf. as to duty of lawyer to disclose to courts any adverse decisions, 35 A. B. A. J. 876 (1949).

[9] Sidney Bartlett in Speeches 41, at 43 (1913).

[10] Pp. 65-66 (1924).

[11] Self-Cultivation in English 15 (1897).

Modernization Of The Law

Administrative Law

The advent of the New Deal administration of President Franklin D. Roosevelt brought with it a proliferation of independent regulatory agencies created to aid in the solution of the myriad social and economic problems which were the progeny of the years of depression. The legal profession has not been noted for its receptivity to social reform. It was, therefore, no surprise that the growth of administrative power was greeted by the bar associations with something less than enthusiastic acclaim. The agencies were the outgrowth of social reform, hence the proponents of the status quo directed their attacks against them, confident in the belief that to destroy the agency would prevent the reform.

Vanderbilt regarded the growth of administrative law as the most important legal development of the twentieth century. He believed, however, that without proper judicial safeguards, administrative law constituted a threat to individual liberty. This view was contrary to the opinion prevailing at the time in academic circles. Some of the outstanding scholars in the field of administrative law thought that the administrators could be trusted to render decisions that were wise and just and should not be bound by a rigid framework of legalistic formalism which might impede the creativity required to provide solutions for the complex problems with which they were faced.

The scholarly defenders of the administrative process served on the Attorney General's Committee on Administrative Procedure which, in 1941, issued its memorable report on the functioning of the various regulatory agencies. Vanderbilt was one of the three members of the Committee who joined in a minority report calling for reforms. These reforms were later embodied in the Federal Administrative Procedure Act. Excerpts from the Report occupy an important place in the casebook on Administrative Law, edited in 1947, by Vanderbilt and Carl J. McFarland, one of those who had joined him in the minority report.

Professor Walter Gellhorn has written that in recent years the infringement of individual rights by administrative action in cases involving security risks, passports, deportation orders, etc., has awakened the scholars to the realization that all may not be well with administrative law and that, as a consequence, "the defenders and detractors of the administrative process have all but exchanged roles." Vanderbilt did not change his position. He had been right from the beginning.

The Administrative Procedure Act was signed by the President on June 11, 1964. From February 1 to February 7, 1947, Vanderbilt, then Dean of New York University Law School, gathered together at the school outstanding experts to discuss with governmental personnel, attorneys at law, and faculties of the law schools, the application of the Act and its impact on the federal administrative agencies. The Proceedings with notes were subsequently published in a 630-page volume. Vanderbilt's contribution to this book follows.

LEGISLATIVE BACKGROUND OF THE FEDERAL ADMINISTRATIVE PROCEDURE ACT *

I.

The year 1946 was marked by the passage of three very important pieces of legislation in the field of administrative law— the Legislative Reorganization Act,[1] the Federal Tort Claims Act,[2] and the Federal Administrative Procedure Act.[3] The last mentioned of these Acts has been aptly described as the most significant and far-reaching legislation in the realm of federal judicial administration since the Judiciary Act of 1789.[4] It is the purpose of these remarks to place the new Act in its proper historical setting, leaving to succeeding speakers the analysis of the Act, a critique of it and the study of its impact on the more important federal administrative agencies.

---

* Federal Administrative Procedure Act and the Administrative Agencies. (Warren, ed. 1947). Proceedings of An Institute conducted by the New York University School of Law.

First of all, in seeking to orient the Act in the field of administrative law, it is worth while to observe what, in concentrating our attention on the federal administrative agencies and the modern view of administrative law, we are otherwise all too likely to forget: administrative law in the original and proper sense of the term as defined by Goodnow, the pioneer American scholar in the field, is "that part of the law which fixes the organization and determines the competence of the authorities which execute the law, and indicates to the individual remedies for the violation of his rights." [5] In that sense administrative law not only dates back to the Year Books but it is still an integral and substantial part of the common law. By means of the extraordinary legal remedies—habeas corpus, quo warranto, certiorari, mandamus, prohibition—and the equitable injuction, not to mention suits for damages, every subordinate official was held to his appropriate sphere in the body politic as well as to the proper exercise of his power within that sphere to the end that there may be what the English have called the Rule of Law and what we have customarily referred to as "a government of laws and not of men." These writs or their modern statutory substitutes, to which must now be added the recent remedy of the declaratory judgment, still serve their ancient purposes and to an extent undreamed of by most law students, whose only law happens, unfortunately for them, to be law school law. As Maitland said, speaking in lectures on Constitutional History of England delivered in 1888:

> If you take up a modern volume of the reports of the Queen's Bench division, you will find that about half the cases reported have to do with rules of administrative law; I mean with such matters as local rating, the powers of local boards, the granting of licenses for various trades and professions, the Public Health Acts, the Education Acts, and so forth. Now these matters you cannot study here; they are not elementary, they are regulated by volumes of statutes. Only do not neglect their existence in your general conception of what English law is. If you do, you will frame a false and antiquated notion of our constitution. That constitution does not now-a-days consist merely of king and parliament, privy council, courts of law and some purely executive officers, such as sheriffs, obeying their commands. We have changed all that since the first Reform Act. The governmental powers, the sub-

ordinate legislative powers of the great officers, the Secretaries of State, the Treasury, the Board of Trade, the Local Government Board, and again of the Justices in Quarter Sessions, the Municipal Corporations, the Guardians of the Poor, School Boards, Boards of Health and so forth; these have become of the greatest importance, and to leave them out of the picture is to make the picture a partial one-sided obsolete sketch.[6]

The practical importance, even today, of administrative law in the traditional sense is just as important as it was when Maitland spoke and it cannot be ignored in any realistic study of government. Examples of administrative law in this original sense still abound in the federal reports, though they are naturally much more frequent in the states. Even suits for damages against public officials persist: only last year the United States Supreme Court held that the federal courts had jurisdiction over a suit for damages against agents of the Federal Bureau of Investigation resulting from alleged unlawful searches and seizures in violation of the Fourth Amendment and from alleged false imprisonment in violation of the Fifth Amendment.[7]

Currently, however, particularly in the federal field, a different and narrower definition of administrative law is in wide use. Administrative law, according to the Attorney's General's Committee on Administrative Procedure, is the law applicable to agencies which have "the power to determine, either by rule or by decision, private rights and obligations." [8] It contemplates agencies exercising not only executive powers but subordinate legislative or judicial powers or both. It is to such agencies with broad commingled powers rather than executive agencies pure and simple that the new Federal Administrative Procedure Act is primarily addressed.

The term "administrative law" is also used loosely to refer to all of the law made by administrative agencies and officials by rule or regulation as well as by decision or announcement of policy, but this use of the term is popular rather than legal. In its essence administrative law, either in its traditional common-law sense or its more recent meaning as relating to agencies exercising commingled powers of investigation, prosecution, rule-making and adjudication, relates to procedure and remedies rather than to substance. It would be humanly impossible for anyone to know the federal administrative law in the popular sense; it is decidedly possible since the passage of the Federal Administrative Procedure Act for any competent lawyer to comprehend federal administrative law in its technical, legal sense.

II.

The Federal Administrative Procedure Act owes its existence to the phenomenal growth of the administrative agencies. The Final Report of the Attorney General's Committee on Administrative Procedure [9] traces the origin of three agencies to the First Congress, finds eight more coming into existence before the Civil War, six others, including the Interstate Commerce Commission, in the ensuing period to the end of the century, nine more from 1900 to the end of World War I, and a like number from 1918 to the beginning of the Great Depression, and 17 more from 1930 to 1940—51 agencies in all, of which 22 are outside the regular executive department and 29 within.[10] World War II utilized or evoked a host of agencies, many of which came within the meaning of an administrative agency as defined by the Attorney General's Committee.[11] Of these agencies 9 antedated 1940,[12] 15 were created in 1940,[13] 44 in 1941,[14] 48 in 1942,[15] 28 in 1943,[16] 19 in 1944,[17] 19 in 1945,[18] and 20 even in 1946 [19]— in all 202 emergency agencies in addition to the 51 peacetime tribunals.

Nor does the number of administrative agencies tell the whole story. The vast increase in civilian employees from 1,703,099 in January, 1942, to 3,649,769 in November, 1945,[20] reflects the vast increase in jurisdiction and functions of the administrative agencies. Each successive administrative agency, moreover, under the grant of rule-making power in its enabling act, developed its own peculiar procedure, most of which, to be sure, followed in the main accepted patterns with minor but, to the practioner, troublesome variations.

It may be helpful to trace the movement for administrative reform in England. There, as in the United States, the growth of the new administrative order has been the subject of sharp attack.

There the leadership in the conflict was taken, not by, as in this country, the organized bar, but by the Lord Chief Justice and some of the members of the teaching profession.[21] In 1929 Lord Chief Justice Hewart of Bury published *The New Despotism*,[22] a slashing attack on the bureaucrats, whose creed he forcefully stated for them:

1. The business of the Executive is to govern.

2. The only persons fit to govern are experts.

3. The experts in the art of government are the permanent officials, who, exhibiting an ancient and too much neglected virtue, "think themselves worthy of great things, being worthy."

4. But the expert must deal with things as they are. The "four-square man" makes the best of the circumstances in which he finds himself.

5. Two main obstacles hamper the beneficent work of the expert. One is the sovereignty of Parliament, and the other is the rule of law.

6. A kind of fetish-worship, prevalent among an ignorant public, prevents the destruction of these obstacles. The expert, therefore, must make use of the first in order to frustrate the second.

7. To this end let him, under Parliamentary forms, clothe himself with despotic power, and then, because the forms *are* Parliamentary, defy the Law Courts.

8. This course will prove tolerably simple if he can (a) get legislation passed in skelton form, (b) fill up the gaps with his own rules, orders and regulations, (c) make it difficult or impossible for Parliament to check the said rules, orders and regulations, (d) secure for them the force of statute, (e) make his own decision final, (f) arrange that the fact of his decision shall be conclusive proof of its legality, (g) take power to modify the provisions of statutes, and (h) prevent and avoid any sort of appeal to a Court of Law.

9. If the expert can get rid of the Lord Chancellor, reduce the Judges to a branch of the Civil Service, compel them to give opinions beforehand on hypothetical cases, and appoint them himself through a business man to be called "Minister of Justice," the coping-stone will be laid and the music will be the fuller.[23]

Nor was he alone in his views. In *Bureaucracy Triumphant*[24] Professor C. K. Allen of Oxford, reviewing this work and Dr. F. J. Port's *Administrative Law*[25] sustains the Lord Chief Justice's philippic, in essence, by concluding:

> We remain unconvinced, then, of the necessity for specialist tribunals and a specialist administrative law. Unless we are prepared to admit that the whole constitutional centre of gravity has moved from the legislature to the executive; unless we are willing to be governed not by ourselves but through our representatives but by officials who are responsible to no electorate; unless, in short, we are disposed to revise the whole theory and practice of the constitution which has so long been our boast; unless we are prepared to go thus far, then what is most urgently needed, and what is in no sense beyond practical possibility, is to make administrative powers as responsible *de jure* as it is efficient *de facto*. And this we believe will be done only by means of a wholesome body of administrative law developed in harmony with the traditional principles of the general legal system.[26]

It has been the fashion in certain circles in this country to belittle the Lord Chief Justice's broadside, but it is interesting to to note that the rumors of the publication of his book led Lord Chancellor Sankey to appoint an able committee with Lord Donoughmore as chairman to investigate the legislative and judicial powers of ministers and to report on safeguards "to secure the constitutional principles of the Sovereignty of Parliament and the Rule of Law." The Report of the Committee on Ministers' Powers, published in 1932,[27] lists fifteen important recommendations for changes under delegated legislation [28] and eleven more under judicial or quasi-judicial powers.[29] After quoting at length from the Lord Chief Justice's work, the Report concludes:

> Our Report draws attention to certain parts of that machinery which are capable of improvement, and certain aspects of its working where specific safeguards are needed. At the same time we say deliberately that there is no ground for public fear, *if* the right precautions are taken. None the less the public should be grateful for outspoken criticism, even if exaggerated and we think that the critics whose warnings—and it may be attacks—led up to our investigations performed a useful service.[30]

It is significant to note, however, that Sir Cecil T. Carr, writing his *Concerning English Administrative Law*[31] in 1941, states that the recommendations of the Committee have received scant attention and is able to record only four slight changes looking toward compliance with them.[32]   The direct effect of the Report of the Committee on Ministers' Powers has been negligible. If its conclusions are sound—and they never have been questioned —there must have been much more than smoke to justify the Lord Chief Justice's attack.   In *Law and Orders*, published in 1945, Professor C. K. Allen has returned to the attack in a scathing indictment of the British bureaucracy in wartime, a book which American lawyers, interested in liberty, would do well to read.

Quite different has been the course of events in this country. Here the law schools, by and large, have neglected administrative law despite the pioneer work of Goodnow at Columbia, Freund at Chicago, Frankfurter at Harvard and Dickinson at Pennsylvania.[33] As late as 1934 only forty of the eighty law schools belonging to the Association of American Law Schools gave any course in the subject, and most of these courses were elective or postgraduate, interesting a select, but numerically negligible, group of students.[34]   Despite the agitation of the American Bar Association and the press for administrative reform, by 1938 only 52 out of 82 taught the subject.[35]   Law teachers, like lawyers generally, cannot easily give up their age-old intellectual habit of seeking all wisdom in the volumes of decisions reported in the English language, of provincial indifference toward the way other nations have solved similar problems, of a peculiar sort of unspoken contempt for legislation as a type of inferior law until such time as it shall have been construed by the courts, and of reluctance to apply the disciplines of economics and sociology to legal problems.

The credit for the reform of administrative procedure, as well as for saving the nation from the recall of judges, the recall of judicial decisions, and thirty years later from the court-packing plan, and for bringing about the exercise of the rule-making power in the federal courts in both civil and criminal cases, must be given to the practicing lawyers of the country working through the American Bar Association. A special committee on administrative law was appointed in 1933. Its annual reports have been veritable mines of information in a field where, until the Attorney General's Committee made its report, information was by no means easy to obtain.[36] In its successive studies the committee has also advocated various methods of solving the problems of administrative law.

As the work of the special committee progressed, other agencies lent a hand. In 1937 the President's Committee on Administrative Management recommended the complete separation of investigative-prosecuting functions and personnel from adjudicating functions and personnel.[37] In 1938 and 1939 the committee on administrative agencies and tribunals of the Section of Judicial Administration of the American Bar Association made its reports dealing particularly with state administrative law and submitted a model bill in that field.[38] The final report of the Attorney General's Committee on Administrative Procedure appeared in 1941 and submitted two bills, one by the majority, the other by the minority.[39] The legislative bill of the minority which was approved by the American Bar Association has furnished the substance of the new Federal Administrative Procedure Act. The National Conference of Commissioners on Uniform States Laws worked from 1940 to 1946 on a model state administrative procedure act which has been finally approved by the Commissioners but not yet published.[40] There have been several state reports, notably the Jacobs-Vogel report in New Jersey in 1941,[41] the Benjamin Report in New York in 1942,[42] and the Report of the Judicial Council of California on Administrative Agencies Survey in 1944.[43] All of this has been grist for the federal legislative mill.

III.

The first federal proposal for general administrative procedural reform seems to have been the Norris bill in 1929 for a separate administrative court.[44] A proposal for an administrative court of appeal was also made by Dr. Port in England the same year.[45] In 1936 the Logan bill[46] proposed the establishment of a Federal Administrative Court, having both trial and appellate divisions. Sessions of the trial division were to be held anywhere in the United States. The appellate division was to review all issues both of fact and of law and was to be permitted to take additional testimony. Its decision was to be final, subject to review by the Supreme Court by writ of certiorari. The Logan bill was drafted along the lines of the earlier recommendations of the special committee on administrative law of the American Bar Association. In 1936 the special committee approved in principle the establishment of a Federal Administrative Court but withheld approval of any pending bill. In 1937, however, the special committee abandoned its advocacy of the administrative court and since that date has concentrated on the improvement of administrative procedure. Senator Logan and Representative Celler introduced bills providing for the administrative court in 1938. Hearings were held on the Senate version of the bill, but no action was taken.

The first of the so-called administrative law bills was S. 915, introduced in the first session of the Seventy-sixth Congress in 1939 by Senator Logan. Representative Celler introduced an identical bill in the House. This Logan-Celler bill represented the first introduction in Congress of the American Bar Association legislative proposals on this subject, the bill having been formally approved by the Association in January, 1939. S. 915 was reported by the Senate Committee on the Judiciary, with amendments, on May 17, 1939. It was passed by the Senate on July 1, 1939, but was restored to the calendar by adoption of a motion to reconsider. Congressmen Walter at that time introduced H. R. 6324, which was practically indentical with the Senate bill as amended and passed.

Meantime the Attorney General's Committee on Administrative Procedure had been appointed in February, 1939. It requested the committees of the Congress to defer action on any of the administrative law bills until after the completion of the Committee's work. H. R. 6324, which came to be known as the Walter-Logan bill, was reported to the House, with slight amendments, on July 13, 1939. It was passed by the House on April 21, 1940, and sent to the Senate. Reported to the Senate on May 9, 1940, it passed, with amendments, on November 26, 1940. The Senate version was agreed to by the House on December 2, 1940. This bill was vetoed by the President on December 17, 1940, the veto message stating that it was deemed advisable to await the report of the Attorney General's Committee, at that time engaged in its study of the administrative agencies. The President's veto was sustained by the House.

Both the majority and the minority of the Attorney General's Committee had set forth model bills, and bills patterned after these models were introduced into Congress in 1941. The Senate Judiciary Committee held extensive hearings on three bills[47] but suspended consideration in that summer in view of the imminence of war and the then declared national emergency.

In 1944 interest in the admiinistrative processes was revived, particularly in view of the actions of some of the wartime agencies, and the bill approved by the American Bar Association was introduced as S. 2030 and H. R. 5081. No action was taken on these bills but a revised and simplified bill, S. 7 and H. R. 1203, the McCarran-Sumners bill, was introduced in 1945. This bill received much attention. First, the Committees on the Judiciary of the Senate and the House requested the administrative agencies to submit their views on the bill in writing. Then in May the Senate Committee published the bill as introduced and a tentatively revised bill in parallel columns. Next the administrative agencies and all other interested persons were invited to comment on the revised text. Then these comments were analyzed by the Committee's staff and a second pamphlet was issued in June, 1945, setting forth in parallel columns: (1) the text of the bill as introduced, (2) the text of the tentatively revised bill previously published, (3) a general explanation of provisions with references to the report of the Attorney General's Committee on Administrative Procedure and other authorities, and (4) a summary of views and suggestions received. The Attorney General designated representatives of his Department to obtain and to correlate the views of the administrative agencies and to discuss the matter with other interested persons. Thereafter a bill was drafted. The Attorney General submitted a favorable report on the bill. Most significant are the committee reports and the Congressional debates on the bill as it passed the Senate on March 12, 1946, and the House on May 24, 1946, without opposition in either house. President Truman signed the bill on June 11, 1946.

The painstaking work of the Committees on the Judiciary of each house, as incorporated in their reports, and the cooperation of the Attorney General did much to account for unanimity of legislative opinion on what had for years been a controversial issue, but there can be no doubt that the desire of the members of Congress to pass the bill on the subject, even thought it might fall short of the perfect statute that individual members of Congress might desire, was an important factor in eliminating any possible opposition. In the debates in each House it was made amply clear that if the new Act should in anywise fail to protect individual rights, Congress was prepared to return again to the consideration of the problems of administrative procedure.

IV.

Nor did the Act satisfy everyone outside of the Congress. There are many who favor a complete separation of the investigating, prosecuting, and rule-making functions from adjudication, such as has long existed in the instance of the Bureau of Internal Revenue and the Tax Court. The minority of the Attorney General's Committee took the position that:

> in cases involving factual issues between the investigating or prosecuting agents of the Government and private parties, the same agency should not issue complaints, prosecute the proceedings thereunder, and adjudicate the cases where there is no opportunity for the citizen to have a readjudication by an independent tribunal. This is the typical situation where the prosecutor-judge combination is criticized. In practice, it takes two forms—either the agency initiates proceedings on its own motion, or private parties make complaints and the agency then makes those complaints its own (as often happens in prosecuting attorneys' offices). But these differences in form are not significant. Here we think complete separation, with adjudication by wholly independent agencies, is normally to be preferred.[48]

The President's Committee on Administrative Management was of the same view:

> Furthermore, the same men are obliged to serve both as prosecutors and as judges. This not only undermines judicial fairness; it weakens public confidence in that fairness. Commission decisions affecting private rights and conduct lie under the suspicion of being rationalizations of the preliminary findings which the Commission, in the role of prosecutor, presented to itself.[49]

The minority of the Attorney General's Committee conceded that there were obvious difficulties in the separation of functions in areas of administrative law in which the practice of administrative discretion is large, as in passing upon licenses or applications for benefits.[50] It also stated that an administrative agency may properly adjudicate cases between two private parties, rather than between the Government and a party as in the instance of the reparation cases of the Interstate Commerce Commission.[51] In testifying before a subcommittee of the Judiciary Committee of the Senate, I added a third exception to the doctrine of complete separation of functions: one of the chief reasons justifying the Congress in setting up administrative agencies with commingled powers is that Congress does not have the detailed information in the field it is seeking to regulate to enable it, even if it had time at its disposal, to draft the necessary regulations. This detailed knowledge can best be accumulated through one body conducting investigations, prosecuting complaints, adjudicating cases and making rules. This does not, however, justify the commingling powers *ad infinitum,* but only for limited periods varying from two to three to five years while the Commission was accumulating experience for competent rule-making.[52] Subject to these exceptions, in the opinion of many, the reasons for complete separation of functions are still controlling. The present Act represents the best compromise that adherents of this school of thought believed themselves able to obtain.

On the other hand, there have been fears expressed by some that a general act governing administrative procedure might interfere with the flexibility of the administrative process or, indeed, to quote the agitated language of some, "put it in a strait jacket." In this connection it may be well to recall similar misgivings of a century or more ago when courts were consolidated, law and equity merged and the forms of action abolished, but they proved groundless. It may be well to remind ourselves that chancery practice has more than once required revision to save itself and that the Star Chamber, though it served an extremely useful purpose in preserving law and order in a turbulent period—indeed, Maitland suggests that it saved the English constitution [53] — brought about its own undoing by its excesses. Executive justice, we need always to remember, tends to be heady. Whichever school of thought one may adhere to, it is conceded on all sides that the present Act is in line with the general tendency, illustrated in the judicial field by the Federal Rules of Civil Procedure and the Federal Rules of Criminal Procedure, to simplify and streamline the rules of adjective law.

Procedure

"Perhaps no man in the history of American law has more thoroughly dedicated himself to procedural reform than has Chief Justice Vanderbilt of New Jersey." (Professor Harold G. Reuschlein in Jurisprudence—Its American Prophets). For his accomplishments in bringing New Jersey from procedural darkness into the forefront of advanced judicial administration and procedure, Vanderbilt is compared to David Dudley Field in the Field Centenary Essays, a compilation of scholarly reports which celebrated the one hundred years of procedural reform commencing with the Field Code.

Vanderbilt often lamented the "allergy" of lawyers to procedural change. There is an awareness that substantive law must be adapted to the needs of the times but, he charged, outmoded procedures of yesterday, under which our courts are struggling to decide the controversies of today, meet with inertia and indifference on the part of the lawyers. He called upon the law schools to assume responsibility in acquainting the student at the outset with basic problems of procedure. He asked that procedure be taught in a way which will relate to what actually occurs in the courtroom rather than as a set of technical rules. To further this objective, and using the Federal Rules as a base, he published his **Cases and Other Materials on Modern Procedure and Judicial Administration.** Judge Harold Medina of the United States Court of Appeals in his review of the book said:

Chief Justice Vanderbilt approaches the subject from a number of entirely new angels. He would have procedure taught "at the outset" of the student's course in law school; he would make it modern and up-to-date, with only such historical references as are essential to an understanding of the subject; he would intermingle civil and criminal procedure so that they would appear, as they truly are, part of a single integrated system; and he would arouse the zeal and enthusiasm of the student by giving him first of all some understanding of the great battles which have been fought for procedural reform, and a matter-of-fact survey of many practical and intensely interesting current problems having to do with the selection of judges and general jury panels, the education of lawyers, the Canons of Ethics, the integration of courts and so on.

CASES AND OTHER MATERIALS ON MODERN PROCEDURE AND JUDICIAL ADMINISTRATION *

I. THE IMPORTANCE OF PROCEDURE IN THE WORK OF THE PRACTICING LAWYER AND IN THE STUDY OF LAW

Procedure in the widest sense of the term—judicial, legislative and administrative—is an integral part of every attorney's daily work, whether or not he is a trial lawyer. Even an office practitioner who never goes to court always works, or at least he always should work, with the thought in mind that his labors may some day be put to the acid test of litigation. It will do a lawyer little good to know all the substantive law in the books if he does not

* Cases and Other Materials on Modern Procedure and Judicial Administration 1-27. N.Y., Washington Square Pub. Corp. 1952.

know how it is actually applied in practice. The courtroom thus being implicit in all sound legal work, it necessarily follows not only that the courses in substantive law should be studied in the light of this controlling fact, but also that procedure should be recognized as the core of the law school curriculum. Skill in procedure, in research as to both facts and law, and in legal reasoning are the chief instruments in the lawyer's kit. With them he is equipped to solve any problem in the law. But while legal reasoning has long been stressed in the law schools, and while experience in legal research is recognized as the great reward of work on a law review, the art of research as to facts and, to a large degree, the essentials of procedure have not only been neglected, but procedure has generally been looked down on by law students and, it must be added, by most law teachers and many practitioners.

This professional allergy to procedure is the more curious in view of the important part that procedure plays in a lawyer's life. It is by no means uncommon for a client to know more about the substantive law of his business and, indeed, of the very problem that brings him to his lawyer than his lawyer does—in fact, the better the client, the more likely is this to be the case—but he wisely comes to his lawyer for advice on procedure in the courts, before legislative committees and in the administrative agencies. Is it not obvious, therefore, that any member of the bar who cannot give his client expert and realistic counsel on matters of procedure is not worthy of being called a lawyer? Nor will he attract intelligent clients or keep them long, for his advice will not stand the test of the judicial, the legislative and the administrative forums. Over the centuries, moreover, much of our substantive law has grown out of judicial procedure and has been in large measure molded by it. "Whenever we trace a leading doctrine of substantive law far enough back, we are very likely to find some forgotten circumstances of procedure at its source." [1] This process, furthermore is still going on from day to day. A rule of the substantive law in action, as every practitioner knows, is likely to be quite a different thing from the same rule as aid down in the law books, and it may well prove elusive to one who is not versed in both the science and the art of procedure.[2] The growing law does not develop in a vacuum. It is fought out in the very real struggles of human beings in the trial courts and refined and systematized in our appellate tribunals, and it is therefore quite beyond the comprehension of those who do not understand the judicial process in action.

But there are deeper reasons for the systematic study of the principles of procedure than the desire to excel in giving one's clients the highest kind of professional service. No substantive rights, not even the rights guaranteed by the federal and state constitutions, are really assured to one until he is vouchsafed the most fundamental right of all—the right to a fair trial in both civil and criminal cases. Of what real avail is a suit for the breach of a contract or a libel action for injury to one's reputation, if the judge on the bench or the jury in the box or one's attorney at the counsel table is either incompetent or corrupt, or if the system of procedure under which they attempt to function is dilatory, cumbersome or exceedingly expensive or unduly restricts the search for truth? Even today after several centuries of development in the law a fair trial is not always assured in its entirety by our constitutions, statutes, rules of court, decisions and practice. As every lawyer knows and as every law student should quickly learn, the right to a fair trial is still being developed in the courts.[3] More progress, to be sure, has been made in this vital matter in the last fifteen years than in the entire preceding century, yet much remains to be secured. Every lawyer has a definite professional stake in the orderly and complete development of the right to a fair trial, just as every honest litigant has a personal interest in it. Indeed, it is fundamental in our civilization. On it in the last analysis depends popular respect for law, and without general respect for law our kind of government cannot long survive. One of the most important aspects of the study of procedure for the individual student, therefore, is to learn to what extent the right to a fair trial is protected by constitution, statute, rule of court, court decision and practice in the jurisdiction in which he intends to practice, and how much is yet to be achieved, for on his admission to the bar he, too, will be charged with the duty of perfecting it. It will doubtless come as a shock to many law students to see how far short of fair standards the courts of their own state fall, but the shock is essential to a realization of the challenge that defective standards impose on him. As Sir Maurice Sheldon Amos aptly puts it, "Procedure lies at the heart of the law." [4]

Quite as fundamental as the right to a fair trial in the protection of all our substantive and procedural civil rights is the due enforcement of the criminal law. It will do one little good to obtain his just deserts in the civil courts, if he is deprived of them through some unpunished breach of the criminal law. Many lawyers and most people take the enforcement of the criminal law for granted, but this, it is submitted, is scarcely warranted by the facts. Year after year the Director of the Bureau of Federal Investigation has reported on the extent of crime in the United States. He tells us:

> Every 5 minutes during 1950 someone in the United States was feloniously assaulted or killed. During each average day 146 persons were robbed and the cars of 468 others were stolen. With the passing of each day 1,129 places were entered by burglars and in addition every 30 seconds on the average throughout the year a larceny was recorded. [5]

These reports take on additional significance when it is recalled that in September, 1949, the National Municipal Association, representing 9,500 municipalities, petitioned the Department of Justice of the United States to investigate the taking over of municipal governments in many localities by organized gangs of criminals. [6] The hearings and reports of the Kefauver Committee, appointed by the United States Senate to investigate these charges, have demonstrated that the evil has not been overstated. [7] With these things in mind there should be no dissent from the proposition that it is quite as essential for the lawyer to understand criminal procedure and the enforcement of the criminal law as it is for him to know the civil law and practice. Manifestly the essentials of civil and criminal procedure should be studied together, for not only do they have much in common, as a glance at appendix D will show, [8] but they are interrelated historically. The first aim of the law, both civil and criminal, has always been to preserve order. Historically the King's Peace [9] was no mere phrase, but a very real factor in the lives of men. The common origin of the law of crimes and of torts is attested by the language of indictments and of the original writs by which the earlier tort actions were commenced.[10] It is important that we see clearly that it is only the rights that can be adequately enforced in or civil and criminal courts that constitute the sum of our actual freedom. Without such enforcement our alleged rights become a snare and a delusion. In this connection we shall do well to keep in mind the pointed warning of Mr. Justice Brandeis that "In the development of our liberty, insistence upon procedural regularity has been a large factor."[11]

To maintain that procedure should be the core of the legal curriculum does not mean, however, that the law school should attempt to teach the minutiae of practice at common law or in equity or of the procedures that have grown up in many states through the overamendment of what were once relatively simple codes, each amendment being an attempt to cure some real or fancied defect of the original rule and all to often leading in turn to another series of amendments designed to overcome its real or fancied shortcomings. On the other hand, the overemphasis on courses expounding the substantive law of our commercial civilization to the neglect of the fundamentals of the science of procedure is as unjustifiable and as shortsighted as it would be to omit clinical demonstrations and laboratory work in the education of a prospective surgeon in favor of a mere series of lectures on human anatomy and physiology. Procedure, it is important to stress, is the prime bread-and-butter subject of the practitioner. He must know it intimately both as a science and as an art, but the law school does its duty to its students if it inculcates in them the essentials of the science and prepares them for the later study of it as an art in their practice. It is intolerable, however, that law students should be allowed to graduate from law school or to be admitted to the bar without having learned the fundamentals of taking a civil and a criminal case through the courts. They must know more than the bare bones of the law; they must understand it in action as a living, growing institution. Once they have learned the principles of the science of procedure, they are ready for the mastery of it as an art; without such knowledge they may spend their lives, to quote Bolingbroke, " in a mean but gainful application of all the little arts of chicane," but they will not be lawyers.

Yet, so great has been the ascendancy of the courses in private substantive law for the last three quarters of a century that procedure has been neglected in most law schools. In my time in law school three hours for a single semester sufficed to teach Ames' *Cases on Pleading,* the leading casebook of half a century ago. This casebook did not touch on the jurisdiction or the organization of the courts, or on the qualifications of judges, of jurors or of members of the bar, or on how defendants were brought into court, or on how rules of procedure came into existence. Pleading was the all-important topic. Pretrial procedures were not discussed—indeed, some of them had not yet been developed—nor was the student instructed in what happened at the trial or in subsequent proceedings to review errors committed there or to satisfy the judgment obtained by the successful party. Pleading was the beginning and the end of our course in procedure and even what consideration was given to it was confined to civil actions at law—criminal procedure, equity pleading and probate practice being altogether ignored. Many of the cases assigned for study, moreover, seemed remote from the realities of life; indeed, the only things that I remember with any distinctiveness from our study of demurrers, traverses, pleas in confession and avoidance, novel assignment and departure (the chief topics we studied) are that it was demurrable to plead that one threw a stone gently,[12] but that it was not demurrable to plead that the events alleged occurred on the Island of Minorca, to wit, at London, in the parish of St. Mary le Bow in the ward of Cheap,[13] provided one did it under a videlicet! All of this seemed to me then, and after thirty-four years of practice largely in the courts followed by some years on the bench still seems to me, an utterly inadequate preparation for understanding what is going on in the courts today. Yet while we were being fed these meager rations, we were solemnly enjoined by our instructor and the textwriters to which we were referred to peruse the precedents of special pleading in *Williams' Saunders Reports* in order to transform ourselves into modern Daniel Websters.[14]   Indeed, on the very title page of our casebook was the admonition in law French from Littleton's *Tenures* (1481), which for the convenience of the modern student I venture to translate:

> And know ye this, my son, that this is one of the most
> honorable, laudable and profitable things in our law; to

have the science of well pleading in actions real and personal; and therefore I counsel thee especially to set all thy courage and care to learn that.[15]

Fortunately, before we attempted to comply with this onerous admonition some of us hit upon Lord Chief Justice Coleridge's address to the law students of Birmingham, and there we learned on high authority that special pleading had disappeared from the English common law just in time to avoid ruining it.[16] Accordingly, we confined our efforts to a perusal of McKelvey on *Common Law Pleading,* a work which paralleled Ames' *Cases* with such remarkable fidelity as to endear its author to every law student who possessed the wisdom to conserve his "courage and care" for more auspicious objectives.

I would not leave the impression that the men who revolutionized legal education by the introduction of the casebook system were not masters of procedure, for Langdell's *Summary of Equity Pleading* (1877) and Ames' *Legal Essays* [(1913)] are convincing proof to the contrary. Ames was primarily interested, however, in teaching the fundamental subjects of the substantive law and the course in pleading was intended chiefly as an aid to the better understanding of the cases studied in the courses in substantive law. In this attitude he was but following the tradition of the early American law schools that procedure could best be learned through a clerkship in a law office under an able preceptor who would take a personal interest in the professional education of his apprentice. This method, while attractive in theory, has long since proved untenable in practice. The practioner who had mastered the judicial process in its common-law, equity and probate branches in both the trial courts and on appeal—in short, an all-around lawyer— was and still is a rather exceptional figure at the bar. He is likely, in addition, to be an exceedingly busy man. Even if he had the time to instruct his clerks, the chances are that he would prove to be more interested in discussing his own experiences in the art of trying cases than in expounding the essentials of the science which in the public interest should govern such proceedings. That anything approaching a science or art of procedure has survived this process of instruction is proof both of the tough fiber of the law and the ingenuity of the profession. All too often the young lawyer has been left to learn his procedure at the expense of his clients. The unethical nature of this course becomes apparent if we ask ourselves what we, or the community, would think of a physician who learned the basic techniques of his profession at the expense of his patients. However this may be, one will not find a page devoted to procedure in all of the four stout volumes of Kent's *Commentaries*, the great classic from which our professional forebears gained their knowledge of the principles of American law. Nor are the reasons for this omission far to seek. Procedure at common law was an agglomeration of traditions, fictions, decisions, rules of court, statutes and medieval scholastic logic culminating in the absurdities of special pleading against which Lord Chief Justice Coleridge inveighed to the delight of a new generation of law students. It simply did not lend itself to orderly academic presentation. Says Holmes, "When I began [1864] the law presented itself as a ragbag of details," [17] and to no branch of the law was his observation more peculiarly applicable than to procedure.

The defects of the course in procedure of a half century ago were not merely in the omission of topics essential to an understanding of the work of the courts or in the inclusion of the technicalities of an overrefined system of special pleading. Indeed, no subject in the law school curriculum has been more sinned against than procedure, for in addition to the crimes of omission and inclusion I have mentioned, procedure was, and in most schools still is, made to bear a heavy teaching burden that should have been assumed long since by the substantive law courses in contracts, property and torts. Nobody will gainsay the importance to an understanding of our common-law system of a knowledge of the essentials of the forms of action at common law, for as Maitland has truly said, "The forms of action we have buried, but they still rule us from their graves." [18] They rule us, however, not as procedure but as substantive law, and the discussion, therefore, of debt, covenant and assumpsit should be primarily the responsibility of the instructor in contracts while trespass, case, trover, detinue and replevin should be left to the course in torts, and ejectment should be a charge on real property. To cast the burden of teaching these important but to us strange concepts of centuries ago on the introductory course in procedure was to make assurance doubly sure that it would be the most unpopular as well as the least effective course in law school. Yet so ingrained is the custom in the law schools that it is almost too much to hope that the courses in substantive law will soon assume their rightful responsibility for teaching the forms of action unless teachers of procedure rise up and refuse to do so.

What procedure has been taught, moreover, has traditionally been presented historically. Lawyers incline by training as well as by temperament to rely on experience and authority. It is this instinct that tends to give stability to the law. It is a great source of the strength of the common law, unless it is pushed to the extreme of ignoring either contemporaneous facts at hand or valuable experience to be gained from other jurisdictions. In the field of procedure, however, this predilection for the historical approach has unfortunately led the beginning student in the law over a rough road all the way from trials by ordeal, by battle and by compurgation (ideas quite foreign to his thinking and experience) to the gradual development of trial by jury, but rarely has he been told how a modern jury panel is summoned or a grand jury selected, though in these seemingly simple processes there are grave constitutional questions lurking which should be dealt with in any thoroughgoing course in procedure. Then he has been drawn through the technicalities and complexities of the various forms of action at common law without having them related intimately and in detail to the principles of contract, tort and property he was studying in other courses, although, as we have observed, these subjects of the substantive law owe a large part of their modern content to the characteristics of these very forms of action. All this learning of centuries ago baffles the neophyte in the law at a time in his studies when what he most needs from his course in procedure is a clear-cut presentation of what actually is going on in the courts today, in order to understand the decisions that he is reading in his casebooks on the substantive law. Failing to get these things in his courses in procedure, is it to be wondered then that he joins with his fellows in condemning the course in procedure as the most unsatisfactory course in the curriculum? Every principle of sound psychology dictates the desirability of starting off the student with the relatively simple and fundamental concepts of modern procedure rather than with the obsolete and complicated system of practice that prevailed in earlier days and that is entirely alien to his life and thinking. It seems to me that much of the confusion and the perplexity that have been taken for granted by law school faculties as the inevitable lot of the beginner in the law could be obviated if he were introduced at the earliest possible moment to the essentials of modern procedure. One great by-product of such a study of practice would be that he would understand more easily the procedural aspects of the cases he was studying in his other courses and thus be free to concentrate in those courses on the problems of substantive law.

I would not have it thought that I am opposed to teaching a law student in due season the essentials of the history of procedure, not, of course, from the standpoint of a legal antiquarian, but as an indispensable prerequisite to a thorough understanding of the development of the law. First, however, I would introduce the student to the best simplified practice of today through the rules of court in which it is embodied and the leading cases interpreting these rules. Having once grasped the fundamentals of modern procedure, he can then explore with more understanding and zest the history of how our present-day procedure came to be what it is—and incidentally be thankful for having been spared learning the cumbersome technicalities of by-gone ages as set forth in Tidd's *Practice*,[19] Chitty on *Pleading*,[20] and Daniell on *Equity Pleading and Practice*,[21] or as laid down in some of our complicated state codes of procedure. In this historical phase of his study he will be interested to see how often what now purport to be new ideas are really very old ones with new names, stripped, fortunately, of the techicalities with which they had become encumbered over the centuries and rededicated to a more efficient use. I would also have the student realize from the outset the defects as well as the merits of the procedure of the particular state in which he expects to practice law. He should study the procedure of the state of his choice not as something superior to the practice of all other jurisdictions and therefore set apart, or as something absolutely perfect and therefore fixed and immutable, but rather as a working system that no matter how good it is needs constantly to be developed in competition with the best that has been achieved elsewhere. In short, he should be concerned not only with what the law of procedure in his state is and with the essentials of what it has been, but also with what it should be. Procedure, it is always well to remember, is merely a means to an end, albeit a most important means, as we shall see, insofar as a man's life and liberty and his property are concerned. Lawyers constantly draw on the best experience of other states in dealing with matters of substantive law; why, therefore, should we be provincial as to our procedure?

Until recently the materials for the kind of a course in procedure that I have been describing have not been available. With the adoption in 1938, however, of the Federal Rules of Civil Procedure and in 1944 of the Federal Rules of Criminal Procedure, and with the extensive revision of the Federal Rules of Civil Procedure in 1947 and 1948 after a decade of use, we can at long last introduce the law student at the outset of his studies to a simple system of modern procedure that is in force in the federal courts throughout the country and is fast being accepted on the civil side in the several states. Arizona, Colorado and New Mexico were the first states to take this advanced step, adopting the federal rules as governing their own civil practice in 1940, 1941 and 1942 respectively. More recently Delaware, Minnesota, New Jersey and Utah have adopted the federal rules practically in toto, and a substantial portion of the federal practice has been adopted in California, Connecticut, Florida, Iowa, Maryland, Missouri, New York, North Dakota, Pennsylvania, South Dakota, Texas and Washington. In addition many other states have adopted individual rules from the federal system.[22] The federal civil rules are finding acceptance in other jurisdictions for good reasons. First, these rules embody the work over several years of outstanding experts selected by the Supreme Court of the United States for their familiarity with the best available practice everywhere. They were aided by the federal bench and the bar of the entire country to whom successive drafts of the rules were submitted for comment and criticism. Second, they provide not only the simplest, but the most flexible and workable system of procedure that the common law has known. Third, and most important, the fundamental premise of the federal rules is that a trial is an orderly search for the truth in the interest of justice rather than a contest between two legal gladiators with

surprise and technicalities as their chief weapons, an outmoded
point of view that unfortunately still lingers on in all too many
states. But sound as the federal rules are, these considerations
alone would not bring their acceptance elsewhere, for, as I have
just indicated, we are little given to borrowing from state to state
in matters of procedure. Fortunately, however, for the ultimate
adoption of the federal civil rules throughout the country, they
are in open competition in every state with the local practice in
peculiarly favorable circumstances. The run of civil cases in the
federal courts is likely to be more important than the run of civil
cases in the state courts. The best lawyers in each state are likely
to appear in important litigation and thus become familiar with the
federal practice. They have often been forced against their initial
impulses to admit the superiority of the civil practice in the federal
courts and so been brought to urge its adoption locally.[23]   Nor
has the process been wholly involuntary. Many suits may be
brought either in the federal or the local courts. The 'shopping'
for the best rule of law for the purposes of one's case that was
possible under *Swift v. Tyson*[24] until it was overruled by *Erie
Railroad v. Tompkins*[25] has been followed in recent years by
shopping for the best rules of procedure[26] and, it may be added,
for the best judges, jurors and judicial admistration for one's
particular case. Because of this open competition in every state
the basic pattern of the federal civil rules is bound ultimately to
prevail throughout the country.[27]   For all of these reasons it
seems advisable to introduce the law student at the outset of his
course to the Federal Rules of Civil and Criminal Procedure. Not
only will he learn the simplest, most flexible and best system of
procedure now available and that is now being extensively used
in this country and that will ultimately prevail in its essentials
everywhere, but he may use the federal rules as a basis of comparison with the procedure of his own state. Singularly enough,
despite their obvious availability the Federal Rules of Civil Procedure have seldom been made the basis of an introductory course
in practice, nor indeed have they even been taught in the law
schools generally at any stage in the curriculum, preference being
still given in most law schools to the local practice. And so far
as I know, the Federal Rules of Criminal Procedure have never
been presented with the Federal Rules of Civil Procedure, related

though they are at so many points. Indeed, they seem never to have been even printed together, so general is the neglect of criminal procedure.

Nor has there been available until recently any convenient approach to the crucial topics of practice and procedure in the several states from a comparative point of view. Generally local practice has been taught as a watertight compartment in the law, carefully separated from substantive law on the one hand and from the practice of other states on the other. Now we have at our disposal through the recommendations and reports of the seven great committees of the American Bar Association on the Improvement of the Administration of Justice, which were unanimously adopted by the American Bar Association with one very slight exception in 1938 (the same year that the Federal Rules of Civil Procedure became effective), a clear statement of "the *minimum* requirements that are needed in a *practical* way" to make our procedural law workable in the twentieth century.[28] The status of the procedural law of each of the forty-eight states and the District of Columbia with respect to each of the recommendations of the American Bar Association committees is reflected in *Minimum Standards of Judicial Administration*,[29] which is the joint product of the research of the National Conference of Judicial Councils and the Junior Bar Section of the American Bar Association. In that volume are numerous maps graphically indicating the degree of acceptance of each of these standards of procedure in the several states. Most of these maps have been reproduced in this casebook to enable the student to grasp at a glance not only the status of the standards throughout the country on each topic but also the degree of their acceptance in his own state. Thus the student, while learning the federal system of procedure, will at the same time be introduced to the essentials of the practice in his own state in comparison with the federal rules and the standards of judicial administration approved by the American Bar Association, which naturally have much in common with the federal rules, and the practice prevailing in all other jurisdictions. He will see clearly that in many jurisdictions our procedural law falls far short of meeting "minimum requirements that are needed in a practical way." So far as I know this is the first attempt that has been made to present procedure from a comparative point of view on a nationwide scale. The great virtue of the comparative approach to procedure is that it furnishes the necessary guide for improvement in the law, for what has been made to work successfully in one state may be made to work elsewhere.

In short, the approach to the problems of procedure should not only be comparative but also critical. As students of the law we are as much concerned with what the law should be as with what it is or has been. Such an approach is not generally possible in the rush of a modern law office. It is to the law schools, therefore, that we must look for the systematic development of procedure in the future, even though it must be admitted that in the past they have not often lived up to their responsibilities in this field. Legal education over the past three quarters of a century has emphasized only the What (the principles of law) and the Why (legal reasoning). If legal education is not to continue to be surpassed by medical and engineering education, it must deal increasingly with the How (legal skills) and the Whither (what the law should be if the law is best to serve society). There is no more useful or easier place to begin such a study of the law than in the field of procedure. Indeed, we cannot hope for the effective development of the substantive law until our procedural law is perfected and the right to a fair trial adequately secured, for the effectiveness of the law can be fairly judged only in action.

II. THE PLACE OF THE FEDERAL RULES OF CIVIL AND CRIMINAL PROCEDURE IN THE MOVEMENT FOR JUDICIAL REFORM

The significance of the Federal Rules of Civil and Criminal Procedure can best be understood by considering briefly the nature of the practice that preceded them. Common-law procedure had its sources in customs, rules of court, judicial decisions (especially such as resorted to fictions), legislation, and in this country constitutional provisions. The resulting olla-podrida—it could not truthfully be called a system—of technical, cumbersome, expensive and dilatory precepts of practice was attacked more than once in England before it yielded in some measure to common sense and reason in the third quarter of the nineteenth century. When reform finally came, it was due in large part to the determination of laymen to be rid of the accumulation over centuries of much intolerable legalistic junk that served only to prevent the effective administration of justice.[30] It should not be thought that earlier attempts had not been made to simplify procedure. Thus Lord Mansfield, the greatest of English judges, renowned throughout the common-law world for introducing the law merchant and quasi contracts into the body of our substantive law, crashed through the incredible techniques for procrastination [31] of the bench and bar of his day (1756-1788) and despite the vast increase in the judicial work of his court finished it all term after term before rising.[32] After Mansfield's death the old habits of delay and of decisions on technicalities and points of pleading rather than on the merits reappeared, ultimately in the aggravated form known as special pleading. To realize what the procedural jungle at common law was like the student should thumb through (but not read) the sturdy volumes of Williams' *Notes to Saunders Reports,* of Tidd, and of Chitty. Fortunately F. W. Maitland, the most brilliant of the English legal historians, has sketched about all that the modern student needs to know of common-law procedure in seven brief lectures on *The Forms of Action at Common Law,* which is reprinted as appendix A [33] and to which cross references will be made at appropriate points throughout this casebook.

Supplementing or restricting—depending on the point of view of the litigant—the law enunciated in the common-law courts was the great body of equity jurisprudence that developed over the centuries, chiefly in the Court of Chancery, side by side with the common law. Complaints in Chancery regarded equity as supplementing the common law, because it gave them rights or remedies that they did not have in the common-law courts; defendants in Chancery were quite naturally inclined to look on equity as restricting their common-law rights. The practice in the Court of Chancery was derived in large measure from civil-law procedure as administered in the English ecclesiastical courts, for the chancellors for centuries were all churchmen, but it was also influenced in some degree by the practice of the common-law courts. The differences between procedure at common law and the practice in Chancery

were, however, striking and fundamental. The law judges tried
their cases, except such as involved prerogative writs, with a jury;
the chancellor sat without a jury. In the law courts the evidence
was adduced in open court and subject to cross-examination in
public; in Chancery it was taken privately by depositions before
examiners with a view to "scraping the defendant's conscience,"
reduced to writing and later read by the chancellor in chambers.
The law courts ordinarily did not issue commands but merely
rendered judgment, leaving it to the successful litigant himself to
pursue the execution necessary to satisfy his judgment; the chancellor, in contrast, not only issued decrees directed to the defendant,
but he commanded obedience to them and punished any violation
of his mandates by imprisonment and also, if necessary, by the
sequestration of the defendant's assets. The law courts because of
the limitations of the jury were not equipped to decide controversies
involving a variety of issues or a considerable number of parties
with conflicting interests; the machinery of Chancery, on the other
hand, was admirably adapted to disposing of such litigation. In
general the law courts did not issue preventive remedies, but merely
entered judgment after wrongs that had been committed; Chancery,
however, not only enjoined threatened torts but prevented forfeitures
and often settled doubts as to the meaning of wills and trusts. The
law courts rendered judgment on the issue of liability as it existed
when the action was started; Chancery's decree was molded to fit
the facts as they existed at the time the decree was entered. In
general the common law was constrained by forms and tradition;
equity looked to the substance and to the realities of the situation.
The chief things that procedure at law and in equity had in com-
as they finally developed were their defects. Procedure in Chancery, while originally quite simple, ultimately became even more
technical, cumbersome, expensive and dilatory than that of the
law courts, as a leafing through of the massive volumes of Daniell
(again not to be read) or a perusal of Charles Dickens' account
in *Bleak House* [34] of the proceedings in the celebrated suit of
Jarndyce v. Jarndyce will demonstrate. The most penetrating account of Chancery practice is to be found in Langdell's *A Summary
of Equity Pleading,* excerpts from which are printed in appendix
B [35] and to which cross references will frequently be made.

In England both in the law courts and in Chancery the fight for procedural simplicity was a long one, culminating in the drastic simplification in the structure of the courts in 1873 and in the return to the courts in 1875 of the rule-making power over judicial procedure.[36] In this country, because of the antipathy toward all things English folowing the American Revolution (several states actually passed legislation forbidding the citation in their courts of English decisions handed down or statutes passed since 1776),[37] one would have expected an early movement for the simplification of practice in the courts. Instead, the conservatism of the bar toward their hard-learned procedure on the one hand and their preoccupation on the other hand with adapting the fundamentals of substantive law [38] to the needs of a new country served to divert their attention from the absurdities of the existing procedure except as they came face to face with them in simplifying outmoded parts of the substantive law. An outstanding example of this process is to be found in the Revised Statutes of 1828 in New York, where the English law of real property, based as it was on principles of feudal law that were deemed peculiarly inappropriate in a new state where feudalism had no place, was swept aside in favor of a relatively simple statutory system of property rights. In the course of this process the ancient real actions for deciding title to real property were simplified and John Doe and Richard Roe, the perennial straw men of the possessory action of ejectment, were discarded as unnecessary fictions. The scope of the Revised Statutes was so extensive and the results of the labors of the revisors so far-reaching as to excuse the failure to deal with procedure except incidentally.[39]

The great need a century ago for reform in procedure is graphically portrayed in the article by Lord Chief Justice Coleridge,[40] previously alluded to:

In 1847 the Common Law rested mainly, thought not exclusively, upon special pleading, and truth was investigated by rules of evidence so carefully framed to exclude falsehood, that very often truth was quite unable to force its way through the barriers erected against its opposite.
Plaintiff and defendant, husband and wife, persons, excepting Quakers, who objected to an oath, those with an interest, direct or indirect, immediate or contingent, in the

issue to be tried, were all absolutely excluded from giving evidence. Nonsuits were constant, not because there was no cause of action, but because the law refused the evidence of the only person who could prove it. I do not speak of Chancery, which had defects of its own, because I pretend to no more knowledge of Chancery practice than is picked up by a common lawyer who, as he rises in his profession, is taken into Courts of Equity to examine a witness or to argue a case upon conflicting facts. Questions as to marriage, and as to wills, so far as they related to personal property, were under the jurisdiction of courts called ecclesiastical, with a procedure and principles happily of their own, and presided over by judges not appointed by the Crown. The Admiralty jurisdiction, at all times of great, in time of war of enormous, importance, was in practice committed to an ecclesiastical judge. Criminals, except in high treason and in misdemeanor, could be defended by counsel only through the medium of cross-examination. Speeches could be delivered, with the above exceptions, only by the prisoners themselves. . . .

Such, in rude outline, was the Bar when I joined it. The system had its great virtues, but it had its great and crying evils; and they were aggravated by the powerful men who at that time dominated Westminster Hall, and whose spirit guided its administration. . . . The ruling power in the Court in 1847 was Baron Parke, a man of great and wide legal learning, an admirable scholar, a kind-hearted and amiable man, and of remarkable force of mind. These great qualities he devoted to heightening all the absurdities, and contracting to the very utmost the narrowness, of the system of special pleading. The client was unthought of. Conceive a judge rejoicing, as I have myself heard Baron Parke rejoice, at non-suiting a plaintiff in an undefended cause, saying, with a sort of triumphant air, that "those who drew loose declarations brought scandal on the law." The right was nothing, the mode of stating everything. When it was proposed to give power to amend the statement, "Good Heavens!" exclaimed the Baron, "think of the state of the Record!"—*i.e.*, the sacred parchment, which it was proposed to defile by erasures and alterations. He bent the whole powers of his great intellect to defeat the Act of Parliament which had allowed of equitable defences in a Common Law action. He laid down all but impossible conditions, and said, with an air of intense satisfaction, in my hearing, "I think we settled the new Act to-day, we shall hear no more of Equitable defences"! And as Baron Parke piped, the Court of Exchequer followed, and dragged after it, with more or less reluctance, the other Common Law Courts of Westminster Hall. Sir William Maule and Sir Cresswell did their best to resist the current. Cresswell was a man of strong will, of clear, sagacious, sensible mind, and a sound lawyer; Sir William Maule seems to me on reflection, and towards the close of a long life, on the whole the most extraordinary intellect I ever came across. . . . Baron Parke was, in a legal view, his favorite aversion. "Well," I have heard him say, "that seems a horror in morals and a monster in reasoning. Now, give us the judgment of Baron Parke which lays it down as law." With the advent of Lord Campbell to the Chief Justiceship, a great lawyer, not wedded to the narrow technicalities, which he thoroughly understood, but did not admire, came to the assistance of good sense and justice. But for some time he struggled in vain against the idolatry of Baron Parke to which the whole of the Common Law at that time was devoted. Even so very great a lawyer and so independent a man as Sir James Willes dedicated a book to him as the judge "to whom the law was under greater obligations than to any judge within legal memory." One of the obligations he was very near conferring on it was its absolute extinction. "I have aided in building up sixteen volumes of Meeson & Welsby," said he proudly to Charles Austin, "and that is a great thing for any man to say." "I dare say it is," said Austin; "but in the Palace of Truth, Baron, do you think it would have made the slightest difference to mankind, or even to England, if all the cases in all the volumes of Meeson & Welsby had been decided the other way?" He repeated his boast to Sir William Erle. "It's a lucky thing," said Sir William, as he told me himself, "that there was not a seventeenth volume, for if there had been the Common Law itself would have disappeared altogether, amidst the jeers and hisses of mankind," "and," he added, "Parke didn't seem to like it."

Peace be with him. He was a great lawyer, a man of high character and powerful intellect. No smaller man could have produced such results. If he ever were to revisit the glimpses of the moon one shudders to think of his disquiet. No *absque hoc,* no *et non,* no colour, express or implied, given to trespass no new assignment, belief in the great doctrine of a negative pregnant no longer necessary to legal salvation, and the very nice question, as Baron Parke is reported to have thought, whether you could reply *de injuria* to a plea of deviation in an action on a marine policy not only still unsolved, but actually considered not worth solution! I suspect that to the majority of my hearers I am talking in an unknown tongue, and it is strange that in the lifetime of one who has not yet quite fulfilled the appointed span in human life such a change, such a revolution in a most conservative profession should be actually consummated. . . .

And with these men the system under which they flourished has gone to rest too. Parties are examined, husband and wife are heard, special pleadings finds no refuge upon the habitable globe, except, as I believe, in the State of New Jersey,[41] in America. Law and equity are concurrently administered; marriage, wills, Admiralty cases are dealt with by the profane hands of judges with not a flavour of ecclesiasticism about them. Of the administrators of the new system, those who made it, and those who now preside over or contend under it, the living and the lately dead it is not for me to speak.

In this country the great reform movement aiming at codification not only in procedure but for the entire body of law, is forever linked with the name of David Dudley Field. He almost succeeded in becoming the American Justinian[42] and even though his codes dealing with the substantive law were defeated in New York and not adopted in most other states, he dominated American procedure for at least three quarters of a century.[43] Despite the general nineteenth century antipathy to legislation[44] the Field Code of Procedure was promptly adopted by the New York Legislature in 1848 and it quickly spread to other jurisdictions, being accepted in more than thirty different states.[45] Its central thesis was the merger of law and equity and the substitution of one civil action for all the forms of action at common law and for the several kinds of bills in equity.[46] This thesis marked the end of both fictions[47] and special pleading and paved the way for the substitution of the practice of giving the facts in "a plain and concise statement . . . , without unnecessary repetition,"[48] and in such a manner as to enable a person of common understanding to know what is intended.

Despite the virtues of the Field Code it was manhandled in both the legislature and the courts. Field's draft of a more complete code of procedure was rejected in 1876 in New York in favor of the revised code of Montgomery H. Throop. By the process of legislative tinkering heretofore mentioned, the 391 sections of the original Field Code grew by the year 1880 to more than 3,400 sections. Even if the courts had looked favorably on the successive codes, which they did not,[49] their complexities were such that conflicting decisions interpreting them were inevitable. Attempted reforms by commissions in 1895, 1900 and 1915 failed of passage, and finally the legislature created its own committee, which reported a detailed civil practice act, which was enacted in 1920. Many of its good provisions were offset by retaining many of the mistakes of the past. Nor was the experience of New York unique; such difficulties seem to be inherent in the legislative process of formulating rules of procedure.

It was not until well after the turn of the twentieth century that American judges and lawyers generally began to take real interest in the problems of judicial administration. As late as 1906 Dean Roscoe Pound's famous address before the American Bar Association at St. Paul on *"The Causes of Popular Dissatisfaction with the Administration of Justice"* elicited hostile, almost virulent, criticism, although the address was merely a factual and analytical presentation of the problems of judicial administration. The dramatic story of its reception by the American Bar Association has been told by another great legal scholar, Dean John H. Wigmore, in an article appropriately entitled *"The Spark That Kindled the White Flame of Progress."*[50] Dean Pound's address is a classic. It deals with fundamentals that are essential to a sound understanding of the work of the courts and of the intimate relation between procedure and justice. With Dean Pound's permission it is printed here as chapter II along with Dean Wigmore's article. If I had my way, I would make it prescribed reading once a year for every judge, practicing lawyer, and law professor and law student on the day he returns from his summer vacation and starts a new year of professional activity. It should be added that since 1906 the American Bar Association has made honorable amends for the reception of Dean Pound's speech by furnishing the leadership that has brought about the drafting and promulgation of the Canons of Professional and Judicial Ethics, led the fight against Theodore Roosevelt's campaign for the recall of judges and of judicial decisions, raised the standards of legal education throughout the country, agitated for years for the Federal Rules of Civil Procedure, opposed President Franklin D. Roosevelt's proposal for packing the United States Supreme Court, aided in the establishment of the Administrative Office of the United States Courts and in the movement for the promulgation of the Federal Rules of Criminal Procedure, and brought about the passage of the Federal Administrative Procedure Act.

We are especially concerned here with the campaign that led to the promulgation of the Federal Rules of Civil Procedure. In 1912 Thomas W. Shelton of Norfolk, Virginia, was appointed chairman of the American Bar Association Committee on Uniform Judicial Procedure.[51] For nearly twenty years,[52] with untiring energy he led a crusade for an act to give the United States Supreme Court the same rule-making power in actions at law that it had long exercised in equity proceedings, thus seeking to avoid the evils of the Conformity Act[53] which required litigants to follow the state practice. Year after year he faced the adamant opposition of Senator Thomas A. Walsh, chairman of the Senate Judiciary Committee.[54] After Shelton's death his successor as chairman of the committee in 1930 reported to the Association his pessimism as to the possibilities of obtaining such an enactment.[55] Two years later his successor, a federal district judge, reported his personal opinion that the rule-making power was undesirable, and the following year on his recommendation[56] the committee was discontinued. But in 1934 the same bill, sponsored this time by Attorney General Homer S. Cummings[57] became law.[58] Never will one find a more perfect illustration of the soundness of the advice given by General Jan Smuts to the students at Oxford, "When enlisted in a good cause, never surrender, for you can never tell what morning reinforcements in flashing armor will come marching over the hilltop."

The United States Supreme Court promptly appointed an Advisory Committee with former Attorney General William D. Mitchell as its chairman and authorized it to prepare rules abolishing separate procedure in law and equity in the federal courts.[59] The Committee deserves as much credit for the methods employed by it as for the excellent rules that it drafted, for it solicited suggestions from individual judges and lawyers throughout the country and from committees organized by every state bar association and and important city bar association as well as in every federal district. Through the aid thus obtained as well as through the knowledge and experience of its members, the committee had at its disposal the best practice of the several states and diligently sought to utilize it. Tentative drafts of proposed rules were submitted for the criticism of these cooperating committees and of the bench and bar of the country generally, so that the final draft of the Federal Rules of Civil Procedure may be said to embody the experience not only of an unusually able advisory committee but of the legal profession throughout the entire country. This method of procedure has become standard for later committees, both federal and state, that have undertaken similar responsibilities. The rules themselves, which were promulgated in 1937, effective in 1938, were a model of simplicity and flexibility. As has already been stated, they have been made the basis of reform in several states [60] and it may safely be said their influence in the states will be of a continuing nature. In 1946 the Advisory Committee, having been continued by the Supreme Court, submitted its recommendations for amendments to the rules based upon almost a decade of experience with them. Acting on these recommendations the Supreme Court adopted amendments to 33 of the 86 original rules, the amendments becoming effective on March 19, 1948,[61] and later adopted additional amendments to 24 of the rules, effective October 20, 1949.[62]

Much as the Federal Rules of Civil Procedure had been needed, there was an even greater necessity for the reform of criminal procedure. Due to the outstanding example of the Federal Rules of Civil Procedure and the favorable attitude of Attorney General Jackson the victory for the reform of criminal procedure was as swift as the war for reform of civil procedure had been prolonged and difficult. The bill recommended by the Section of Criminal Law of the American Bar Association authorizing the Supreme Court to act was passed within a year,[63] and in February, 1941, the Supreme Court appointed an Advisory Committee.[64] Several drafts were prepared and distributed in the same manner as in the case of the civil rules and received the careful attention of lawyers everywhere. Many of the criminal rules involved difficult constitutional questions as well as a careful balancing of the public interest and private rights. The rules in final form were promulgated by the Supreme Court on December 26, 1944,[65] and though the Judiciary Committees of the Congress had the power, as with the civil rules, to hold hearings and consider the criminal rules, they did not do so.

There is one interesting incident in connection with the criminal rules that deserves recounting here because it illustrates how continuous is the struggle for a fair trial. Among the rules recommended to the Supreme Court by its Advisory Committee was one aimed at the elimination of the practice prevailing in certain districts of the government submitting a so-called "confidential brief" to the trial ourt without furnishing the defendant or his counsel with a copy. Often these briefs went far beyond a statement of the government's view of the law of the case and detailed the evidence the government hoped to elicit from its witnesses. The unfairness of this practice is obvious, yet for some reason not disclosed to the Advisory Committee the Supreme Court deleted the proposed rule. Months later one of the Justices told me that the Court did so because it felt that the rule was an affront to the dignity of the trial judges (!), though the rule was in fact directed to the attorneys and not to the trial courts. The matter, however, did not end there, for some of the federal judges continued their opposition to the practice with the result tht we find recorded in the Report of the Annual Conference of Senior Circuit Judges held in October, 1946, a minute reading:

> The Conference, after consideration of the report of the Committee appointed to study the subject matter, disapproved the practice, prevalent in some districts, of trial

judges in criminal cases receiving from the attorney on
one side a brief or trial memorandum that has not been
furnished to the attorney on the other side, and recommended the immediate discontinuance of such practice.[66]

Another battle for the right to a fair trial had been won. So far
as I know, this was the first time that the senior circuit judges
have, in effect, overruled the Supreme Court, but of the soundness
of their decision there can be no doubt. The incident is also significant as an example of the difference between law in the books
and law in action. A study merely of the history of the Federal
Rules of Criminal Procedure would show the recommendations to
the Supreme Court by its Advisory Committee of a rule against
attorneys submitting confidential briefs and the Court's rejection
of the proposed rule. From the books alone therefore the inference
might be drawn that the Supreme Court still approved of confidential briefs. Yet the action taken by the Judicial Conference
in 1946, without amending the rules, did away with a bad practice
by administrative action.

The student may well ask, "What are the advantages of
judicial rule-making over statutory enactments in the formulation
of procedure?" That question has never been better answered than
in an article by Dean Roscoe Pound a quarter of a century ago.[67]
Rules of court, he points out, have great advantages. Not only
are they made by experts, but they are interpreted and applied by
judges who are sympathetic with them. Changes may be made
whenever occasion may require without waiting for stated legislative
sessions and without overburdening already overworked legislators.
Finally, procedure may be made subsidiary, as it should be, to the
substantive rights of the litigants. The courts may avoid the snarls
of procedural red tape and concentrate on the real questions at issue.
Indeed, writes Dean Pound, "All experience shows that while
statutory procedure runs to details, becomes elaborate and over-
grown, and is of necessity rigid and unyielding, procedure prescribed
by rules of court tends continually to become simple, adapted to
its purposes, and adaptable by the simple process of judicial amendment to new situations and needs of practice." [68]

In examining any set of court rules of procedure the heart
of the inquiry is to ascertain the spirit that actuated their form-

ulation and that should govern their enforcement. Conceivably a set of court-made rules might result in a procedure as vexatious, as dilatory, as expensive and as technical as the practice in the worst days of special pleading at law or of delays in Chancery. Indeed, the Hilary Rules, promulgated in England in 1834 as a first step toward procedural reform, had exactly that effect,[69] but fortunately for the administration of justice the spirit of the federal rules is otherwise.[70]   Rule 1 of the Federal Rules of Civil Procedure provides, "These Rules . . . shall be construed to secure a just, speedy, and inexpensive determination of every action"; and Rule 2 of the Federal Rules of Criminal Procedure reads, "These Rules are intended to provide for the just determination of every criminal proceeding. They shall be construed to secure simplicity in procedure, fairness in administration and the elimination of unjustifiable expense and delay." One of the chief objects of this casebook will be to bring out the means whereby these highly desirable objectives are accomplished at each stage of a judicial proceeding. In general it may be said that the underlying principle of both sets of rules is that a trial is an orderly search for truth in aid of the administration of justice rather than a battle of wits between counsel. A few simple and flexible rules have been preferred to a detailed regulation of every step of procedure. Much is left to the sound discretion of the trial judge instead of hampering him with statutory provisions that he must follow even if they inevitably work injustice in a particular case. In general the rules have regard for principles of justice giving emphasis to substance rather than mere form.

The federal rules are part of our "written law," which also embraces constitutions, treaties, statutes, ordinances and regulations, as distinguished from the unwritten or common law which is stated in judicial decisions. Each branch of the written law has its own style. Constitutions properly deal with fundamentals in a broad way, treaties generally use the involved language of diplomacy, statutes, ordinances and regulations are likely to be detailed and rigid in their provisions, but rules of court, in contrast, are generally written in a more flowing style than statutes with fewer definitions, for the reader is supposed to know the meaning of the words of art used therein. Like all written law, however, it is inevitable that

they become coated with a judicial gloss. We should always remember, however, in studying the rules and decisions construing
them that the rules come first, that the decisions construing them
may vary from case to case with different sets of facts and that
in determining the meaning of the rules intent prevails over content
and any reports or commentaries of the draftsmen are likely to be
of as much significance as judicial decisions.[71]

III. *THE MAJOR PROBLEMS OF PROCEDURE*

Procedure under the federal rules, or indeed in any system,
is largely concerned with answering ten major questions having
to do with the progress of a case from inception to conclusion, and
with solving four sets of major problems revolving around the
manpower of the courts.

The ten major questions having to do with the progress of a
case are:

1. In what court may the plaintiff bring his suit? Here we
are dealing with the vital question of *Jurisdiction*. Ordinarily
the power of a court to hear and determine a cause may be
questioned at any time. To enable a court to act, it must
acquire jurisdiction over the subject matter of the suit and
the person against whom or the thing with respect to which
judgment is sought.

2. Who should or may bring suit, and who should or may be
sued? Here we are concerned with the complicated question
of *Parties*.

3. Where the parties may be reached may often determine
the question of *Venue*, *i.e.*, the county or district in which the
suit may be brought.

4. How can the plaintiff bring the defendant or the subject
matter of the suit into court? Here we are concerned with
Process, such as a summons, arrest or attachment.

5. Before the parties can intelligently state their respective
positions, they must perforce know what kinds of relief the
court may award, *i.e.*, *Remedies*.

6. How do the parties get their respective positions in the
controversy before the court? Here we have to do with the
statements of the respective parties, known as the *Pleadings*.

7. The parties having stated their respective positions, how
do they prepare for trial? The several *Pretrial Procedures*

(such as demands for admissions, interrogatories, depositions, discovery, inspections, examinations, and finally the pretrial conference), while known in varying degree in earlier systems of procedure, have reached their highest development in these modern rules of court because of the new spirit of searching for truth which characterizes them.

8. How do the parties litigate and the courts determine the issue or issues presented by the pleadings? The *Trial* represents the culmination of all of the preceding preparations and normally results in a *Judgment* for or against the moving party or parties.

9. Since the losing party may conceive that he has just ground for complaint as to the result of the trial, the question arises how may the outcome of the trial be reviewed? *Judicial Review* may take the form of a motion addressed to the trial court for judgment notwithstanding the verdict or for a new trial and the like, or of an appeal to a higher court.

10. After a case has been finally disposed of in the trial court or the appellate court, the final question is, how can the prevailing party have satisfaction of its judgment? The answer is by one or more of several kinds of *Execution* and proceedings in aid thereof.

We must never forget that justice is administered by men. The kind of justice administered necessarily depends on the kind of men administering it. The four great sets of problems relating to the manpower of the courts are therefore next to be considered:

1. The first concerns the judiciary. How are judges selected? What is their tenure of office? Is their salary an adequate compensation today in comparison with what lawyers make? What standards govern their conduct? The problems of *Judicial Selection, Tenure, Salaries* and *Ethics* go to the heart of any judicial system. The efficacy of a judical system and of the body of jurisprudence enunciated through it depends in large measure on the character and the professional qualifications of the judges selected to man the system. The accepted standards of judicial conduct have been set down in the Canons of Judicial Ethics of the American Bar Association and should be known by every law student.

2. It will do a litigant little good to have his case tried before the ablest judge on the bench by competent lawyers, if the jurors who are chosen to pass on the facts are not both honest and intelligent. In the enforcement of the criminal law the selection of a proper grand jury is quite as important as the

choice of a proper trial jury. The *Selection of Jurors* is therefore a vital matter in the due administration of justice.

3. Cases in the trial courts are not tried by judges and juries alone. Lawyers play an essential part not only in presenting the evidence to the court through witnesses and documents but also in arguing the facts to the jury and the law and the facts to the court both at the trial and on appeal. A judicial system in the long run can be no better than its bar. Every law student should know as soon as possible what are the professional responsibilities of *The Legal Profession*. Fortunately he is aided in determining his ethical responsibilities by the Canons of Professional Ethics formulated by the American Bar Association and adopted by the bench and bar of many states. With these canons he must become acquainted.

4. To have the judges, jurors and lawyers work together effectively in a judicial system requires *Judicial Administration*. This involves the coordination of every branch of the judicial establishment; the collection of judicial statistics from the judges and court clerks and the compilation and periodical publication of these judicial statistics, so as to obtain an accurate over-all picture of what is going on currently in the courts; the assignment of the judges where they are most needed and to the kind of work for which they are best fitted; the drafting and promulgation of rules of court governing the practice before both trial and appellate tribunals, and the setting up of judicial conferences made up of the judges and representatives of the bar and of the legislature to consider such amendments to the rules and practice as experience proves necessary and to advise generally with respect to the administration of justice. Strangely enough in a country distinguished for managerial talent and executive technique, the art of judicial administration is still in its infancy here.

Each of these ten fundamental questions and four sets of subjects should be approached in the spirit of our modern rules of court—that a trial or an appeal is not a sporting event in which the rival lawyers are the leading players but an orderly search for the truth in aid of the administration of justice. This, in turn, involves a firm grasp of the fundamental axiom that the courts exist not for the benefit of judges and lawyers, though they often seem to think so, but primarily for the litigants, and that the test of every rule of court should be not what is most convenient for the judges and lawyers but what is best for the litigants. This is not an easy idea for some judges and lawyers to grasp, but it is fundamental to any real progress in judicial administration. Specifically, at each point the inquiry should be, does this step contribute as much as possible to a fair trial? Viewed in this light it is hoped that the student will no longer think of procedure as "adjective" or subordinate law in comparison with "substantive" law, but rather that he will recognize that procedure and judicial administration are integral elements of first importance even in an office lawyer's work, and that all legal rights depend directly on the right to a fair trial under sound rules of procedure administered by honest, intelligent and competent judges, jurors and lawyers.

Finally, it should be pointed out that there are specialized branches of law, such as probate, admiralty, divorce, bankruptcy and condemnation proceedings,[72] involving generally the administration of a *res*, the procedure of which does not fall within the scope of this book.

Criminal Law And Procedure

Vanderbilt discerned a causal connection between the minor position to which criminal law and procedure had been relegated in the law school curriculum and the general breakdown of the administration of criminal justice. He believed that the law student, in addition to his study of the basic principles of criminal law, should be made aware of the problem of organized crime in our society and the methods proposed to cope with it. Vanderbilt's theory was that the elevation of the subject of criminal law to a position of greater importance in the legal curriculum would immeasurably increase its effectiveness as an instrument of social control. The severe time limitation imposed by the three-year curriculum has up to now prevented the theory from being tested, but recent developments in the field lend encouragement that Vanderbilt's hope may some day be realized. The Ford Foundation has given a substantial grant to the National Legal Aid and Defender Association. One of the three purposes of the grant is "to aid law schools through fellowships and student internships to interest outstanding law school graduates in the defense of accused persons and to strengthen the curriculum in the law school."

It was in the procedural aspects of criminal law that Vanderbilt's influence made its greatest impact. Antiquated rules of criminal procedure had long constituted road blocks preventing expeditious trials in the federal courts. After the adoption of the rules of civil procedure in the federal district courts, it seemed logical to prepare comparable rules of criminal procedure. In 1941 the United States Supreme Court appointed an advisory committee for their preparation and named Vanderbilt the chairman. The rules formulated by the committee, which went into effect in 1944, have thoroughly modernized federal criminal procedure.

The introduction to the American Bar Association Report of the Commission on Organized Crime reflects his ideas on criminal law and its administration.

His 1946 report of the experiment which he helped introduce in Essex County, under which every member of the Essex County Bar agreed to serve without compensation as counsel for indigent criminal defendants, was the first plan developed in this country, and foreshadowed the case of Gideon v. Wainwright, 372 U. S. 335 (1963), which is the subject of an informative book by Anthony Lewis, "Gideon's Trumpet." The title of the report is **An Experiment in the Trial of Indigent Criminal Cases.**

THE NEW FEDERAL CRIMINAL RULES *

The federal courts have set the pace in the task of improving the administration of justice not only for most of the state courts, but, in some respects, for the federal administrative tribunals as well.[1] There are few, if any, judicial structures as free from complexity as the federal courts. In the work of attending to the business and administrative affairs of a judicial system, moreover, no state has an organization comparable to the Administrative Office of the United States Courts.[2] Furthermore, in the adaptation of relatively simple rules to the work of governing court procedures, few jurisdictions have achieved the simplicity and efficiency of the Federal Rules of Civil Procedure.

The work of the Advisory Committee of the United States Supreme Court on Federal Rules of Criminal Procedure is not, it will be seen, an isolated effort to improve procedure; on the contrary, it is an integral part of a broad program for simplicity and efficiency in all branches of judicial administration. The federal system of courts did not attain its present symmetry of district courts, circuit courts of appeals, and a Supreme Court without considerable experimentation. The Administrative Office of the United States Court was born of turmoil.[3] The act granting the rule-making power in civil cases to the Supreme Court was passed only after a crusade by the bar lasting thirty years.[4] In contrast, the act conferring on the Court the rule-making power in criminal cases up to verdict [5] was passed without opposition, largely as a result of the example of the Civil Rules and of the Act of 1934 conferring on the Court rule-making power in criminal cases after verdict.[6] The Supreme Court's broad rule-making powers now cover not only traditional civil and criminal proceedings but also such fields as bankruptcy and copyright cases.

Many lawyers conceive of procedure as static, but nothing could be further from fact. The Criminal Appeals Rules of

---

* 51 Yale L. J. 718-722 (1942).

1934 were a noteworthy achievement in simplifying procedure;
yet the treatment of exceptions in the Federal Rules of Civil
Procedure of 1938 [7] seems definitely to be a step in advance
of the Rules of 1934. The Civil Rules, in turn, now seem to
be obsolescent with respect to such an important matter as
the record on appeal when compared with the practice that
has been adopted in the circuits on the Atlantic seaboard of
printing merely the parts of the record to which counsel desire
to call the reviewing court's attention.[8] This process of
continuous growth in matters of procedure has been recognized
by the Supreme Court in designating the members of its
Advisory Committee on Rules of Civil Procedure as a continuing committee.[9]

The Advisory Committee on Rules of Criminal Procedure
commenced its work in February, 1941, and the members of
the Committee are now considering the third tentative draft.
The Committee has had invaluable assistance from committees
appointed by the district judges on the recommendation of
Chief Justice Hughes and similar committees of state and local
bar associations. With the work of the Committee still in the
formative state and not yet in shape to submit to the Supreme
Court, it would be manifestly improper to discuss its contents
in detail. But there is no impropriety and perhaps some advantage in directing attention to some of the considerations
that have impressed the Committee as it has proceeded with
its work.

The first impression concerns the enormous number of
legal barnacles that encrust the subject of criminal procedure.
Legal barnacles are not, however, a peculiarity of criminal
procedure alone; they seem to thrive in all branches of adjective law.[10] The first task in procedural reform is to dis-
tinguish between the essential and the adventitious and to
eliminate the latter.

Essentially criminal procedure is, or at least seems to be,
more simple than civil practice. Perhaps this impression is
engendered by the fact that much of the pleading on the
criminal side of the trial court and many of the motions are

oral as distinguished from the formal written documents on the civil side.

These observations as to encrusting technicalities and essential simplicity apply as much to state courts as to the federal system. There are two peculiarities of criminal procedure in the federal courts, however, that immediately distinguished it from the corresponding practice in the state courts. The first distinction is to be found in the wide differences in the communities to be served by the federal courts. A set of rules may be very satisfactory in a large urban center where there is a considerable number of judges sitting the year round and yet be quite intolerable in a rural district where the terms of court last but a week or two once or twice a year. The generality of the Federal Rules of Criminal Procedure should be such as to encompass suitable practice in each type of community.

Then, too, there is a vast difference between the rather simple common law crimes under state law and most of their statutory crimes, on the one side, and the complicated federal statutory crimes, on the other. A set of rules that may be admirably adapted to the trial of issues ranging from assault and battery to murder may not be at all suited to the disposition of such involved proceedings as anti-trust or mail-fraud cases. A case that may take months or even years for trial is likely to require rules different from one that may be disposed of in half a day.

In drafting rules for criminal cases we must also take into account the fundamental difference in constitutional problems between criminal procedure and civil practice. Federal rules of criminal procedure must meet the test of a considerably larger number of constitutional provisions than do civil rules. Obviously, criminal procedure was much more in the minds of the draftsmen of the first ten amendents to the Federal Constitution than was civil practice. But today the constitutional provisions relating to civil litigation are much better known to laymen and lawyers alike than the constitutional safeguards designed to protect the accused in a criminal proceeding. In quiet times the constitutional safeguards of an accused seem relatively unimportant, but in times of crisis their significance is greatly enhanced, and the Government often feels hampered by them. At all times, however, they are indispensable to the accused; any set of rules of criminal procedure must conform to them in letter and in spirit. Fundamentally what is sought is what a recent writer has called "the Right to a Fair Trial." [11] It is significant that even in England there should still be doubt as to just what a fair trial means.

In a world torn by international conflict, with national defense our primary responsibility at the moment, there may be lawyers as well as laymen who wonder why time and thought should now be devoted to the formulation of federal rules of criminal procedure. They should be reminded that these rules will expedite the prompt and efficient trial not only of ordinary criminals but of the many persons suspected of being saboteurs or enemy agents. But, even more important, they should be reminded that the international conflict is essentially a struggle between law and order on the one side and brute force on the other. Our type of civilization depends on "equal justice under law." The present international struggle is not merely political; on the contrary, our primary goal is the preservation of freedom in our own country and its restoration elsewhere. One has but to look back to the many criminal prosecutions arising in World War I to realize that in times of crisis there is always a tendency to disregard the individual's civil rights and liberties. In our zeal to achieve ultimate victory, we must not cast aside the very thing we are fighting for.

FOREWORD: ORGANIZED CRIME AND LAW ENFORCEMENT *

. . . Popular dissatisfaction with the administration of the criminal law has been kindled and rekindled through the years since Roscoe Pound's address at St. Paul's in 1906 by periodic breakdowns in criminal law enforcement and the ensuing examinations of their causes. Through the years the American Bar Association, and other organized bar groups as well, have carried the torch and served as an instrument of reform. Reform in the law and even more so in its administration is a slow process. Not until after World War I did Dean Pound, by his pioneer survey of the administration of criminal justice of a single city, provide chapter and verse for his conclusions. The Cleveland Crime Survey, published in 1922, was the first in a series of state and city studies from Oregon to Missouri, from New York to Illinois. By the time of the investigations of the National Commission on Law Observance and Enforcement, commonly known as the Wickersham Commission, in the early thirties, the defects noted by these surveys had grown to cancerous proportions in the nourishing soil of Prohibition.

On the procedural side the American Law Institute had long since been at work on its Model Code of Criminal Procedure. Althogh this Code broke new ground in simplifying our procedural methods for dealing with crime, it has never found acceptance due in part to the general lack of both public and professional interest in the criminal law enforcement, due also to the growing distaste for rigid procedural codes. The failure of state legislatures to adopt this code, however, did not prevent other efforts at reforming our archaic criminal procedure. The promulgation of the Federal Rules of Criminal Procedure by the Supreme Court is a major achievement in this direction. This technique of reforming criminal procedure by rule of court rather than by legislative code has more recently been followed by the National Conference of Commissioners on Uniform Laws, which at the request of the American Law Institute reworked the Code of Criminal Pro-

---

* American Bar Association Commission on Crime. II Organized Crime and Law Enforcement XV-XXVII (American Bar Association, 1953).

cedure into Uniform Rules of Criminal Procedure, which were adopted at the Institute's last meeting for recommendation to the several states.

In 1937, the American Bar Association turned to an overall survey of the administration of justice both civil and criminal in the several states. This survey, under the general chairmanship of Judge John J. Parker, formulated fifty-six specific recommendations as to the minimum requirements for the sound administration of justice. A review of the extent to which these have been adopted in the forty-eight states was published a few years ago.

In the mid-thirties problems of criminal law enforcement were very much the concern of the American Bar Association. The major part of the 1935 annual meeting was given over to their consideration. Dean Pound, with years of investigation into the actual operation of criminal justice behind him, returned to the scene of his earlier foray to argue the need for changes in substantive criminal law, which he ranked behind personnel, administration and procedure in the list of factors demanding consideration in a program of improvement. George Z. Medalie, a distinguished prosecutor from New York, discussed methods of making criminal law enforcement more effective at the local, state and federal levels. Justin Miller, chairman of the Attorney General's Advisory Committee on Crime, reviewed the Attorney General's program for crime control and Earl Warren, then a youthful attorney from Alameda County, California, advocated the return of common law powers to the state attorney general to remedy the deficiencies in criminal justice in this country. Judge John J. Parker's plea for the enforcement of professional ethics had relevance to the concern for criminal law, because of the prevailing suspicion, then as now, that unethical practitioners played an important role in the breakdown of criminal justice. This preoccupation with criminal justice was an obvious result of the conflicts and investigations that attended the failure of Prohibition.

As the shadow of impending war grew darker, however, this preoccupation lost its force. But it as been revived again with a great sense of shock. A year after the end of World War II, J. Edgar Hoover, the Director of the Federal Bureau of Investigation, warned us that we were nearer to the days of gang control than we were a year after World War I, and this despite the absence of Prohibition. In 1949 the American Municipal Association, a voluntary organization of several thousand public officials, expressed concern in a petition to the Attorney General over the control of local government by national crime syndicates. The Attorney General's Conference on Organized Crime followed and then in due course the hearings of the Senate Committee to Investigate Organized Crime in Interstate Commerce, which under the chairmanship first of Senator Kefauver and then Senator O'Conor supported the charges of the American Municipal Association in terrifying detail. The American Bar Association is again, as in the mid-thirties, concerned with the pressing problems of the criminal law. Its Commission on Organized Crime proposed remedies which were firmly grounded in the investigations and researches of the past thirty years and constituted another landmark on the road to reform Dean Pound had opened that August day of 1906.

Reform becomes a matter of urgency when we learn from the survey of organized crime in the summer of 1952, presented in this volume, that large scale criminal gangs did not die with the exposure of their leaders to public scrutiny, nor as the result of such attractive panaceas as compelling gamblers to register with the Federal government. A sampling of informed opinion throughout the country clearly indicates that the resurgence of organized crime is to be expected and that the results of the recent investigations will prove to have been purely temporary unless public opinion, aware of the danger, forces official vigilance, official action, and such changes in our laws and their administration and procedure as will stimulate the choice of officials of integrity and enable them to act effectively.

Investigation may establish the need to do something; unfortunately, it does not necessarily make action inevitable. The failure of the Congress to implement the program of the Kefauver-O'Conor committee is a case in point. Between investigation and action there is still an important intermediary point: the formulation of a program of action. It is here that the present volume, which sets forth four model acts designed to correct defects in our substantive law, administration and procedure, of which organized crime has been able to take advantage, has its greatest value. With these four model statutes, the Commission on Organized Crime comes to grips with major aspects of the problem of reducing the threat of organized crime to this country.

The Commission acted first on the finding of the Senate Committee that organized crime draws its major revenues from the operation of gambling enterprises. In part the operation of these enterprises was facilitated by defective gambling laws. A study in forty-eight states made by the Commission last year revealed the widespread failure of legislation to keep pace with the realities of modern gambling operations. Having rejected the legalization of gambling as a solution to the problem of preventing gambling from enriching organized crime, the Commission had no alternative but to draft a modern, effective gambling statute. With an act of this character on the books, law enforcement agents are provided with an instrument that facilitates the elimination of professional gambling operations and which deprives officials when confronted with wide-open gambling activities of the familiar and sorry excuse of deficient laws.

Despite its brilliant device of an all-inclusive definition of proscribed gambling activities, the act is not wholly original. In fact, much of its usefulness derives from judicious borrowings. It has incorporated in one statute those methods for eliminating organized, professional gambling that states with the best records for the enforcement of anti-gambling laws have found most successful. One such measure, for instance, is the authority to revoke the business license of any enterprise upon whose premises gambling is permitted. Several states have found this an effective means of preventing taverns, restaurants and other establishments from sheltering gamblers. Imitation of procedures effective elsewhere may be the simplest method of reform as we have discovered in New Jersey in our experience with the nonfixable traffic violations ticket which we borrowed in large measure from certain cities in Michigan.

The Commission also turned its attention to the prosecutor and the organization of his office because of their key role in the control of organized crime. The organization of criminal prosecution throughout the country has felt the influence of the Jacksonian concept of the equal qualification of all men for office. This concept may have brought progress in an earlier day of relatively isolated communities but it has had a different and evil effect in a technological civilization of large cities spread over a continent which can be covered in twelve hours by airplane. The Jacksonian philosophy resulted in the recruiting of prosecutors by popular election for short terms. Today the exercise of the prosecutor's function in areas of large population by untrained, inexperienced and shifting personnel, dependent for its future upon the favor of a political organization often open to underworld influences, menaces the public welfare. In Jackson's day, even state capitols were so far away in time from cities within their own borders that routine control or supervision of administrative work of the prosecuting attorney by a higher state official was either difficult or impossible. Thus geography fostered the political philosophy of home rule and eliminated in most states the common law concept of the local prosecutor as the subordinate of the Attorney General in the enforcement of a uniform policy throughout the state. In proposing a model Department of Justice Act the Commission on Organized Crime does not suggest that our traditional reliance on local home rule be scrapped, but simply asks us to consider whether we cannot strengthen it by resorting to the older tradition of the common law.

The Act gives the Attorney General in each state, or a comparable state official, the indispensable authority to maintain that supervision over the prosecution of criminal cases, or that authority to intervene in any particular case or class of cases, which is necessary if uniform standards of criminal law administration are to be maintained throughout a state. The Act makes it possible for the Attorney General, or the supervising official acting in his place, to make such necessary studies and surveys as will improve the functioning of the machinery of criminal prosecution. The Act also provides effective removal procedures to take care of inefficient or corrupt prosecutors. Here again the Act lays less claim to originality than to a judicious choice of the best existing state practices.

We also see the effect of outmoded Jacksonian doctrines when we examine the administration of police departments. Here local home rule and freedom from outside supervision have reached the stage of shibboleths. The Jacksonian idea that any man can handle any public job and that special preparation in the performance of public functions is not necessary has been the chief barrier to effective police training. The Model Police Council Act formulated by the Commission makes a real break with tradition in police work. It provides a state agency to take some responsibility for standards of police work throughout the state. The periodic inspections of police departments and follow-ups of such inspections, the power to make surveys and studies with a view to consolidation of police departments and police services, the power to inspect and approve police training schools, the requirement that only persons who have graduated approved training schools may be appointed to police departments, the subsidy for police training—all these give a state the means to improve police performance within its borders.

One of the most startling aspects of recent investigations has been the manner in which the constitutional privilege against self-incrimination, devised as a defense for the honest citizen against a despotic government, has been converted into a shield by underworld characters against any inquiry into their activities. The statement "I refuse to answer on the ground that it will tend to incriminate me," which is reminiscent of the great English constitutional struggles of the seventeenth and eighteenth centuries, has been mouthed over and over again by arrogant gang bosses and their underlings, derisive of law enforcement. Their right not to answer has necessarily been upheld by the courts, so long as the answer might give even the remotest clue to criminal activities. Under our system of law information about crime may be compelled only through an adequate grant of immunity from prosecution and punishment. The Model Witness Immunity Act, drafted by the Commission, therefore fills a real need in our law enforcement procedures. It applies to all offenses and makes possible a constitutionally adequate grant of immunity under proper safeguards to those whose testimony may be more important than their incarceration. It makes it possible to compel the testimony of underlings against major leaders in criminal conspiracies.

At this point the Commission on Organized Crime touches not only on the power of the underworld but upon that companion menace in American life today, the communist conspiracy. The communists, like the hoodlums in organized crime, have managed to distort the mechanics of criminal law and criminal procedure to their own purposes. Communists are quick to take advantage of the civil rights they would be the first to destroy if they came to power. Like the mobster, the Communist has been shielded from scrutiny by the constitutional guarantees against self-incrimination. Public exasperation is mounting at the recurrent sight of communist or communist sympathizer, underworld leader or underling and their political associates taking refuge from the consequences of their acts, in a constitutional phrase meant for the protection of the innocent.

These model acts, it may be seen, are no mere exercise in bill drafting. They offer practical solutions for difficult problems of the criminal law and criminal law enforcement which have engaged attention for years and decades. They were prepared with the thoroughgoing cooperation of committees of the National Conference of Commissioners on Uniform State Laws and the Council of State Governments as well as of many individual law enforcement officials. They were submitted to thorough analysis and debate last September before being adopted as Model Laws by the Conference of Commissioners on Uniform Laws and before being approved by the American Bar Association.

The next move is up to the states. The Commissioners on Uniform State Laws will place the Acts before the legislatures in the several states for consideration. Here the final and the only effective action can take place. In every state where they are considered a careful comparison with existing laws will be necessary. Thus the consideration of the Model Acts will bring about that very self-scrutiny by the states of their own criminal law procedure, administration and enforcement, which must everywhere be the first step in effective reform.

Will the Model Acts be adopted despite their departure from the notion that long cherished principles of government can only be carried out in ways that have prevailed for the last century? I can only point in hope to the experience of two states, my own state of New Jersey and the state of California. After years of research and planning New Jersey by its Constitution of 1947 transformed one of the most complicated and antiquated systems of courts in this country into one of the simplest. The change has won wholehearted public approval as a heavy backlog of old cases disappeared and new ones began to move along briskly because of the application of simple, modern judicial and new court administrative methods. Following our constitutional convention the legislature did a very remarkable thing which I think should be an inspiration to proponents of criminal law reform all over the country. It has been a tradition throughout the country that nothing can be done about the justice of the peace, who dated back to the twelfth century. He was an institution. He had to be tolerated. In many instances he was incompetent, unversed in the law he sought to administer, and with the advent of the automobile his usefulness was ended. It created problems with which he could not cope. Accordingly in New Jersey a single legislative bill tolled his departure without any public mourning whatsoever. The public is ready for forward-looking changes in the administration of justice and it is no longer bound by tradition where it can be shown that tradition is not only outworn but harmful.

The experience of California is equally pertinent to the problems posed by this book. Seventeen years ago Governor Earl Warren of California, then a district attorney, argued before the American Bar Association that every state should under normal conditions have supervisory powers over all law enforcement agencies within its borders and certain direct enforcement powers for use when local law enforcement fails. This he stated would not violate the American concept of local self-government. Later as Attorney General and then as chief executive, he took the leadership in establishing just such a system in California, where it receives much credit for the existing high level of law enforcement there. California, too, is one of the states which has made good use of model laws. It has adopted the Model Youth Correction Authority Act, formulated by the American Law Institute, and found it so satisfactory a method of dealing with young offenders that it has adopted the same concept in prescribing for the treatment of its adult offenders.

The administration of justice can never hope to reach perfection. There must be a continual process of reappraisal of existing conditions. Our court reorganization plan in New Jersey met this necessity by providing for an annual judicial conference which brings together not only members of the judiciary but the law enforcement officials, representatives of the bar, the deans of accredited law schools and a group of interested laymen to discuss current problems of the administration of justice in the courts and to make recommendations for improving our practice, procedure and administration. Because of the constructive results of these annual conferences, I am glad to see that this same principle of the recurrent conference for continuous self-examination and self-improvement has been incorporated in the Model Acts on police and prosecution.

The Commission under whose direction these latest reforms were prepared was of such caliber as to guarantee practical realistic proposals for improvements in law enforcement. Working under the chairmanship of the late Judge Robert P. Patterson until his unfortunate death last January, the Commission continued its devoted attention to the task at hand under another of its members, a distinguished lawyer from Memphis, Walter P. Armstrong, Jr.

It is no cause for surprise but must certainly be a source of satisfaction to Dean Pound as the moving spirit of a half-century of
reform that this latest attack of the American Bar Association on
problems of criminal law administration has from start to finish
been directed by a former pupil and protege, Judge Morris Ploscowe
of New York City. The work of the Commission to determine
from the Senate investigation the causes of the current breakdown
in criminal justice, and to construct practical remedies, is done.
The road to reform now lies through forty-eight state capitols.
There the challenge presented by these model acts must be met,
by legislators, lawyers, and laymen alike, who wish to see the
administration of the criminal law restored to its true purpose—
the protection of the rights and liberties, the property and life of
the law-abiding citizen.

AN EXPERIMENT IN THE TRIAL OF
INDIGENT CRIMINAL CASES *

What is believed to be an unique experiment by which the
organized Bar will seek to discharge its obligation imposed both
by the standards of the profession and the responsibility of its
individual members as officers of the court, will be undertaken at
the opening of the September term of the criminal courts of Essex
County, New Jersey.

During the summer the final details of a plan in which every
member of the Essex County Bar Association has agreed to serve
without compensation as counsel in turn to indigent defendants in
criminal cases, assisted by law school students, will be worked out.
The broad features of the plan already have the unanimous approval
of the members of the Association and the Deans of the Law
Schools located near the County Court House in both New York
and New Jersey.

---

* 32 A.B.A.J. 434-435 (1946).

The plan, believed to be the first developed in this country, was worked out by the trustees of the Association in cooperation with Common Pleas Judge Richard Hartshorne, and his colleagues on the bench of the Essex Common Pleas, after the Association had frowned upon a proposal that it sponsor the creation of a Public Defender program for the county.

Under the plan both young practitioners and experienced older lawyers have agreed to represent as a public service those who are without funds, except in homicide cases where under the State Statutes the Court is permitted to allow a counsel fee paid by the county.

Realizing that many of these men are far too busy to do all of the necessary pre-trial work including the investigation of witnesses, etc., Judge Hartshorne conferred with the Deans of the Law Schools to see whether it might not be to the advantage of the students to do this work under the direction of the assigned counsel. He reported his finding that not only did the Deans believe this practical experience would be of great value to those still in the Law Schools, but also that the students themselves were willing to devote this extra time in order to obtain practical experience in the preparation and trial of criminal cases.

A survey of the indigent cases in the County Courts from April, 1945, to April, 1946, showed a total of 216 different defendants with a total of fifty-one resultant trials. With more than a thousand members of the Bar Association, it is expected that each lawyer will be assigned but once in five years and of these assignments a trial will result but once in twenty years. The present number of available students in New York University, Columbia, Newark University, Fordham University and John Marshall Law Schools is sixty-three, so that each law student will be given practical experience in less than four cases a year and a participation in less than one trial a year.

With four judges sitting in the criminal courts, the membership of the Bar Association and the list of the law school students will be divided equally so that each can make his own assignments. While the assignments generally will be made in alphabetical rotation, some adjustments will be made so that the more experienced members of the Bar will have charge of the more difficult cases. In cases of exceptional difficulty, additional counsel and students may be assigned.

The Court, the Essex County Bar Association and the Law School Deans have expressed their view that in providing this public service to those unfortunates who have not the necessary funds to provide their own counsel, they will be discharging the obligation imposed by both the Federal and the New Jersey State Constitutions which guarantee to every man the right to be represented by counsel.

They also expect that this method of assigning counsel will prove to be much fairer and will end the burden which has been carried in the past by a few members of the profession who have voluntarily represented these indigents. While, as indicated, the members will be called upon alphabetically, a few returned servicemen who are desirous of being assigned probably will be placed at the head of the list.

Although the County Courts in New Jersey have long been regarded as free from so-called "ambulance chasers," or lawyers who sought these assignments in order to obtain some small fee from relatives wherever possible, it is said to be the belief of the Court that this method of handling assignments will tend to prevent any such attempts being made.

For the older practitioners, many of whom have not represented a defendant in the criminal courts for many years and some, indeed, not at all, far from being a routine chore, should prove to be an interesting experience. It is in the criminal courts, dealing with the most unfortunate group of our citizens, that the human problems arise with all of their tragedy and pathos. For those who have long breathed the rarified atmosphere of specialized civil practice both in the courts and in their offices, these cases in which a defeat means the loss of a man's liberty, perhaps for many years, should bring forth all of the skill of the defense counsel. Frequently the surgeon finds the work in the hospital wards far more interesting than the treatment of those whose financial position has given them all of those things which make for good health. So with the criminal courts. Here it is traditional that the lawyer carries the responsibility not only of saving a man's liberty but also of seeing that ultimate punishment is not upon the defendant's family.

In a sense this whole program is looked on by its sponsors as being but one phase of the responsibility of the Organized Bar to be the Public's lawyer. It is anticipated also that there will be reflected to the Bar some measure of good will, from the public, engendered by having some of the most capable members of the Bar willing and assigned to represent those accused persons who are least able to pay for legal assistance of that quality.

Substantive Law

The major portion of Vanderbilt's accomplishments in the reform of the law lies within the contiguous realms of procedure and judicial administration. But reform in these areas he regarded as merely preliminary to what he termed the "great task of the law in the second half of the twentieth century," the simplification and the modernization of the substantive law to make it more responsive to, in the words of Mr. Justice Holmes, "the felt necessities of the times." With Pound and Cardozo, he saw the tremendous task at hand resulting from rapidly expanding governmental activities and changing traditions in individual rights and liberties. He warned that "impending changes in the law may be intelligent, based on all the available facts and grounded on a social insight into the virtues as well as the infirmities of human nature, or they may be a haphazard, unthinking revolt against the existing order."

The Cook Lectureship on American Institutions at the University of Michigan is designed to provide the constructive thinking of the best minds of our times on American institutions. Arthur T. Vanderbilt's Cook Lectures, **Men and Measures in the Law,** delivered in 1948, are concerned with the functioning of the legal order.

He sketches the course of reform in substantive and procedural law through the centuries. Revealing deficiencies, he constructively suggests means by which the legal order may meet its obligations to improve the future. In his Lecture III, entitled **The Growth of Substantive Law,** Vanderbilt describes the methods of developing substantive law by means of legislative reform. Asserting that the growth of law also revolves around individuals, he gives insight into the personalities of some of the great English and American reformers of the past. What is needed, he states, is a body in each state trained continually to study, overhaul, revise and consolidate the statutory substantive law.

Vanderbilt, the Chief Justice, was no less an advocate of substantive law reform than Vanderbilt, the lawyer and academician. His dissent in **Fox v. Snow,** in which he deals brilliantly with the problem of stare decisis and the genius of the common law inherent in its capacity for growth has been referred to by Professor W. Barton Leach as "the most quoted dissent since Holmes."

THE GROWTH OF SUBSTANTIVE LAW *

In this lecture I shall comment on the growth of substantive law, reserving the more difficult matters of procedural law and the improvement of the administration of justice for subsequent discussion.

In viewing the broad sweep of Anglo-American legal history over the centuries it is surprising to note how much of the growth of the law revolves around individuals. Some

---

* Men and Measures in the Law 67-97 (Knopf, 1949). William W. Cook Foundation Lectures.

of these individuals who are pre-eminent in the history of the law have been kings or presidents, some judges, some writers, some both judges and writers. In the group of kings and presidents among the outstanding figures are Edward I, often called the English Justinian,[1] Theodore Roosevelt, Woodrow Wilson, and Franklin D. Roosevelt. Among judges we must list Coke, Mansfield, and Stowell in England, along with the giants of equity, Bacon, Nottingham, Hardwicke, and Eldon, and in this country Marshall, Kent, and Story. Coke's claim to fame is based on his services as a judge, as a writer of legal classics, but above all as a courageous parlimentary leader. Stowell shares with Mansfield the credit for developing a new body of substantive law, prize law, but Mansfield's domain was far broader. The development of a body of prize law, moreover, was inevitable in Stowell's time, but Mansfield's contributions in the main involved a deliberate choice on his part as to whether large bodies of law such as the law merchant and quasi-contracts should be incorporated in the common law. Equity was molded not by one man but by several, the chief being Bacon, Nottingham, Hardwicke, and Eldon in England, Kent and Story in America. No judge has ever equaled Marshall in his contributions to the field of public law. With both Kent and Story reputation as jurist is merged in pre-eminence as writer. Among English law writers Glanvil and Bracton, Littleton and Fortescue, Coke and Bentham stand out. Blackstone, in respect to influence, belongs to America as much as to England. In this country Kent and Story were the leaders among the writers who made law but as surely as Story is entitled to be called the father of conflict of laws should Dillon be given credit for the law of municipal corporations and Keener for quasi-contracts. Nor is the list closed; what renowned executives, great jurists, and distinguished writers have done in earlier ages and often in the grand manner still remains to be repeated on innumerable fronts and in each state by their modern successors.

Not all of the great achievements in the law, however, may be traced to individuals. Much has been accomplished by small groups of men working together. The barons at Runnymede forcing Magna Carta on a hostile king, and the Founding Fathers in Independence Hall drafting the Federal Constitution, are outstanding examples of group accomplishments.

The first thing that strikes one studying the broad course of the growth of our substantive law is the important place of legislation. At no time was this more true than in the reign of Edward I. Sir Matthew Hale, equally distinguished as a judge and as a law writer (1609-76), credits Edward with "the very scheme, mould and model of the common law," [2] and describes his influence on English jurisprudence in these significant words:

> Yet the Laws did never in any one Age receive so great and sudden an Advancement, nay, I think I may safely say, all the Ages since his Time have not done so much in reference to the orderly settling and establishing of the distributive Justice of this Kingdom, as he did within a short Compass of the Thirty five years of his Reign, especially about the first Thirteen Years thereof.[3]

Lest it be thought that I am returning to the Dark Ages for an example of the influence of a single man, let me quote the concluding paragraph of Pollock and Maitland's *The History of English Law Before the Time of Edward I,* on his present-day significance for all of us:

> It was the critical moment in English legal history and therefore in the innermost history of our land and our race. It was the moment when old custom was brought into contact with new science. Much in our national life and character depended on the result of that contact. It was a perilous moment. There was the danger of an unintelligent "reception" of misunderstood and alien institutions. There was the danger of a premature and formless equity. On the other hand, there was the danger of a stubborn *Nolumus,* a refusal to learn from foreigners and from the classical past. If that had not been avoided, the crash would have come in the sixteenth century and Englishmen would have been forced to receive without

criticism what they once despised. Again, we have stood at the parting of the ways of the two most vigorous systems of law that the modern world has seen, the French and the English. Not about what may seem the weightier matters of jurisprudence do these sisters quarrel, but about "mere matters of procedure," as some would call them, the one adopting the canonical inquest of witnesses, the other retaining, developing, transmuting the old *enquete du pays.* But the fate of two national laws lies here. Which country made the wiser choice no Frenchman and no Englishman can impartially say: no one should be judge in his own cause. But of this there can be no doubt, that it was for the good of the whole world that one race stood apart from its neighbours, turned away its eyes at an early time from the fascinating pages of the *Corpus Iuris,* and, more Roman than the Romanists, made the grand experiment of a new formulary system. Nor can we part with this age without thinking once more of the permanence of its work. Those few men who were gathered at Westminster round Pateshull and Raleigh and Bracton were penning writs that would run in the name of kingless commonwealths on the other shore of the Atlantic Ocean; they were making right and wrong for us and for our children.[4]

Although a few statutes of the Tudor period are still important, we may move on three centuries before we come to other great legislation that arrests our attention. The Petition of Right,[5] the statutes that establish the control of Parliament over taxation, direct and indirect, the legislation abolishing Star Chamber and other administrative courts,[6] and the Habeas Corpus Act[7] were all passed by Parliaments bitterly opposed to the aggressions of the Stuarts. All of these acts were victories of the common law through Parliament over the absolutistic pretensions of the Stuarts. Foremost among the small group of parliamentary leaders in the early part of this movement was Coke, advocating in the House of Commons the principles he had championed on the bench before he was summarily dismissed as Chief Justice of the Court of King's Bench by James I for refusing to submit to his command not to proceed with the hearing of a case involving the King's prerogative.[8] The triumph of the parliamentary forces was due to his moral courage as much as to his vast knowledge of the law and the justice of his cause. In admiration of his public service we can afford to forget some of his personal meanness. Can there be any doubt that the example set by him and his parliamentary associates was a source of inspiration to the revolutionary patriots of America a century later? These constitutional gains of Englishmen were crowned in the Glorious Revolution of 1688 by the Bill of Rights and the Act of Settlement, which marked, among other things, the achievement of the independence of the judiciary.[9]

We may skip nearly two centuries more before we come to the era of social reform signalized by the passage of the long overdue Reform Act of 1832. This era of unprecedented legislation, rivaled only by that of Edward I, was the result primarily of the changed living conditions brought on by the industrial revolution. It was delayed for nearly half a century through fear that the excesses of the French Revolution might sweep across the English Channel, but the delay at least served the good purpose of making the statutory program more thoroughgoing than it otherwise would have been. Jeremy Bentham died at the advanced age of eighty-four, the day before the Reform Act received the royal assent, but more than any other man he was responsible for it and the ensuing legislative program that transformed the daily life of the English people as well as ancient notions of the sphere of governmental activities. From the anonymous publication in 1776 of his *Fragment of Government* — at first variously attributed to Mansfield, Camden, and Dunning,[10] so excellent were its contents — to the time of his death he strove to induce his countrymen to look at the facts of government realistically and to measure the worth of every political institution by the utilitarian test of the greatest good to the greatest number. So great was his influence that Sir Henry Maine has termed Benthamism the English counterpart of the *jus naturale* of the Roman Law.[11] Bentham was the guiding spirit of his age. His disciples had long known what some other law reformers have not always seemed to grasp — that it is not enough merely to have good ideas; the ideas must be exploited. In bringing the Reform Act into existence they had themselves come into power as the leaders of the new Parliament. Their accession to office gave them new resources. As Sir Cecil Thomas Carr, the distinguished editor of the English *Statutory Rules and Orders* and of the *Revised Statutes,* graphically describes it:

The new Parliament (and its successors), impulsive, rather undisciplined, and very serious, knew that the country expected it to experiment and to risk the impact of State interference upon individual liberties. A series of non-party royal commissions and committees explored social conditions; their disclosures shocked public opinion and revealed the gap in the local administration of those times between efficient government in some places and scandalous neglect in too many others. Parliament, fortified by the reports and recommendations of these exploratory bodies, gave a smooth passage to several controversial Bills which were in no way the product of the government machine. And so Britain got a quick and quiet revolution in the laws of factories, poor relief, municipal corporations, prisons, and presently public health, while striking changes were also being made in civil procedure and summary jurisdiction and mitigation of savage punishments. This reinforcement of the governmental process by a concentration of the intelligence of men of independent mind, not always attached either to Parliament or to political parties, is an object lesson to which our eyes turn in these no less stimulating times.[12]

This vast statutory program ushered in modern administrative law. The success of social reform depended upon uniformity of administration throughout the country, and uniformity of administration in turn necessitated a tremendous increase in the activity of the central government. This increased activity of the central government meant paid professional officials replacing local amateurs. It also required much delegation of legislative power to these professional officials, for Parliament could not be expected to legislate on the intricacies of such a complex legislative program. The delegation of legislative power in turn involved grave questions of what were proper standards of administrative action. Most of all did it lead to the bureaucratic attitude in government. It is not easy to convey the reforming spirit of this new age in a few words, but Carr has hit it off in a brief paragraph describing Bentham's literary secretary, Edwin Chadwick:

He was a great investigator of social conditions, a great writer of bluebooks, and a great sanitary reformer. One modern historian has attributed to him the vices as well as the virtues of the official mind — rigidity, ruthlessness, a certainty that he was right, and a conviction that his opponents represented merely "sinister interests." Another has written of him that, born in 1801 in a Lancashire farmhouse where the children were washed all over every day, he made it his life's object to wash the people of England all over every day by executive order. Let us dwell rather upon his virtues. He was seized when young with what he called the "sanitary idea" — the idea that unhealthy conditions produced disease, and disease produced poverty. When he was not busy with other crusades, such as pensions for teachers, public promenades, physical training for trade unionists, and employers' liability for blameless accidents (our workmen compensation of today), he was devoting himself to every kind of sanitary research and improvement, whether it was housing, sewerage, water supply, prevention of epidemics, disposal of the dead, registration of the causes of death, or the cure of intemperance. At the age of eighty-six, when he wrote a vigorous essay advocating the uses of tricycles by the police, he pointed out that not only would the constables thus have the legs of the criminals but they would also find tricycling a valuable sanitary exercise. When he died in 1890, a postmortem examination would surely have revealed that word "sanitary" graven upon his heart.[13]

It will not do, however, merely to smile at the reformers. In a single generation they turned the criminal law from what Dr. R. M. Jackson has called "more brutal and savage than that of any civilized country"[14] into a system of law enforcement that has become the envy of all mankind. They did more to alleviate the condition of the poor and the underprivileged than had been accomplished in centuries. They not only awakened the conscience of England; they cast it into statutory mold.

Thus we have had exemplified the three chief instruments of legislative reform: first, the ruler, aided, of course, by experts; second, a small group of legislative leaders; and third, a broad popular movement sparked by the ideas of genius and fanned into flame by ceaseless agitation. In contrast with such epoch-making statutes is ordinary legislation, which has always involved the influence of pressure groups and legislative logrolling. We too often think of logrolling as a vulgar process, a product of our modern materialistic age. To illustrate its persistence even in the most spacious days, let me quote some genteel correspondence between the great Lord Chancellor Hardwicke and Lord Fitzwilliam:

> Lord Fitzwilliam presents his compliments to the Lord Chancellor, and will be glad of the disposal of the encumbency of Rawmarsh at the next vacancy.

> The Lord Chancellor presents his compliments to Lord Fitzwilliam, and has other views as to the disposal of the benefice of Rawmarsh.

> Lord Fitzwilliam presents his compliments to the Lord Chancellor, and will for the future manage for his own benefit his political influence in the West Riding of Yorkshire.

> The Lord Chancellor presents his compliments to Lord Fitzwilliam and the benefice of Rawmarsh will be at his disposal at the next vacancy.[15]

This exchange of greetings is matched in thought, if not in felicity of phrasing by the famous query in a letter addressed by William Jennings Bryan, when Secretary of State, to the Receiver of Customs in San Domingo:

> . . . can you let me know what positions you have at your disposal, with which to reward deserving Democrats? . . . You have had enough experience in politics to know how valuable workers are when the campaign is on; and how difficult it is to find rewards for all the deserving.[16]

The era of social reform in England has been a more or less continuous process since 1832, with an especially large wave of legislation from 1906 to World War I. All of these statutes find their source, as Dicey has pointed out in his *Law and Public Opinion in England*,[17] in popular sentiment, which as in the Benthamite period was very largely the result of endless discussion and agitation, but without any single inspiring genius such as Bentham. The socialist government that swept into office following World War II has undertaken further social experiments in a series of nationalization acts covering the Bank of England, the coal industry, civil aviation, communications, electric power, and transportation.[18]   It is interesting to observe that over the past three quarters of a century many of the social reforms of England, with more or less regularity, have found their way across the Atlantic. The recent nationalization acts of the present socialist government of England raise the interesting question whether this sequence will still continue. Or does, perchance, the adoption of the Federal Administrative Procedure Act of 1946 [19] mark a turn in the tide of legislative opinion not only as to the conduct of our own bureaucracy, but also with respect to the further acceptance here of English social experiments?

In modern times it is rare, indeed, that an individual has been able to make himself felt in Parliament as the sponsor of private bills. Sir A. P. Herbert is an interesting exception to the general rule. Long a member of the staff of *Punch,* as well as a barrister of the Inner Temple, he published in 1934 *Holy Deadlock,* a legally accurate novel, in which he satirized the divorce law of England.[20] The following year he was elected to the House of Commons to represent Oxford University. He promptly introduced a bill to meet the deficiencies in English divorce law. Ordinarily a private member's bill has very little chance of passage because of the exigencies of the government's legislative program. His wit and his skill at popularizing his cause eventually won the day. His bill was passed as the Matrimonial Laws Act, 1937, but is popularly known as the Herbert Act. Divorce in England and Wales is governed by it.[21]

In the United States social legislation began long before the English Reform Act of 1832. In the period following the American Revolution down to the Civil War important legislative reforms aimed at advancing the rights of the individual. In part this legislative movement was in response to the political philosophy of the seventeenth and eighteenth centuries, which was dominated by the idea of perfecting the individual. In part the new legislation reflected the conditions of frontier life, characterized by simple economic and social conditions. Self-reliance was the predominant virtue, equality of opportunity the grand objective. Fortunately the interest of the individual in acquiring property subserved the social interest of conquering the wilderness. The Bill of Rights of the Federal Constitution, drafted by George Mason of Virginia and ratified in 1791, and the corresponding provisions in the several state constitutions [22] were hardly more fundamental than the disestablishment of churches, which began in Virginia in 1786; [23] the abolition of slavery in the northern states from 1781 to 1804; [24] the legislation providing for the abolition of entail in Virginia in 1776 and of primogeniture in Georgia in 1777; [25] the grant of universal manhood suffrage, beginning in Vermont in 1777; [26] free compulsory public education, instituted in Massachusetts in 1852,[27] though urged long before by Jefferson; [28] and the abolition of the disabilities of married women, starting in New York and Pennsylvania in 1848.[29] These reforms, seeking to equalize and advance the individual as such, reflected in large measure the political ideals of Thomas Jefferson. Only one of them was in any sense socialistic; in free public education for the first time in this country we find the state, through legislation, giving positive aid to the individual rather than merely removing negative obstacles. Even free education was first proposed as a means of advancing the individual; its ultimate effect on society was deemed secondary. In practically all of this legislation the United States was well in advance of England.

The period following the Civil War was marked by a tremendous increase in legislative activity, the importance of which has tended to be underestimated in both the professional and the popular mind by reason of the attention focused throughout this period on the judiciary and particularly the United States Supreme Court. Legislation directed at business, such as the Sherman Act, aimed primarily at preventing monopoly.[30] Railroad legislation, exemplified by the Interstate Commerce Act, sought to eliminate the evils of monopoly.[31] Tariff legislation was offset by labor and immigration legislation.[32] Gradually the original sanctions for the enforcement of legislation by the criminal law came to be superseded, or at least supplemented, by the newer methods of administrative regulation. Conservation legislation seeking to put an end to the wasting of natural resources did not gain a foothold until the turn of the century.[33] The "Square Deal" of Theodore Roosevelt forecast the "New Freedom" of Woodrow Wilson with its Federal Reserve System, Federal Trade Commission, and the Clayton Act.[34] The financial crash of 1929 paved the way for the social program of the "New Deal," which was really a continuation of the "Square Deal" and the "New Freedom." The "Square Deal," the "New Freedom," and the "New Deal" were emphatically the work of individual leaders. The hegemony of the executive had arrived. The forces that have produced a large part of our social legislation, however, have been the same as those which led to the English Reform Act of 1832 and the burst of legislation that followed in its train. As John Dewey, the philosopher, has pointedly observed:

> Quite aside, however, from the allegation that "Big Business" plays the tune and pulls the strings to which bosses dance, it is true that parties are not creators of policies to any large extent at the present time. For parties yield in piece-meal accommodation to social currents, irrespective of professed principles. As these lines are written a weekly periodical remarks: "Since the end of the Civil War practically all the more important measures which have been embodied in federal legislation have been reached without a national election which turned upon the issue and which divided the two major parties." Reform of civil service, regulation of railways, popular election of senators, national income tax, suffrage for women, and prohibition are supported to substantiate the statement.[35]

Substitute Theodore Roosevelt, Woodrow Wilson, and Franklin D. Roosevelt for Edward I, the Founding Fathers at Philadelphia for the barons at Runnymede, and Thomas Jefferson, the political philosopher, for Jeremy Bentham, and you have the three chief methods of achieving social reform clearly illustrated in the course of American legislation, along with the inevitable activities of pressure groups and logrolling omnipresent in ordinary legislation.

So much for the manner in which substantive changes in the law have been effected by statute. Even before our national Constitution was adopted, the writers of the *Federalist* papers, though they could not possibly anticipate the plethora of legislation that afflicts us, gave voice to their well-grounded fears:

> It will be of little avail to the people, that the laws are made by men of their own choice, if the laws be so voluminous that they cannot be read, or so incoherent that they cannot be understood; if they be repealed or revised before they are promulgated, or undergo such incessant changes, that no man who knows what the law is today, can guess what it will be tomorrow.[36]

For our legislative ills we have only ourselves to blame. When Boswell reported to Dr. Johnson that a friend had told him that any plodding blockhead could excel in the legal profession, the good doctor expostulated: "Why, Sir, in the *formulary* and *statutory* part of law a plodding blockhead may excel; but in the *ingenious* and *rational* part of law a plodding blockhead never can excel." [37] It is this disparaging attitude toward legislation, to which I have already alluded more than once, that is chiefly responsible for the generally low estate of our statute law. Our attitude, of course, has been utterly irrational in view of the enormous importance of legislation over the centuries. All too slowly are we coming to realize that too much care cannot be given to the drafting of legislative bills, both with respect to their content and technical style as well as to the periodic — indeed, the continuous — overhauling of the entire statute book now made in but a few states.[38] The work of drafting a bill or revising a statute or perfecting a code is infinitely more difficult than that of preparing a brief or writing an opinion or even a textbook. All of these activities call for an accurate knowledge of the law and insight into its application. In addition not only must the lawyer laboring in the legislative field have the rare gift of peering into the future, but he must also be peculiarly endowed with the art of precise expression.[39] Nearly all states now have legislative reference bureaus.[40] Some states go beyond mere library service and provide technical research for the legislators in the form of elaborate briefs.[41] Most states also offer their law-makers bill-drafting facilities,[42] generally as part of their legislative reference bureaus. In spite of all these precautions the legislative product varies from the skillfully wrought bills of the National Conference of Commissioners on Uniform State Laws, one of the most successful of American efforts at co-operation in the law, to the slipshod, litigation-producing draftsmanship of pressure groups, of which some of the state fair-trade acts constitute a horrible example. In 1931 the first fair-trade act was enacted in California;[43] it embodied in one section language that was not only grammatically incorrect but utterly lacking in meaning.[44] This California act, as amended in 1933,[45] was blindly copied verbatim in Iowa, Maryland, New Jersey, New York, Oregon, and Pennsylvania without correction of the error.[46] It was only after lititgation arose in some of the blundering states,[47] in which the Illinois statute,[48] which had corrected the error, was contrasted with the offending acts, that amendment necessarily followed. However, the egregious blunder of this paragraph still remains on the statute books in Iowa.[49]

Even if all of our legislation were well drawn, the problems of our statute book would still be with us. There remains the perennial need of cutting out the deadwood by repealers and republishing only that which is still living. By this process in England in the 1860's 118 volumes were trimmed to 18.[50] Without periodic revision the mass of our statutes would, indeed, be forbidding. Revision, however, is but a first step in making our statute law available to the profession and the public. Especially in the field of local public law do statutes on various topics tend to grow like mushrooms. Unless all of the statutes on a given subject are occasionally merged into a single statute, they will perforce constitute a labyrinth in whose mazes even the most skillful lawyer may well become lost. This process of consolidation is a much more difficult task than that of revision.[51] It should be the work of lawyers who are trained in the arts of legislation and in addition thoroughly familiar with the actual operation of the laws in question. A rare example of what can be accomplished in this field is the recent consolidation of the Education Law of New York under the direction of Dr. Frank P. Graves, a competent lawyer who was for nineteen years Commissioner of Education for the State of New York.[52] Some of the finest legislative work of this type was done by able jurists in the period following the American Revolution in adapting to the needs of the new states the laws of England and of the respective colonies. The laws of New York were successively compiled by such persons as Samuel Jones and Richard Varick in 1789, and James Kent and Jacob Radcliff in 1801, and were re-examined and revised from 1825 to 1828 by Benjamin F. Butler, John Duer, John C. Spencer, and Henry Wheaton.[53] William Paterson, Governor and Chancellor of New Jersey, later a justice of the United States Supreme Court, spent eight years, from 1792 to 1800, in preparing a revision of the statutes of England and of New Jersey, which the legislature enacted into law.[54] In Connecticut former Chief Justice Zephaniah Swift was chairman of a legislative committee that published an invaluable revision of the laws of his state in 1820-3.[55]

What is most needed in each state is an agency that would be charged not only with the proper drafting of every bill that is introduced in the legislature, but with the *continuous* revision of the statutes as they appear on the statute books. In several states, notably Wisconsin and Kentucky, such action has been undertaken. There the entire statute book has been overhauled up to a certain date, and the work of revision and consolidation, the pruning of outmoded enactments, the combination of similar statutes, and the correction of stylistic errors, together with topical consolidation, is a continuous task, carried on by a trained body especially charged with these responsibilities. Moreover, the public and the profession are further aided by the provision for the biennial republication of the statutes in these states,

thus making available in most useful form the complete
statutory law. The result of the continual work of statutory
consolidation is best illustrated in Wisconsin, a pioneer in this
activity, in which state, during one five-year period, the volume
of the statutes increased only by sixteen pages.[56]

Codification goes a step further than consolidation in
dealing not only with statutes but with the decisions of the
common law with a view to incorporating all of the law of
any subject in systematic written form. In its most ambitious
aspect it seeks to cover the entire law written and unwritten.
As might be expected, Jeremy Bentham was its great advocate.
The very words "codify" and "codification" were coined by
him.[57] It was he who inspired Edward Livingston to draft
his penal code, which was finally completed in 1825, but never
enacted into law. Livingston also composed a Code of Civil
Procedure regulating Louisiana practice and completed a revision of the Civil Code which became law in that state.[58]
The great name in American codification, however, is David
Dudley Field. From 1839, when he had been admitted to the
bar only eleven years, to his death, in 1894, he not only worked
on the drafting of his codes, but agitated for them. His Code
of Civil Procedure was adopted in New York in 1848 and
rapidly spread westward, finding acceptance in whole or in part
in twenty-four states. His Penal Code was adopted in 1881,
but his Civil Code was twice rejected by the Assembly, thrice
passed by it, twice with the concurrence of the Senate, only
to be vetoed each time by the Governor.[59] The battle was
bitterly fought between Field and James C. Carter, representing
the Association of the Bar of the City of New York.[60]
Field almost became the American Justinian. Largely through
the influence of his brother, Mr. Justice Stephen J. Field, of
the United States Supreme Court, all five of Field's codes, the
Codes of Civil and of Criminal Procedure, and the Political,
Civil, and Penal Codes, were adopted in California.[61]

Codification in England took a different turn. Macaulay
the historian, labored for years on what ultimately became
the Indian Penal Code, replete with definitions and concrete

examples.[62]   Sir James Stephen, after years of experience in India, came back to England in 1872 fired with the possibility of codification at home, but his draft of a penal code was lost in the House of Commons.[63]   Codification in England received a new impetus when Sir Frederick Pollock,[64] influenced by Macaulay and Stephen, made a digest of the law of partnership in 1877 which later became the Partnership Act of 1890. Influenced in turn by Pollock's Digest, in 1878 Sir Mackenzie Chalmers had made a digest of the law of negotiable instruments, which became the Bills of Exchange Act. He also drafted the statutes codifying the law of the sale of goods in 1893 and the law of marine insurance in 1906.[65] With these, codification became almost a dead letter in England.[66] Professor Munroe Smith with his customary clarity has pointed out the parallel between Anglo-American and Roman legal development, showing that codification is most likely to prevail in the field of the organization of government, including the definition of the powers of public officers, both general and local, as well as with respect to the law of crimes and criminal procedure.[67]

A fourth method of improving statutes is of more recent origin. In 1934 Lord Chancellor Sankey appointed a Law Revision Committee made up of members representing every branch of the legal profession "to consider how far, having regard to the statute law and to judicial decisions, such legal maxims and doctrines as the Lord Chancellor may from time to time refer to the committee may require revision in modern conditions." The committee before the war had reported on eight matters that had been referred to it, and seven of their reports were accepted by Parliament. They covered such important matters as contribution between joint tort-feasors, the liability of a husband for the torts of his wife, the maxim that a personal action dies with the person, and the statute of limitations. The Lord Chancellor has also appointed other committees such as the Company Law Reform Committee, most of whose recommendations were embodied in statute in 1947, the Alternative Remedies Committee, whose recommendations for the abolition of the doctrine of common employment have also become law, and a committee to consider the law of libel and slander. There is still another committee on the practice and procedure of the Supreme Court of Judicature.[68] In New York, owing in large part to the influence of Mr. Justice Cardozo's plea for "a ministry of justice," [69] a Law Revision Commission was created in 1934, which has done more work in this field than has been done in all the rest of the states combined, as its annual reports attest.[70]

These perennial problems of the science of legislation give weight to the recent words of Sir Hartley Shawcross, the English Attorney General, that

> . . . by the end of the 1914-1918 war it had become very obvious that the necessity for strong government was accompanied by the need of a civil service experienced in the technique both of preparing legislation for submission to parliament, and of administering such legislation when its principles were enacted. . . .[71]

When he speaks of Civil service, he, of course, has in mind the English practice whereby examinations govern all appointments up to and including under-secretaries under a competitive system that ensures not only the broadest liberal education but also technical skill. These are matters that have been relatively neglected in this country, particularly at the higher levels, until comparatively recent times, though now progress is being made, noticeably in the selection of hearing commissioners under the Federal Administrative Procedure Act under the aegis of the United States Civil Service Commission.[72] But even superior official personnel will not avail, as I have intimated before, in the face of a general professional distaste for statute law. What is most needed is a rational attitude toward legislation as a mode of law-making. This, it would seem, must be sought first of all in the law schools.[73]

As I turn from legislation to the broad field of judicial decisions, I am confronted with an embarrassment of riches. One might select cases illustrating the gradual growth of the law to meet new conditions, such as Judge Cardozo's great decision in *MacPherson* v. *Buick Motor Co.*,[74] granting redress against a manufacturer to a person injured by latent defects in an article purchased at retail, when the defect might have been discovered if the manufacturer had exercised vigilance. Or one might consider a case like *Funk* v. *United States,* where Mr. Justice Sutherland, speaking for the Court, enacted law as truly as any legislature ever does. The background of this case is that Congress, unlike most state legislatures, had failed to abolish the ancient common-law rule that precluded a wife from testifying in behalf of her husband in a criminal proceeding against him, though it had done away with many other common-law disabilities of witnesses. Weary of waiting for Congress to act, the Court proceeded to dispose of this common-law disability saying: "That this court and the other federal courts, in this situation and by right of their own powers, may decline to enforce the ancient rule of the common law under conditions as they now exist we think is not fairly open to doubt." [75]

These two cases illustrate the two fundamental kinds of growth in the common law in modern times, the arch-demons of fiction having long since been slain by Bentham, and equity having in most jurisdictions been fused into the common law. But instead of seeking to study the growth of the law in individual cases, would it not be more profitable to turn our attention to the judge who has made the most extensive contributions to the growth of law and, what is even more to the point, made it largely as a matter of free volition. Stowell, it is true, made the prize law of England, and Marshall set the course for our constitutional law, but they were both confronted with specific cases calling for decisions in their respective fields. Mansfield, by his liberal judicial attitude, encouraged the bringing of cases that led to his development of the action of *indebitatus assumpsit,* the creation of the doctrines of quasi-contract and restitution, and the incorporation of the law merchant into the common law. One cannot imagine any other judge of his time who could or would have done so. Certain it is that there were many judges and lawyers who did not look at all with favor on his importation of equitable principles into the law, but his efforts to avoid

legal technicalities and to adapt the law to the needs of the
period appealed greatly to the common sense of businessmen.
The reception of the law merchant into the common law of
England is the work of his peculiar genius, as was his contribution to the improvement of the administration of justice, an
aspect of his activities too long neglected by a profession
preoccupied with private substantive law, but of which I shall
necessarily speak in my next lecture.

Lord Mansfield has fascinated me since the first day I
encountered him in my law school course on contracts. I had
more or less successfully navigated the course through Offer
and Acceptance without having been asked to accept too much
that to my youthful mind seemed irrational, but as I traversed
the dismal swamp of Consideration, I felt as if I had been
left to myself without a map or compass or means of communication with the strange forms around me. When at length
I turned the page to *Pillans* v. *Van Mierop*,[76] I knew that
I was in the presence of a great mind who, fortunately for me,
spoke a modern language I could understand. Why shouldn't
a promise in writing intended as a business transaction be
good, regardless of consideration? It made sense to me, and
it accorded with the civil law. A few pages later on I felt
almost a personal sense of injury when I discovered in *Rann*
v. *Hughes* that the House of Lords had overruled *Pillans* v.
Van Mierop, declaring that:

> All contracts are, by the laws of England, distinguished
> into agreements by specialty, and agreements by parol;
> nor is there any such third class as some of the counsel
> have endeavored to maintain, as contracts in writing.
> If they be merely written and not specialties, they are
> parol, and a consideration must be proved.[77]

Imagine my delight in discovering two years later in the
summary to Dean Ames's *Cases on Bills and Notes*[78] his
convincing demonstration that beyond the peradventure of a
doubt negotiable instruments were and always have been
specialties in the English law though not under seal, Chief
Baron Skynner and his brethren to the contrary notwithstand-

ing. It is interesting to note that the English Law Revision Committee in one of its reports has sided with Lord Mansfield.[79] When in due season I came to the cases on conditions in contracts in our casebook, Mansfield's opinions in *Kingston* v. *Preston*[80] and *Boone* v. *Eyre*[81] stood out like beacon lights in the midst of much murky thinking. To study his decisions in Keener's *Cases on Quasi-Contract* was a rare treat, rivaled only by the pleasure of reading by myself his contributions in Wambaugh's *Case on Insurance.*

I am never quite certain whether I am moved more by his opinions or by the dazzling achievements of the man himself in spite of seemingly insuperable obstacles. William Murray, the later Lord Mansfield, was born in 1705,[82] a younger son of a poor Scotch peer, in a family tainted with the Jacobite heresy. He attended the grammar school at Perth until the age of thirteen, when at the suggestion of his elder brother James, Secretary of State for the Old Pretender, he was entered at Westminster. His career at Westminster and at Christ Church, Oxford, was distinguished. At Oxford he first crossed swords with William Pitt over a prize poem on the death of George I, and the rivalry there begun continued in the House of Lords until the death of the Earl of Chatham. At Lincoln's Inn his self-education marked the man. At a time when instruction at the Inns of Court was a mere form, he schooled himself to master not only the common law, but international law, *Justinian's Institutes,* the *Corpus Juris Feudalis,* the standard works of his native Scotland — Stair and McKenzie — as well as the *Ordinance de la Marine* for the grasp it might give him of the law merchant. In addition, moreover, to studying special pleading under Denison and conveyancing with Booth, to quote Dr. Johnson, "when he first came to town [he] 'drank champagne with the wits.' He was the friend of Pope."[83] This literary giant thought sufficiently of Murray to inscribe odes to him in imitation of Horace, praising his young friend, only to call forth parodies at the hands of the envious, Scotchman, Jacobite, and one of the wits! In that day with what further handicaps for success in his profession could genius burden itself?

Called to the bar in 1730 at the age of twenty-five, he
soon made a name for himself as a junior in two appeals
from the Court of Sessions of Scotland to the House of Lords.
Within eight years he had made his way to the front and
was appearing in the leading matters of the day, such as
representing the City of Edinburgh in the parliamentary
inquiry into the Porteous riots. In the same year he married
the amiable Lady Elizabeth Finch, daughter of the Earl of
Winchelsea and a descendant of Lord Chancellor Nottingham.
Four years later he became Solicitor General, a position that
he held for fourteen years — "the longest and most brilliant
solicitor generalship recorded in the annals of Westminster
Hall," according to the acidulous Lord Campbell [84] — and
during all of this period he also served as the resourceful
leader of the majority in the House of Commons. In 1754 he
succeeded Sir Dudley Ryder as Attorney General. On Ryder's
death, two years later, in the last days of the ministry of the
Duke of Newcastle, despite the Duke's entreaties that he remain in the House of Commons, he achieved his life's ambition
of becoming Chief Justice of England, a position that he filled
for thirty-two years with the highest distinction.

Although Murray served many years as a parliamentary
leader, his activities as a barrister and his conduct as one of
the chief law officers of the kingdom left little doubt of his
primary interest in the law and its administration. [T]his
selection as Chief Justice was one of those rare cases where
the man, the office, and the times were ideally suited. This
is not to say that his life was no longer crowded with conflict
or beset with controversy, for reforms of the magnitude that
he contemplated were not to be accomplished without violent
objections from the adherents of the established order.

His greatest achievement on the substantive side of the
law was the reception of the law merchant into the body
of the common law. This he was able to accomplish because
of his broad knowledge of Continental authorities in this field,
based on his studies which began during his student days at
Lincoln's Inn. But not content with this learning, he consulted

personally with the merchants to ascertain the customs of their business. Furthermore, to aid in the trial of commercial cases he resorted to the ancient device of a special jury of merchants, but with him the special jury became an established institution of his court. Lord Campbell recalls that several of these gentlemen survived when he began to attend Guild Hall as a student and were designated and honored as "Lord Mansfield's jurymen." [85] Lord Mansfield is said not only to have conversed with them freely in court, but to have won their confidence by inviting them to dine with him.

Even so, Mansfield's task was not an easy one. His predecessors, and even Lord Chancellor Hardwicke, were inclined to admit in each case evidence of relevant mercantile customs, with the result that every such case would be merely decisive of the facts presented in it, without enunciating any general rule. On the other hand, if such evidence of customs were excluded, there was the danger that the law might lose touch with prevailing mercantile practice. Mansfield solved the problem by declining to admit evidence of mercantile customs that had already been established as law, applying them as general rules of law, but if a particular custom had not already been established as law, he would allow evidence concerning it and, if reasonable, would accept it as law. The obscure archaic language that abounded in mercantile documents he construed liberally to meet the true intent of the parties, regardless of the actual words, with the result that in the course of time the construction that he put upon these instruments developed a body of law as to their meaning. The principles developed in his court covered the wide range of commercial law, maritime law, and the law of marine insurance, the details of which cannot be traced here. It is not too much to say that it was he who put all of these subjects on a sound footing in English law. To a very large extent the principles of his opinions have been codified in the British Marine Insurance Act of 1906 and only to slightly less degree have his rulings on negotiable instruments found their way into the English Bills of Exchange Act and the American Uniform Negotiable Instruments Act.

In the field of contract law Mansfield's attempt to harmonize the law of consideration with the Continental law was overruled, as we have seen, but his clear recognition in *Kingston* v. *Preston*[86] that terms in a contract might be concurrent as well as dependent or independent served to advance clear thinking in a complicated phase of the law. It was in the field of quasi-contracts that he made his bravest attempt to change the course of English legal history by seeking to give to the action of *indebitatus assumpsit* the effect of a bill in equity. Although he did not succeed in this goal, *indebitatus assumpsit* did come to cover a wide variety of cases where the plaintiff was allowed a recovery on the ground of the unjust enrichment of the defendant. If he did not succeed in making *indebitatus assumpsit* the equivalent of a bill in equity, he at least introduced into the common law the equitable doctrines of estoppel by conduct, the doctrine of stoppage in *transitu*, and the rule that there is no right of stoppage in *transitu* against the assignee of the consignee. Above and beyond matters of specific rules, he definitely broke the ties of the common law with the formalism of the black-letter law dear to Coke; through him the spirit of equity had entered much of the common law.

There were other spheres in which he was quite unsuccessful in reforming the law. In *Perrin* v. *Blake*[87] he attempted to reduce the rule in Shelley's Case to a rule of construction. This led to a bitter attack on him by Fearne, the author of the well-known work on *Contingent Remainders.* Fearne charged that Mansfield when a barrister had given an opinion on Shelley's Case exactly contrary to his decision as a judge. Mansfield, of course, did not deign to reply.[88] Suffice it to say that his decision eventually was viewed with favor by Parliament, which vindicated his position by abolishing the rule in Shelley's Case in the Law of Property Act, 1925.[89] As to Fearne, Sir Frederick Pollock tells with obvious delight of Macaulay's lament over Fearne's devotion of a life to the barbarous puzzles of contingent remainders.[90]

Mansfield's most unfortunate experiences were in the field of criminal law, but there he also experienced some of his greatest triumphs. Neither the legislature nor the profession has approved his efforts to limit the power of the jury to return a general verdict in cases of criminal libel, which called forth the savage attacks on him of Junius.[91]   When his whole record, however, is reviewed, it may be justly said that no one judge has ever made a greater contribution to our law or done more to raise its moral level. The maxim "Let justice be done though the heavens fall," attributed to him, expresses his aim as a judge. It is what we would expect from the advocate who, when criticized for his moderation in the prosecution of the rebel Scotch lords, could say with dignity:

> If I had been counsel for the Crown against Sir Walter Raleigh, and that unfortunate man had been as clearly guilty of high treason as the rebel lords, I would not have made Sir Edward Coke's speech against him to gain all Sir Edward Coke's estate and all his reputation.[92]

No judge in these days may hope to rival Mansfield's contribution to the growth of the law, but every judge and every lawyer may learn much from his skill in adapting the law to the needs of the times. His judicial work is the outstanding example of the results obtainable from the use of the comparative method in the law.

FOX v. SNOW *

VANDERBILT, C.J. (dissenting)   I am constrained to dissent from the views of the majority of the court, first, because they apply to the case a technical rule of law to defeat the plain intent of the testatrix without serving any public policy whatever in so doing and, secondly — and this seems to me to be even more important — because their opinion involves a view of the judicial process, which, if it had been followed

---

* 6 N. J. 12, 14-28, 76 A. 2d 877, 878-885 (1950).

consistently in the past, would have checked irrevocably centuries ago the growth of the common law to meet changing conditions and which, if pursued now, will spell the ultimate ossification and death of the common law by depriving it of one of its most essential attributes — its inherent capacity constantly to renew its vitality and usefulness by adapting itself gradually and piecemeal to meeting the demonstrated needs of the times.

I.

The controversy in the instant case centers around the third paragraph of the will of Rosa E. Green:

> "Third: I give and bequeath unto my husband, William L. Green, all of the money which I have on deposit at the Paterson Savings and Trust Company, Paterson, New Jersey, however, any money which is in the said account at the time of my said husband's death, the said sum shall be held by my niece, Catherine King Fox, absolutely and forever."

Not only is the meaning of this bequest entirely clear to any mind not encumbered with the involved and technical feudal lore of estates in fee simple, estates in fee tail and estates for life and the medieval doctrines of seisin and possession, but it is consonant with her entire testamentary plan. By the second paragraph of her will she gave her husband a life estate in her homestead with a remainder in fee to the plaintiff, her niece; by the fifth paragraph she named the plaintiff as her sole residuary legatee and devisee; by the sixth paragraph she designated the plaintiff's daughter to take her place and stead in the event that the plaintiff should predecease the testatrix; and by the seventh paragraph she named the plaintiff as her executrix.

By the words in the third paragraph, "any money which is in said account at the time of my said husband's death, the said sum shall be held by my niece, Catherine King Fox, absolutely and forever," the testatrix beyond and doubt intended that her husband could use up the bank account but that if he did not, the plaintiff should take what was left of it on his death. To hold otherwise is to proceed on the untenable assumption that the quoted words are meaningless and to ignore the elementary principle that the provisions of a will are not to be construed as meaningless except on the failure of every attempt to render them effective, *In re Fox,* 4 N. J. 587, 594 (Sup. Ct. 1950); *In re Fisler,* 133 N. J. Eq. 421, 425 (E. & A. 1943); *Shannon v. Ryan,* 91 N. J. Eq. 491, 494 (E. & A. 1920). This principle is an integral part of the most fundamental rule of testamentary construction, *i. e.,* the duty of the court is to ascertain what the intent of the testator was and, then, having ascertained it, to give it effect, *In re Fox, supra,* 4 N. J. 587, 593 (Sup. Ct. 1950); *Blauvelt v. Citizens Trust Co.,* 3 N. J. 545, 552 (Sup. Ct. 1950); *National State Bank of Newark v. Stewart,* 135 N. J. Eq. 603, 605 (E. & A. 1944); *Colwell v. Duffy,* 109 N. J. L. 423, 424 (E. & A. 1932); *Dennis v. Dennis,* 86 N. J. Eq. 423, 429 (E. & A. 1916); *Kent v. Armstrong,* 6 N. J. Eq. 637, 638 (E. & A 1850). The intention of the testator in every case is, of course, subject to rules of public policy and statutory law, *National State Bank of Newark v. Stewart, supra,* 135 N. J. Eq. 603, 605 (E. & A. 1944), but when its objective is lawful, all arbitrary rules of construction must give way, *Colwell v. Duffy, supra,* 109 N. J. L. 423, 424 (E. & A. 1932). The distinction between the construction of wills and the construction of deeds is well summarized in *Shriver's Lessee v. Lynn, et al.,* 43 U. S. 43, 56 (1844):

> "But there is a rule of construction applicable to all instruments, and especially to wills, that is, the intention of the parties, which should control any arbitary rule however ancient may be its origin. * * * Where technical words are used in a deed of conveyance, the legal import of such words must govern. But there is no rule better established than that in giving a construction to a will the intention of the testator must prevail. His expressed intention constitutes the law, unless it shall conflict with some established legal principle."

Even Chancellor Kent concedes that "In the construction of devises, the intention of the testator is admitted to be the pole-star by which the court must steer," but then he inconsistently continues, "yet that intention is liable to be very much controlled by the application of technical rules, and the superior force of technical expressions," 4 *Commentaries on American Law* *537, a rule which may well apply to deeds, but which, as we have seen, has no place in the construction of wills.

In *Smith v. Bell,* 31 U.S. 68 (1832), a case very much like the one now under consideration, Chief Justice Marshall found it possible to give effect to the entire testamentary provision before him. In construing a clause in a will which read:

> "I give to my wife, Elizabeth Goodwin, all my personal estate whatsoever and wheresoever, and of what nature, kind and quality soever, after the payment of my debts, legacies and funeral expenses, which personal estate I give and bequeath unto my said wife, Elizabeth Goodwin, to and for her own use and benefit, and disposal absolutely; the remainder of the said estate after her decease, to be for the use of the said Jesse Goodwin."

the great Chief Justice Marshall had this to say with respect to the intent of the testator, at p. 74:

> "These words give the remainder of the estate, after his wife's decease, to the son, with as much clearness as the preceding words give the whole estate to his wife. They manifest the intention of the testator to make a future provision for his son, as clearly as the first part of the bequest manifests his intention to make an immediate provision for his wife. If the first bequest is to take effect according to the obvious import of the words taken alone, the last is expunged from the will. The operation of the whole clause will be precisely the same as if the last member of the sentence were stricken out; yet both clauses are equally the words of the testator, are equally binding, and equally claim the attention of those who may construe the will. We are no more at liberty to disregard the last member of the sentence than the first. No rule is better settled than that the whole will is to be taken together, and is to be so construed as to give effect, if it be possible, to the whole. Either the last member of the sentence must be totally rejected, or it must influence the construction of the first so as to restrain the natural meaning of its words; either the

bequest to the son must be stricken out, or it must limit the bequest to the wife, and confine it to her life. The limitation in remainder, shows that, in the opinion of the testator, the previous words had given only an estate for life. This was the sense in which he used them."

Instead of following this obviously sound method of testamentary construction our courts have been misled by the complex and artificial rules of the old common law of real property into accepting a technical rule of testamentary construction which gained seeming but altogether undeserved immortality from the opinion of Chancellor Kent in *Jackson v. Robins,* 16 Johns. 537 (N.Y. Ct. App. 1819), wherein he categorically stated at p. 588:

"* * * we may lay it down as an incontrovertible rule, that where an estate is given to a person generally, or indefinitely, with a power of disposition, it carries a fee; and the only exception to the rule is, where the testator gives to the first taker an estate for life only, by certain and express words, and annexes to it a power of disposal. In that particular and special case, the devisee for life will not take an estate in fee, notwithstanding the distinct and naked gift of a power of disposition of the reversion."

The rule was later set down by Chancellor Kent in his *Commentaries* as settled law, 4 *Commentaries on American Law* *270 and *535, and has been followed by the New Jersey courts in a long line of decisions commencing with *Dutch Church at Freehold v. Smock, et al.,* 1 N. J. Eq. 148 (Ch. 1830), and including, *inter alia, Downey v. Borden,* 36 N. J. L. 460 (E. & A. 1872) ; *Tuerk v. Schueler,* 71 N. J. L. 331 (E. & A. 1904) ; *McCloskey v. Thorpe,* 74 N. J. Eq. 413 (E. & A. 1908) ; *Brohm v. Berner,* 95 N. J. L. 85 (E. & A. 1910) ; *Hyde v. Hyde,* 88 N. J. Eq. 358 (E. & A. 1917) ; and *Trafton v. Bainbridge,* 125 N. J. Eq. 474 (E. & A. 1939). It has likewise been subscribed to by courts in other jurisdictions, though significantly not without dissent, 75 A. L. R. 75-111.

If this rule is applied to the bequest here in question, it is apparent that the husband takes a fee and that consequently the limitation over, being inconsistent with the rights of the first taker becomes invalid. But it is also apparent that this result is altogether contrary to the intention of the testatrix as clearly expressed in her will. By a technical rule of construction the latter half of the third paragraph of the will of the testatrix is thus as effectively blotted out of the will as if she had never written it. If the draftsman of the will knew of this technical rule of testamentary construction and still used language in the will which he knew would be abortive because of the rule (an assumption which in this case and doubtless in most cases where such language is used is contrary to fact) a fraud would have been perpetrated on the testatrix. If the draftsman was unaware of this technical rule, the effect upon the testatrix is the same. Of necessity, therefore, the rule operates to perpetrate a fraud on the testatrix.

John Chipman Gray, the foremost American authority on property law, in his *Restraints on the Alienation of Property* (2d *Ed.* 1895) 66, writes:

> "It is to be observed that the rule is not a rule of construction, it is not a rule to carry out the intention of the parties, but its avowed purpose is to defeat that intention."

Because of the fact that in the instant case the clearly expressed intent of the testatrix has been thwarted by this obviously arbitrary and technical rule that owes its continuance to the magic of the name of Chancellor Kent, it is incumbent upon us to inquire closely into its nature in order to determine whether it is a rule necessitated by principles of public policy and founded upon good reason before which testamentary intent should rightly bow, or whether it is merely a rule remarkable only by its ancestry. Gray has stated the alleged reasons for the rule and their complete lack of validity with his customary incisiveness in his *Restraints on the Alienation of Property* (2d *Ed.* 1895), *supra*:

> "What are the reasons given? They are, *First,* that the gift over is repugnant; *Second,* that the passage of a fee simple on death of the tenant intestate to the heirs is a necessary incident of the estate; *Third,* that an executory devise contingent upon a circumstance which it is in the power of the first taker to prevent happening is void. The first is the reason originally given [see *Ide v. Ide,* 5 Mass.

500 (1809)]; the second is the reason given by Fry, J., in *Shaw v. Ford* [7 Ch. D. 669 (1877)]; the third is Chancellor Kent's. But these are only words. They merely mean that the courts have set up a certain rule, and that the proposed provision is inconsistent with it; but why that rule should be set up, what interests are forwarded by it, how it helps the well-being, moral or material, of the community, the courts never show, and, to do them justice, never attempt to show. In the hundreds of pages in the reports on this subject, there is no suggestion that this rule tends to promote any good object." (P. 67.)

Stating that the rule is not a rule of construction to carry out the intention of the parties but that its aim and object is to defeat that intention, he observes:

"The courts always recognize this fact; and that no considerations of public policy are involved is shown by its being perfectly easy to carry out the desired result by a slight change of phrase. If you give a man a fee simple, you cannot provide that if he does not sell or devise it it shall go to T., but if you give him a life estate with power to appoint by deed or will, and in defeault of appointment to T., the gift to T. is perfectly good. In both cases the intention is clear and undisputed; when you defeat the intention in one case, you are defeating exactly the intention that is preserved in the other." (P. 67.)

These observations apply equally to the whole line of decisions in New Jersey which follow Chancellor Kent's rule. One may search them from the case of *Dutch Church at Freehold v. Smock, et al., supra,* 1 N. J. Eq. 148 (Ch. 1830), to *Trafton v. Bainbridge, supra,* 125 N. J. Eq. 474 (E. & A. 1939), without finding any good reason given for this technical rule that is relied upon in derogation of the cardinal rule of testamentary construction of seeking the testator's intent and its corollary that the language of the will is not to be construed as meaningless unless every attempt to render it effective fails.

Nor do Chief Justice Marshall and Gray stand alone in their opposition to the rule. Mr. Justice Holmes, the editor of the 13th edition of *Kent's Commentaries,* has this to say:

"It is difficult to perceive any good reason why the executory devise should not be considered valid, subject to be defeated by a disposition of all the property, just as a remainder after a life estate with a power of appointment is valid, but subject to be divested by an appointment." (Vol. 4 at *270.)

When one recalls that Mr. Justice Story sat with Chief Justice Marshall in *Smith v. Bell, supra,* 31 U. S. 68 (1832), it would appear that the weight of juristic authority as well as sound reasoning are against this rule which inevitably works a fraud on a testator.

That the rule is arbitrary and serves no public policy is perhaps best demonstrated by a few illustrations from our own decisions. In the instant case there was a devise to A generally or indefinitely, with absolute power of disposition, and on A's death a gift over to B. By the operation of Chancellor Kent's rule A gets a fee and the gift over is void, *Downey v. Borden, supra,* 36 N. J. L. 460 (E. & A. 1872); *Tuerk v. Schueler, supra,* 71 N. J. L. 331 (E. & A. 1904); *Hyde v. Hyde, supra,* 88 N. J Eq. 358 (E. & A. 1917). A would not have taken a fee, however, and the gift over to B would have been valid, if the devise had been to A for life, instead of generally and indefinitly, *Pratt v. Douglas,* 38 N. J. Eq. 516 (E. & A. 1884); *Wooster v. Cooper,* 53 N. J. Eq. 682 (E. & A. 1895); *Weaver v. Patterson,* 92 N. J. Eq. 170 (Ch. 1920); *Trafton v. Bainbridge, supra,* 125 N. J. Eq. 474 (E. & A. 1939); or if A's power of disposition had been limited instead of absolute, *Wright v. Wright,* 41 N. J. Eq. 382 (Ch. 1886); *Hensler v. Senfert,* 52 N. J. Eq. 754 (Ch. 1894); or even if the devise had been to A absolutely, or forever, or the like, but with only a power of testamentary disposition, *Kent v. Armstrong, supra,* 6 N. J. Eq. 637 (E. & A. 1850); *Cantine v. Brown,* 46 N. J. L. 599 (E. & A. 1884); *Kellers v. Kellers,* 79 N. J. Eq. 412 (Ch. 1911); affirmed on appeal, 80 N. J. Eq. 441 (E. & A. 1912); or to A absolutely, or forever, or the like, without any mention of a power of disposition, *Jones v. Stites,* 19 N. J. Eq. 324 (Ch. 1868); *West Side Trust Co. v. Guiliano,* 106 N. J. Eq. 475 (Ch. 1930); *Higgins v. Mispeth,* 118 N. J. Eq. 575 (Ct. 1935); but see *Galante v. Silver-*

stein, 98 N. J. Eq. 52 (Ch. 1925); *Kutschinski v. Sheffer,* 109 N. J. Eq. 659 (E. & A. 1932). It is thus obvious that the plaintiff herein is denied her due, not because what the testatrix intended was illegal or impossible, but solely because the verbal formula used to express that intent ran afoul of this idiosyncrasy of the law.

II.

The opinion of the majority of the court, like every other decision in this State on the subject, makes no attempt to justify the rule it perpetuates either in reason or on grounds of public policy. Despite the deleterious effects of the rule and the lack of any sound principle to support it, the majority maintains that it should not be overthrown, because it has been the long established law of this State and because overruling it "would be fraught with great danger in this type of case where titles to property, held by bequests and devises, are involved" by reason of the retroactive effect of all judicial decisions. This view, if it had been consistently applied in the past, wiuld have prevented any change whatever in property law by judicial decisions. There would have been, *e.g.,* no rule against perpetuities, no restraints on the alienation of property, no right to redeem mortgaged premises, no foreclosure of the equity of redemption, and so on endlessly. Every change in the law by judicial decision necessarily creates rights in one party to the litigation and imposes corresponding duties on the other party. This is the process by which the law grows and adjusts itself to the changing needs of the times.

The process is necessarily used not only to create new rights and corresponding duties but, where necessary, to strike down old ones. *Cessante ratione legis, cessat et ipsa lex* (the reason for a law ceasing, the law itself ceases) is one of the most ancient maxims known to our law and it is constantly followed by our courts. Of this maxim it was said in *Beardsley v. City of Hartford,* 50 Conn. 529, 47 Am. Rep. 677, 682 (1883), "This means that no law can survive the reason on which it is founded. It needs no statute to change it; it abrogates itself." The same thought was enunciated by Lord Coke in *Milborn's Case,* 7 Coke 7a (K. B. 1609):

"Ratio legis est anima legis, et mutata legis ratione, mutatur ex lex" (the reason for a law is the soul of the law, and if the reason for a law has changed, the law is changed). "It is revolting," says Mr. Justice Holmes, "to have no better reason for a rule of law than that it was laid down in the time of Henry IV. It is still more revolting if the grounds upon which it was laid down have vanished long since, and the rule simply persists from blind imitation of the past," and "To rest upon a formula is a slumber that, prolonged, means death." *Collected Legal Papers* (1920) 187, 306. Holdsworth, in commenting on this quotation from Mr. Justice Holmes, has described how the Anglo-American system of case law has enabled "the judges, within fairly wide limits, to apply to old precedents a process of selection and rejection which brings the law into conformity with modern conditions." "This process of selection and rejection," he says, "has been applied to the law laid down in the Year Books; and generally the rules there laid down, which are still part of our modern law, have survived because they suit modern needs." *Essays in Law and History* (1946) 161, 162. It is as important to the growth of the law that it should have the inherent power to cast off outmoded or erroneous rules of law as that it have the capacity for developing new doctrines suited to the needs of the times. The only difference between these two phases of the same process is that the one proceeds almost automatically out of sheer necessity and often without any open admission that that new law is being created, while the other involves an open recognition of past mistakes or an express repudiation of a rule once sound but now outmoded. Unfortunately, it is not considered in good judicial taste to overrule erroneous or outworn doctrines *sub silentio*.

To hold, as the majority opinion implies, that the only way to overcome the unfortunate rule of law that plagues us here is by legislation, is to put the common law in a self-imposed straitjacket. Such a theory, if followed consistently, would inevitably lead to the ultimate codification of all of our law for sheer lack of capacity in the courts to adapt the law to the needs of the living present. The doctrine of *stare decisis* neither renders the courts impotent to correct their past errors nor requires them to adhere blindly to rules that have lost their reason for being. The common law would be sapped of its life blood if *stare decisis* were to become a god instead of a guide. The doctrine when properly applied operates only to control change, not to prevent it. As Mr. Justice Cardozo has put it, "Few rules in our time are so well established that they may not be called upon any day to justify their existence as means adapted to an end. If they do not function they are diseased. If they are diseased, they must not propagate their kind. Sometimes they are cut out and extirpated altogether. Sometimes they are left with the shadow of continued life, but sterilized, truncated, impotent for harm." *Nature of the Judicial Process* (1921) 98. All lawyers as well as laymen have a perfectly natural longing to think of the law as being as steadfast and immutable as the everlasting hills, but when we face the realities, we must agree with Dean Pound when he says, "Law must be stable, and yet it cannot stand still." *Interpretations of Legal History* (1923) I, and with Professor Williston when he tells us, "Uniform decisions of 300 years on a particular question may, and sometimes have been overthrown in a day, and the single decision at the end of the series may establish a rule of law at variance with all that has gone before." *Some Modern Tendencies in the Law* (1929) 125. The most drastic and far-reaching example of what Professor Williston had in mind was the overturning of the entire *corpus* of federal common law through the over-ruling of *Swift v. Tyson*, 16 Peters 1 (1842), by *Erie Railroad Co. v. Tompkins*, 304 U. S. 64 (1938).

Particularly in the realm of testamentary construction should the courts feel free to depart from precedent when the dictates of justice and reason demand it. Even Chancellor Kent was of this opinion: "Though we are not to disregard the authority of decisions, even as to the interpretation of wills, yet it is certain that the construction of them is so much governed by the language arrangement, and circumstances of each particular instrument, which is usually very unskillfully and very incoherently drawn, that adjudged cases become of less authority, and are of more hazardous application, than decisions upon any other branch of the law." 4 *Commentaries on American Law* *535. "Blind adherence to precedent as respects the meaning of a particular phrase is fraught with peril to the testamentary design, for, as said, intention is to be gathered from the instrument as a whole, and it rarely happens that the wills are substantially alike." *National State Bank of Newark v. Stewart*, 135 N. J. Eq. 603, 605 (1944). See also Clapp's *New Jersey Practice, Wills and Administration* (1950) 236. Even in England where the doctrine of the judicial infallibility of the House of Lords has prevailed for a century, we find Lord Chancellor Simon declaring in the case of *Perrin v. Morgan* (1943), 1 All E. R. 187, 194, when an ancient and well established rule of testamentary construction was urged upon the court:

> "The present question is not, in my opinion, one in which this House is required on the ground of public interest to maintain a rule which has been constantly applied but which it is convinced is erroneous. It is far more important to promote the correct construction of future wills in this respect than to preserve consistency in misinterpretation."

The dangers that the majority fear, it is submitted, are more apparent than real. The doctrine of *stare decisis* tends to produce certainty in our law, but it is important to realize that certainty *per se* is but a means to an end, and not an end in itself. Certainty is desirable only insofar as it operates to produce the maximum good and the minimum harm and thereby to advance justice. The courts have been reluctant to overthrow established rules when property rights are involved for the simple reason that persons in arranging their affairs have relied upon the rules as established, though outmoded or erroneous, and so to abandon them would result sometimes in greater harm than to observe them. The question whether the doctrine of *stare decisis* should be adhered to in such cases is always a choice between relative evils. When it appears that the evil resulting from a continuation of the accepted rule must be productive of greater mischief to the community than can possibly ensue from disregarding the previous adjudications on the subject, courts have frequently and wisely departed from precedent, 14 *Am. Jur., Courts,* § 126.

What then, are the relative evils in the instant case? First, we should consider the evils that will result from a perpetuation of the rule here involved. It has already been demonstrated that the rule, in each and every instance in which it is applied, results in a complete frustration of the legitimate intention of the testator. It can only operate to take property from one to whom the testator intended to give it and to bestow it upon another.   There is a further evil, moreover, resulting from the very existence of the rule.   As Professor Gray has put it in his *Restraints on the Alienation of Property* (2d ed. 1895) 68, *supra*:

> "It is often a question of the greatest difficulty to determine whether a testator has given a devisee a life estate with general power of appointment, or whether he has given him a fee with an executory devise over in case the first taker shall not dispose of his interest. If it were not for this rule, that question would almost never become material. But now that a testator's intention, if expressed in one form, cannot be carried out, while it can be, if expressed in another, the question becomes of vital importance, and consequently this arbitrary rule is responsible for an enormous amount of litigation."

Bearing out this observation, an annotation in 75 A. L. R. 71-111, entitled "Devise or bequest which does not state character or duration of estate but purports to dispose of what remains at death of devisee or legatee, as creating a fee or life estate," cites 386 cases of which 28 are from New Jersey, and we cannot even hazard a guess as to the number of additional cases, reported and unreported, in which the rule was involved.   That a rule has been so productive of unnecessary litigation is in itself strong proof of its undesirability.

Having considered the evils flowing from continuing to follow the rule, let us now inquire into the evils, if any, which might result from its rejection.   It is pertinent at this point to recall the words of Mr. Justice Cardozo minimizing the effect of overruling a decision: "The picture of the bewildered litigant lured into a course of action by the false light of a decision, only to meet ruin when the light is extinguished and the decision is overruled, is for the most part a figment of excited brains." *The Nature of the Judicial Process* (1921) 122.   The rule in question by its very nature is never relied upon by those who are seeking to make a testamentary disposition of their property, for if the rule were known to a person at the time of the drawing of his will, its operation would and could be guarded against by the choice of words appropriate to accomplish the result desired. This rule is truly subversive of the testator's intent. It is relied upon only after the testator's decease by those who seek, solely on the basis of its technical and arbitrary requirements, to profit from the testator's ignorance and to take his property contrary to his expressed desires. Certainly it is not unjust or inequitable to deny such persons resort to this rule. There are three possible factual situations to be considered in weighing the retroactive effect of overturning this rule. First, where a will has already been the subject of legal proceedings, property rights determined by a judgment entered therein are beyond the reach of any change in the law. Such a judgment is *res judicata*. Second, where a will has been executed, but the testator is still living, or if dead, the clause similar to the one in question has not yet been construed by the courts, the "evil" caused by the overthrow of the rule will be to carry out the testator's intent. No existing will need be changed by a decision doing away with the old rule, since its overturning merely permits the expressed intent of the testator to be given effect. Third, where persons have not now, but may in the future execute wills, no harm can result from overthrowing the rule, for they have neither to forget an old rule nor to learn a new one in order to insure the carrying out of their testamentary plan. In the absence of the rule their intentions, as naturally though perhaps inexpertly expressed, will govern.

Thus it would appear that the dangers envisioned from overthrowing this rule are not present here and that the evils resulting from its continuation are great. This being so, should there be hesitation in rejecting this rule merely because it is old? To recognize a rule solely because it has long been the law "would be to deny every quality of the law but its age, and to render it incapable of progress or improvement. It would be to stamp upon our jurisprudence the unchangeableness attributed to the laws of the Medes and the Persians." *Hurtado v. California,* 110 U. S. 516, 529 (1883). We should not permit the dead hand of the past to weigh so heavily upon the law that it perpetuates rules of law without reason. Unless rules of law are created, revised, or rejected as conditions change and as past errors become apparent, the common law will soon become antiquated and ineffective in an age of rapid economic and social change. It will be on its way to the grave. In the instant case the rule applied by the court below should be rejected and effect should be given to the testator's intention that the plaintiff have the bank account in question.

Constitutional Law

Few scholars had a more thorough knowledge of the Constitution and its history than Arthur T. Vanderbilt. He did not share the illusion that constitutional guarantees could be activated by patriotic speeches or Gladstonian phrases. When abuse of governmental power abridged an individual's freedom, counteraction was required if the values of a free society were to be preserved. Accordingly, when Norman Thomas was denied the right to speak in Jersey City and was "deported" from that locality by Mayor Hague, Vanderbilt, at his own expense, successfully represented Thomas before the United States Supreme Court. Vanderbilt also intervened when Roger Baldwin of the American Civil Liberties Union was convicted of "unlawful assembly" during the strike of the Paterson, New Jersey, mill workers.

Throughout its history, the United States Supreme Court has seldom been free from controversy. In recent years, discussion has centered on the question of the proper role of the Court in our political structure. Some students of the Court, advocates of the doctrine of "judicial self-restraint" (Vanderbilt termed it "judicial deference") believe that the Court should assume a more or less passive role when called upon to decide constitutional issues and not substitute its judgment for that of the popularly elected branches of government. Those opposed to this philosophy, the so-called "judicial activists," are in favor of the Court assuming a more active role, and, by its power of review, implementing the protective provisions of the Constitution. The excerpt from his book on the separation of powers indicates Vanderbilt's opposition to the doctrine of judicial deference. He would have been pleased to learn that the Court finally came around to his way of thinking in the matter of legislative reapportionment. See Baker v. Carr, 369 U.S. 186 (1962). In an introduction to the 1963 edition of Vanderbilt's **Doctrine of the Separation of Powers and Its Present-Day Significance,** Professor Michael Conant of the University of California at Berkeley says: "This volume of lectures . . . is the only modern comprehensive statement and analysis of the constitutional doctrine of the separation of governmental powers . . . it should be required reading for all students of government and law."

Vanderbilt's opinion in **Tudor v. Board of Education** is of more than ordinary interest in view of the pronouncements of the United States Supreme Court regarding prayer in the schools.

JUDICIAL DEFERENCE AS A GRAVE CAUSE OF CONSTITUTIONAL IMBALANCE *

. . . Equally devastating to the individual litigant and the general public are many of the self-imposed limitations on judicial review of issues of constitutionality. Here, too, the doctrine of judicial deference has evolved gradually. Its classic formulation is to be found in the *Ashwander* case:

1. The Court will not pass on the constitutionality of legislation in a friendly, non-adversary, proceeding.
2. The Court will not "anticipate a question of constitutional law in advance of the necessity of deciding it."

---

* The Doctrine of the Separation of Powers 134-140 (U. of Neb. Press, 1953). Reprinted with introduction, 1963. Roscoe Pound Lectureship series.

3. The Court will not "formulate a rule of constitutional law broader than is required by the precise facts to which it is to be applied."

4. The Court will not pass upon a constitutional question . . . if there is also present some other ground upon which the case may be disposed of.

5. The Court will not pass upon the validity of a statute upon complaint of one who fails to show that he is injured by its operation.

6. The Court will not pass upon the constitutionality of a statute at the instance of one who has availed himself of its benefits.

7. "When the validity of an act . . . is drawn in question, and even if a serious doubt of constitutionality is raised, it is a cardinal principle that this Court will first ascertain whether a construction . . . is fairly possible by which the question may be avoided." [107]

One does not have to quarrel with all of these canons to wonder if Chief Justice Marshall's great opinion in *Marbury v. Madison* [108] would not have died stillborn and with it the judicial power to declare an act unconstitutional, if the great Chief Justice had been bound by these principles of self-abnegation. Rather must we not give heed to Marshall's pointed reference to the constitutional requirement that every judge be bound by oath or affirmation "to support this Constitution" [109]—not part of it, but all of it:

> Why otherwise does it direct the judges to take an oath to support it? This oath certainly applies in an especial manner, to their conduct in their official character. How immoral to impose it on them, if they were to be used as the instruments, and the knowing instruments, for violating what they swear to support! [110]

Can there be any doubt that on numerous important issues vital and pressing constitutional questions have gone unanswered because of undue judicial deference? In the *Ashwander* case, for example, stockholders were denied an adjudication of the validity of a contract between their corporation and the Tennessee Valley Authority. But perhaps the most dangerous instance of undue judicial deference, until very recent times, was the decision of the Supreme Court in *Massachusetts v. Mellon*,[111] which challenged the constitutionality of the Maternity Act providing for appropriations of money to be allotted among the several states for the purpose of reducing maternal and infant mortality. The allotment to each state, in accordance with the accepted formula of grants-in-aid, was made conditional on acceptance by the states of the terms of the statute. The states, again in the normal pattern of grants-in-aid, were to contribute financially. Massachusetts claimed that the statute was unconstitutional as a usurpation of power reserved to the states under the Tenth Amendment. It was argued that even though the state had not accepted the Act, is constitutional rights were infringed by the imposition of an option either to yield part of its reserved rights to the federal government or to lose its share of the appropriation. The cases (there was also a suit by an individual taxpayer tied with the state suit) were "disposed of for want of jurisdiction without considering the merits of the constitutional questions." [112]   With respect to Massachusetts the Court said:

> In the last analysis, the complaint of the plaintiff State is brought to the naked contention that Congress has usurped the reserved powers of the several States by the mere enactment of the statute . . .; and it is plain that that question, as it is thus presented, is political and not judicial in character, and therefore is not a matter which admits of the exercise of the judicial power.[113]
>
> No rights of the State falling within the scope of the judicial power have been brought within the actual or threatened operation of the statute and this Court is . . . without authority to pass abstract opinions upon the constitutionality of acts of Congress.[114]

The plaintiff taxpayer alleged that the effect of the statute would be to take her property, under the guise of taxation, without due process of law. Here, too the Court declined to pass on the merits of the petition and asserted that an action does not lie by a taxpayer to test the constitutionality of an appropriation measure. Mere suffering "in some indefinite way in common with people generally" [115] is not sufficient interest, it was said by the Court, to invoke its jurisdiction. The substance of the plaintiff's complaint was stated by the court to be:

Merely that officials of the executive departments of the government are executing and will execute an act of Congress asserted to be unconstitutional; and this we are asked to prevent. To do so would be not to decide a judicial controversy, but to assume a position of authority over the governmental acts of another and co-equal department, an authority which plainly we do not possess.[116]

The net result is that notwithstanding the fact that the constitutional issue was raised by the only parties who could possible object to the act, the United States Supreme Court avoided deciding it and thereby left unanswered one of the most important constitutional questions ever presented to it. By an act of self-imposed judicial deference the Court has rendered immune from attack the flood of legislative appropriations that have created an imbalance between the states and federal government never dreamed of by the Founding Fathers or the judges who spoke of "an indestructible Union, composed of indestructible States." [117]

Professor Oliver P. Field has summarized with restraint yet with clarity the situation in which the Court finds itself in applying its canon of "interest" for testing unconstitutionality:

The Court is still struggling with the problem of "interest" on the part of those who seek to challenge the validity of statutes. Little can be done to extricate the law from the bog into which it has fallen on this point so long as the idea prevails that constitutionality should be sparingly dealt with by the courts. It should be just the opposite, but with statutes or rules of limitation as to the time in which it could be done.[118]

The doctrine of judicial deference has also served to prevent citizens from obtaining their full voting right. In *Colegrove v. Green* [119] the Supreme Court held itself without jurisdiction to decide a controversy involving the apportionment scheme of Illinois with respect to seats in Congress. The effect of the Illinois apportionment act was to give the citizens in some districts a vote disproportionate to that given citizens in other districts. The Court held that to invalidate a state redistricting statute would be to infringe on the exclusive power of Congress and the states to control the election of congressmen, saying:

> The Constitution has left the performance of many duties in our governmental scheme to depend on the fidelity of the executive and legislative action and, ultimately, on the vigilance of the people in exercising their political rights.[120]

In *South v. Peters* [121] the Supreme Court reaffirmed the doctrine of the *Colegrove* case and refused to consider a petition alleging that the county unit system in Georgia was unconstitutionally discriminatory by decreasing the effectiveness of votes from the populous areas. This case also raised the issue of racial discrimination in that the operation of the system permitted a virtual disenfranchisement of Negro voters. In these two cases, out of judicial deference to the action of the two state legislatures, the equal protection clause faded out of the Constitution and with it fundamental rights of citizens of Georgia and Illinois.

Must not situations such as those involved in the *Ashwander* and the *Mellon,* the *Colegrove* and the *South* cases be reconsidered in the light of the enlarged powers of the Congress and of the President and the administrative agencies, all made possible by the new construction placed by the courts on the "general welfare" clause in the tax section of the legislative article of the Constitution? [122] And should not the Court, having made the welfare state possible, permit litigation of the issue of what is and what is not for the general welfare? [123] Has the time not come for a reconsideration of the propriety of the entire doctrine of judicial deference, if the balance contemplated by the Constitution is to be recovered? Should the weakest branch of government on its own initiative weaken itself still further at the expense of the clear rights of citizens under the Constitution?

The responsibility for the growth of federal powers at the expense of the states and for the increase in the powers of the executive branch of the federal government rests, in the first instance, on the Congress and, in the second place, on the federal judiciary. The Congress has delegated vast legislative powers to the executive branch and it has assumed broad powers to promote what it considers to be in the general welfare, all without review by the courts. The assumption by each branch of the government of its full responsibility—but no more—will be no easy task in view of the drift of events, but it is a task nevertheless that must be accomplished if we are to maintain constitutional government.

The doctrine of judicial deference is not the only force working to the disadvantage of the position of the courts. In a representative, democratic government such as ours the power of the judiciary depends largely on its reputation for independence, integrity and wisdom. All too often our judges, even in our courts of last resort, have weakened their position with the public by indulging in politics in clear violation of the Canons of Judicial Ethics [124] as well as of the doctrine of the separation of powers.

TUDOR v. BOARD OF EDUCATION OF RUTHERFORD *

I.

Vanderbilt, C. J.

The Gideons International is a nonprofit corporation organized under the laws of the State of Illinois, whose object is "to win men and women for the Lord Jesus Christ, through * * * (c) placing the Bible—God's Holy Words—or portions thereof in hotels, hospitals, schools, institutions, and also through the distribution of same for personal use." In recent years it began a campaign to make available to pupils in the public schools of this country the so-called "Gideon Bible," which was characterized by the International in its pleadings as "a book containing all of the New Testament, all of the Book of Psalms from the Old Testament, all of the Book of Proverbs from the Old Testament; all without note

---

* 14 N. J. 31, 33-52, 100 A. 2d 857, 858-869 (1953).

or comment, conformable to the edition of 1611, commonly known as the Authorized, or Kings James version of the Holy Bible." In furtherance of this campaign it applied by letter to the Board of Education of the Borough of Rutherford for permission to distribute its Bible to the public schools of that municipality:

"Board of Education
Rutherford, N. J.
Attention: Mr. Guy Hilleboe
Gentlemen:
The Gideons of Passaic and Bergen County, consisting of local business men, hereby offer to furnish, without charge, a volume containing the book of Psalms, Proverbs and the New Testament to each of the children in the schools of Rutherford from the fifth grade up through the eighth grade, and High Schools.
This offer is part of a national campaign conducted by the Gideons International to furnish the Word of God free to the young people of our country from the fifth grade through the high school. If God's word is heard and heeded, if it is read and believed, we believe that this is the answer to the problem of juvenile delinquency.
If your board approves this distribution, we will be glad to have our committee work out the details with the principals of the schools.
　　　　　　Yours very truly,
　　　　PASSAIC COUNTY CAMP OF GIDEONS
　　　　　　　/s/John Van Der Eems,
　　　　　　　　John Van Der Eems,
　　　　　　　　　Treasurer"

The proposal was considered at a meeting of the board of education on November 5, 1951, at which time there was voiced some opposition to the proposal by a Catholic priest and a Jewish rabbi on the grounds that the Gideons' New Testament was sectarian and forbidden to Catholic and Jewish children under the laws of their respective religions. The proposal, however, was passed by the board with one dissenting vote, the resolution adopted providing that "the Gideons International be allowed to furnish copies of the New Testament, Psalms and Proverbs to those pupils who request them." Under date of November 21, 1951 the following request form for signiture of the parents was prepared by the board of education and distributed to the pupils of the public schools of Rutherford:

> "Rutherford Public Schools,
> Rutherford, N. J.
> November 21, 1951

To all Parents:

At the regular meeting of the Board of Education on November 5, 1951, The Gideon Bible Society, presented a request that the New Testament, Psalms and Proverbs be made available, without cost, to all children who wish a copy. The Board approved this request provided the distribution be voluntary. *If you wish a copy of this Bible, will you please sign the slip below and return it with your child to the school he attends by Friday, December 21.*

School ....

....

Please request The Gideon Bible Society to provide my child ...., with a copy of the New Testament, Psalms and Proverbs. This request involved [sic] no obligation on my part or on the part of the Board of Education.

Signed...
Parent or Guardian"

On January 14, 1952 the board of education was advised by its counsel that the proposed distribution was in his opinion legal. At a principal's meeting on February 6, 1952 the following instructions were issued:

"(a) Only names of pupils whose parents had previously signed for the Bibles should be used in any announcement.

(b) Pupils whose parents had signed for Bibles are to report to the home room at the close of the session and no other pupils are to be in the room when the Bibles are distributed.

(c) Any announcement of names for the purpose of reporting after school should not include a reference as to the purpose of reporting."

Prior to the distribution of the books the present action was commenced demanding judgment as to the validity of the distribution under the Federal and New Jersey Constitutions and seeking an injunction against it. On February 19, 1952 the trial judge granted a temporary injunction and by order dated February 29, 1952 restrained the board of education from carrying out the terms of its resolution of December 10, 1951, until further determination of the action. By consent Gideons International was permitted to intervene as a party defendant. After a full hearing the trial judge on March 30, 1953 found in favor of the defendant and vacated the restraint and stay. By consent of the parties, however, the stay has been continued pending appeal. While the appeal was before the Appellate Division of the Superior Court, we ordered certification on our own motion.

The plaintiff Bernard Tudor is an adherent of the Jewish religion, while plaintiff Ralph Lecoque is a member of the Catholic faith, each being a New Jersey citizen and taxpayer of Rutherford and a parent of a pupil in a Rutherford public school. Each contends that the Gideon Bible is "a sectarian work of peculiar religious value and significane to members of the Protestant faith." Mr. Tudor claiming that "its distribution to children of the Jewish faith violates the teachings, tenets and principles of Judaism," while Mr. Lecoque states that "its distribution to children of Catholic faith violates the teachings, tenets and principles of Catholicism." After this action was commenced, the child of plaintiff Ralph Lecoque transferred from the public school to a Catholic parochial school and to the extent that the complaint was based upon his status as a parent, the issue became moot. The State of New Jersey was originally named as a party defendant but the action as to it has been dismissed. The Synagogue Council of America and the National Community Relations Advisory Council have submitted a brief *amici curiae*.

II.

The American doctrine of the separation of Church and State cannot be understood apart from its history for it is the epitome of centuries of struggle and conflict. In 311 A. D. Christians were still being persecuted; but shortly thereafter the Fourth Century witnessed the toleration of Christianity in the Roman world. In 313

A. D. Constantine, the ruler of the West, and Licinius, the emperor of the East, met in Italy and proclaimed the Edict of Milan, which made the toleration of the Christian religion "a part of a universal toleration of all religions, and it establishes absolute freedom of worship," *Innes, Church and State, p.* 23. In 410 A. D. Rome was sacked by Alaric. Italy, as well as Spain and Africa, fell to the Teutonic barbarians, but these conquests did not spell defeat for Christianity. The attitude of the invaders is illustrated by the words of Theodoric, speaking shortly after the fall of Rome:

> "That to pretend to a dominion over the conscience is to usurp the prerogative of God; that by the nature of things the power of sovereigns is confined to external government; that they have no right of punishment, but over those who disturb the public peace, of which they are the guardians; and that the most dangerous heresay is that of a sovereign who separates himself from a part of his subjects, because they believe not according to his belief." *Innes, Church and State, p.* 51.

After the collapse of the Roman Empire the Church remained as the one stable, permanent element in society. Gradually it came to claim not merely equality with the State, but actual superiority. Thomas Aquinas summed up the Church's attitude:

> "The highest aim of mankind is eternal happiness. To this chief aim of mankind all earthly aims must be subordinated. This chief aim cannot be realized through human direction alone but must obtain divine assistance which is only to be obtained through the Church. Therefore the State, through which earthly aims are obtained, must be subordinated to the Church. Church and State are as two swords which God has given to Christendom for protection; both of these, however, are given by him to the Pope and the temporal sword by him handed to the rulers of the State." *Bates, Religious Liberty: An Inquiry* (1945), *p.* 140.

The Church's claim of supremacy did not go unchallenged. Charlemagne, who had been crowned by the Pope, deliberately crowned his own son as successor without consulting the Pope. The struggle for supremacy was on between Church and State, and the history of the Middle Ages in Europe is largely a history of this continuing conflict. The struggles between Pope Gregory VII and Emperor Henry IV in the 11th Century, and between the English kings Henry II and John and Celestine III and Innocent III a century later were but phases of the conflict. The Church reached the height of its supremacy over the State in the 13th Century, under Innocent III, who informed the Patriarch of Constantinople that "the Lord left to Peter (the Pope) the government not of the Church only but of the whole world," and advised Philip Augustus of France that "single rulers have single provinces and single kings have single kingdoms, but Peter, as in the plentitude, so in the extent of his power, is preeminent over all since he is the vicar of Him Whose is the earth and fullness thereof, the whole world and all that dwell therein." *Bates, Religious Liberty: An Inquiry, supra, pp.* 140-141. During his rule Innocent was not only a spiritual leader but he was also the supreme temporal chief of the Italian State, the Spanish Peninsula, the Scandinavian States, Hungary, Bohemia, Poland, Servia, Bosnia, Bulgaria, and the Christian state of Syria, 17 *Encyclopædia Britannica* (14*th ed.*), "Papacy," *p.* 203.

The 14th Century witnessed the growth of new ideas. In 1324 Marsilius of Padua in his *Defensor Pacis* denied the right of the Church to interfere in any matters which were not spiritual. He expounded the very ideas that centuries later were credited to Locke, Montesquieu, Rousseau and Jefferson. Marsilius was far ahead of his age when he claimed that "no man may be punished for his religion." *Acton, History of Freedom in Christianity,* in *Essays on Freedom and Power, p.* 65.

But the doctrine of religious liberty and the separation of Church and State were not established in Europe even with the advent of the Reformation. The Reformation brought forth the more prevalent Erastian doctrine of state supremacy and the use of religion to help carry out state policy. The peace of Augsburg in 1555 was a compromise between Lutherans and Catholics, based on the theory that the religion of a province was to be determined by the religion of its ruler (*cuius regio, eius religio*). To the same effect was the peace of Westphalia in 1648 ending a 30-year religious war which swept Central Europe:

> "Each secular state in Germany was henceforth free to
> profess its existing religion, whether Catholic, Lutheran, or
> Reformed; but no other religion was to be 'received or
> tolerated in the Holy Roman Empire,' and the power of
> the reigning princes to 'reform' their states by driving out
> dissenters was restrained rather than abolished." *Innes,
> Church and State, p.* 157.

In England under Queen Elizabeth the Thirty-nine Articles of the
Church of England were adopted and the supremacy of the Crown
over the Church was clearly established. Bloody struggles between
Anglicans, Catholics and Dissenters continued. By the 17th Century
Catholics were regarded with disfavor and in 1647 the Constitution
established by Cromwell granted religious freedom to all except
Catholics. In the Glorious Revolution of 1689 the Act of Toleration
under William and Mary established religious toleration in England,
but again Catholics were excepted.

By 1787 in Europe no nation had established complete freedom
of worship or the mutual independence of religion and civil government. There had been steps in that direction and there were those
who strongly advocated the separation of Church and State but the
Erastian doctrine still prevailed. In almost every country there was
a state-supported or at least a state-favored religion while the other
faiths were treated with varying degrees of toleration. In Spain
the Inquisition was still in existence in 1787 while at the other
extreme Holland represented the utmost in religious toleration and
freedom for all faiths. In 1784 James Madison summed up the
centuries of bloody religious battles in Europe:

> "Torrents of blood have been spilt in the world in vain
> attempts of the secular arm to extinguish religious discord,
> by proscribing all differences in religious opinions." *Blau,
> Cornerstones of Religious Freedom in America* (1949),
> *p.* 85.

While America has been free from religious wars, our history has
had its dark pages of religious persecution.

III.

Religion was a strong motivating force in the American
colonies. People of all faiths flocked to the New World, many

with the hope that here for the first time they could enjoy religious freedom. Unfortunately to America these earlier settlers also brought the Old World idea of a state-established and state-dominated religion. Many of the original charters granted by the Crown required the settlers to establish a religion that was to be supported by all, believers and nonbelievers alike. Thus, in early Virginia all ministers were required to conform to the canons of the Church of England. Quakers were banished and Catholics were disqualified from public office, while priests were not permitted in the colony. In New York Peter Stuyvesant established the Dutch Reformed Church, which all settlers were required to support. Baptists who attempted to hold services in their homes were subject to fines, whipping and banishment. Quakers were unwelcome and subject to persecution. The Commission of New Hampshire of 1680 provided:

> "And above all things We do by these presents will, require and command our said Council to take all possible care for ye discountenancing of vice and encouraging of virtue and good living; and that by such examples ye infidle may be invited and desire to partake of ye Christian Religion, and for ye greater ease and satisfaction of ye sd loving subjects in matters of religion, We do hereby require and command yt liberty of conscience shall be allowed unto all protest- ants; yt such especially as shall be conformable to ye rites of ye Church of Engld shall be particularly countenanced and encouraged." 2 *Poore, Constitutions* (1878), *p.* 1277.

In New England generally the Calvinist Congregational Church was the established religion.

Religious freedom in the colonies was far from an established fact. In the Massachusetts Bay Colony Anne Hutchinson in 1638 was tried and convicted as a blasphemer and seducer of the faithful and as a teacher of erroneous doctrines, because she held meetings in her home where she advocated the direct intuition of God's grace and love instead of obedience to the laws of the Church and the State. Roger Williams was banished because "he broached and divulged divers new and dangerous opinions, against the authority of the magistrates," 1 *Stokes, Church and State in the United States* (1950), p. 195. Catholics were persecuted and in 1647 the General Court ordered that:

"No Jesuit or spiritual or ecclesiastical person ordained
by the pope or see of Rome shall henceforth come into
Massachusetts. Any person not freeing himself of suspicion shall be jailed, then banished. If taken a second
time he shall be put to death." *Pfeffer, Church, State and
Freedom* (1953), *p.* 68.

Despite these instances of intolerance and persecution there were
successful examples of religious freedom. In 1649, largely due
to the efforts of Cecil Calvert, the second Lord Baltimore, Maryland
granted toleration to all Trinitarian Christians. In Rhode Island
through the efforts of John Clarke, a follower of Roger Williams,
Charles II granted a charter in 1663 which provided for complete
religious freedom. In 1683 Pennsylvania received from William
Penn its "Frame of Government" which stated that all who believed
in "One Almighty God" should be protected and all who believed
in "Jesus Christ the Savior of the World" could hold civil office.

The history of religious freedom in the province of New Jersey
was not fundamentally different from that in the other colonies,
although Stokes states that we "had a better colonial record in the
matter of toleration than most of the colonies." 1 *Church and State
in the United States, supra, p.* 435. The grantees of the Concessions
of 1665, Lord Berkeley and Sir George Carteret, offered liberty of
worship as an inducement to settlers. This was continued under
the Quakers by a law of 1681 in West Jersey and in East Jersey
by a law of 1683. Nevertheless, despite what appeared to be the
establishment of religious freedom in the Province of New Jersey,
*Leaming and Spicer, Grants and Concessions of New Jersey,
1664-1702 (2nd ed.* 1881, *p.* 14), there was strong anti-Catholic
feeling in the colony, and holders of civil office were required to
take an oath against the Pope, *Ibid.* p. 92. By the king's instructions to Lord Cornbury (*Ibid., p.* 633) in 1702 he was to permit
a liberty of conscience to all persons except Paptists. Our Constitution of 1776 provides:

"XVIII. Free Exercise of religion.
"That no person shall ever within this colony be deprived
of the inestimable privilege of worshiping Almighty God in
a manner agreeable to the dictates of his own conscience;
nor under any pretense whatsoever, compelled to attend

any place of worship, contrary to his own faith and judgment; nor shall any person within this colony, ever be obliged to pay tithes, taxes or any other rates, for the purpose of building or repairing any church or churches, place or places of worship, or for the maintenance of any minister or ministry, contrary to what he believes to be right, or has deliberately or voluntarily engaged himself to perform."

But the very next article of this same Constitution, after providing that there shall be "no establishment of any one religious sect in this province in preference to another," goes on to guarantee civil rights and the right to hold office to all who are of the "protestant sect." The exclusion of Catholics from this guarantee of civil rights and from holding civil office was not eliminated until the Constitution of 1844.

Generally speaking, it can then be said that religious toleration varied from one province to another with very few approaching a system of full religious freedom. Pfeffer reviews the religious atmosphere in the colonies:

"Summarizing the colonial period, we may note that the proprietary regimes permitted a considerable degree of toleration, at least in comparison with the other colonies. This difference may be explained partly by the idealism of the proprietors and partly by the economic necessity of attracting large numbers of settlers in order to preserve and make profitable the proprietor's substantial investment. Even in the proprietary colonies, however, the death of the idealistic founder, Calvert, Williams, or Penn, resulted in considerable backsliding, and the imposition of restrictions on civil and religious rights, particularly of non-Protestants. The limited tolerance which did exist did not include Catholics, Jews, Unitarians, or Deists. The variety and degree of discrimination against them varied. Primarily, the discrimination was political—the non-Protestants could not vote or hold office. But the restrictions were not always limited to political disabilities. Public performance of Catholic worship was prohibited almost everywhere, and as late as 1756 the colony which had been founded by the Catholic Calverts enacted a law subjecting Catholics to double taxation. Perhaps the incident that most ironically illustrates the turnabout after the death of the idealistic founder is the action of a Rhode Island court which in 1762 denied the petition of two Jews for naturalization on the ground that to grant the petition would be "inconsistent with the first principles on which the colony was founded.'" *Church, State and Freedom, supra, p. 79.*

It was left to Virginia to lead the struggle for religious freedom and the separation of Church and State. In 1784 there was proposed in its House of Delegates a "bill establishing provision for teachers of the Christian religions." Action thereon was postponed until the next session in order that the bill could be publicized and distributed to the people who could then make known their views. The issue was fought on a very high plane of principle with Thomas Jefferson, James Madison and George Mason aligned with the opposition. It was then that James Madison wrote his famous *A Memorial and Remonstrance* in which he presented his views that religion was not a matter within the scope of civil government. For complete historical background and full text reference is made to Mr. Justice Rutledge's dissenting opinion in *Everson v. Board of Education,* 330 *U. S.* 1, 28, 67 *S. Ct.* 504, 91 *L. Ed.* 711, 730 (1947). At the next session the proposed bill was defeated and in its place an act "for establishing religious freedom" drafted by Thomas Jefferson was passed, the preamble of which stated: "that to suffer the civil magistrate to intrude his powers into the field of opinion, and to restrain the profession or propagation of principles on supposition of their ill tendency, is a dangerous fallacy which at once destroys all religious liberty." The bill further provided "that it is time enough for the rightful purposes of civil government for its officers to interfere when principles break out into overt acts against peace and good order." In his opinion for the court in *Reynolds v. United States,* 98 *U. S.* 145, 163, 25 *L. Ed.* 244, 248 (1879), Mr. Chief Justice Waite states that "in these two sentences is found the true distinction between what properly belongs to the Church and what to the State."

It was a little over a year later that the Convention met in Philadelphia to draft the Constitution of the United States. The Convention failed to include in the proposed Constitution any Bill of Rights or any provision concerning freedom of religion. Although

adopting the Constitution, several states did so only on the understanding that a Bill of Rights would be added including a provision
for a declaration of religious liberty. At the very first session of
Congress the first ten amendments, or Bill of Rights, were proposed
and largely through the efforts of James Madison were adopted,
the First Amendment providing that "Congress shall make no law
respecting an establishment of religion, or prohibiting the free
exercise thereof." It took us over 14 centuries and an incalculable
amount of persecution to gain the religious tolerance and freedom
expounded in 313 A. D. by the rulers of the Roman world.

[1] The First Amendment, of course, applied only to the
Federal Government, but it has been held that upon the adoption
of the Fourteenth Amendment the prohibitions of the First Amendment were applicable to state action bridging religious freedom,
Cantwell v. State of Connecticut, 310 *U. S.* 296, 303, 60 *S. Ct.* 900,
84 *L. Ed.* 1213, 1217 (1940).

IV.

[2] The charge here is sectarianism. The defendant board
of education is accused of showing a preference by permitting the
distribution of the King James version of the New Testament,
which is unacceptable to those of the Jewish faith and, in fact, in
conflict with their tenets. This violates the mandate of the First
Amendment, as incorporated into the Fourteenth Amendment, prohibiting the making of any law "respecting an establishment of
religion," and the requirement of Article I, paragraph 4 of the
New Jersey Constitution that "there shall be no establishment of
one religious sect, in preference to another." By its very terms the
New Jersey constitutional provision prohibits any such religious
preference, while the First Amendment to the Federal Constitution
has been judicially interpreted as so providing. As stated by Mr.
Justice Black in his opinion for the majority of the court in *Everson
v. Board of Education, supra,* 330 *U. S.* 1, 15, 67 *S. Ct.* 504, 91
L. Ed 711:

> "The 'establishment of religion' clause of the First Amend-
> ment means at least this: Neither a state nor the Federal
> Government can set up a church. Neither can pass laws

which aid one religion, aid all religions, or prefer one religion over another. * * *

That Amendment [First] requires the state to be a neutral in its relations with groups of religious believers and non-believers." (330 *U.S.* at *page* 18, 67 *S. Ct.* at *page* 511.)

In *Zorach v. Clauson,* 343 *U.S.* 306, 314, 72 *S. Ct.* 679, 684, 96 *L. Ed.* 954, 962 (1952), Mr. Justice Douglas in his opinion for the majority of the court stated:

"The government must be neutral when it comes to competition between sects."

In *Fowler v. State of Rhode Island,* 345 *U. S.* 67, 69, 73 *S. Ct.* 526, 527, 97 *L. Ed.* 828 (1953), a minister of Jehovah's Witnesses was convicted in the state court for violation of a municipal ordinance prohibiting the addressing of a religious meeting in a public park. The evidence showed that the ordinance had not been construed to prohibit church services of Catholics and Protestants. The court set aside the conviction, saying:

"For it plainly shows that a religious service of Jehovah's Witnesses is treated differently than a religious service of other sects. That amounts to the state preferring some religious groups over this one."

We are well aware of the ever continuing debates that have been taking place in this country for many years as to the meaning which should be given to the First Amendment. There are those who contend that our forefathers never intended to erect a "wall of separation" between Church and State. On the other hand, there are those who insist upon this absolute separation between Church and State. The plaudits and the criticisms of the various majority, concurring, and dissenting opinions rendered by the United States Supreme Court in *Everson v Board of Education, supra,* 330 *U.S.* 1, 67, *S. Ct.* 504, *L. Ed.* 711; *People of State of Illinois ex rel. McCollum v. Board of Education,* 333 *U.S.* 203, 68 *S. Ct.* 461, 92 *L. Ed.* 648 (1948), and *Zorach v. Clauson, supra,* 343 *U.S.* 306, 72 *S. Ct.* 679, 96 *L. Ed.* 954, still continue.

But regardless of what our views on this fundamental question may be, our decision in this case must be based upon the undoubted doctrine of both the Federal Constitution and our New Jersey Constitution, that the state or any instrumentality thereof cannot under any circumstances show a preference for one religion over another. Such favoritism cannot be tolerated and must be disapproved as a clear violation of the Bill of Rights of our Constitutions.

This brings us to the heart of our problem here—namely, whether the resolution of the board of education displays that favoritism that is repugnant to our Constitutions. By permitting the distribution of the Gideon Bible, has the board of education established one religious sect in preference to another? Although as to the Catholic plaintiff this action has become moot due to the withdrawal of his child from the public schools of Rutherford, some testimony was presented at the trial as to his claim of sectarianism so we will at times refer to such testimony in our opinion. Our decision, however, is based upon the claim of the Jewish plaintiff that the resolution of the Rutherford Board of Education constitutes a preference of one religion over the Hebrew faith.

A review of the testimony at the trial convinces us that the King James version or Gideon Bible is unacceptable to those of the Jewish faith. In this regard Rabbi Joachim Prinz testified:

"The New Testament is in profound conflict with the basic principles of Judaism. It is not accepted by the Jewish people as a sacred book. The Bible of the Jewish people is the Old Testament. The New Testament is not recognized as part of the Bible. The teachings of the New Testament are in complete and profound conflict with what Judaism teaches. It presupposes the concept of Jesus of Nazareth as a divinity a concept which we do not accept."

"They are in complete and utter conflict with what we teach, for we teach the oneness of God, which to our—and in accordance with our belief, excludes the existence of a Son of God. We accept Jesus of Nazareth as one of the figures of Jewish history, a Jew born, a Jew, died as a Jew, but we do not accept Jesus of Nazareth as the Christ. * * *

No, it is certainly not a nonsectarian book. It is a book that is—expresses the view of one denomination among the many religious denominations of the world."

Dr. Bernard J. Bamberger, rabbi of the West End Synagogue in
New York City and former president of the Synagogue Council
of America, stated:

> "Well, the New Testament, of course, is itself a complex
> document which contains a great many different writings,
> and so forth. Some of the passages and some of those
> writings are in themselves not necessarily in conflict with
> Judaism, but a very great many of them are in conflict
> with Judaism, first, because they teach certain doctrines
> which are contradictory to doctrines taught by Judaism,
> and also because in certain passages the New Testament
> writers directly attacks certain Jewish beliefs which are
> very sacred to Jews."

He concluded that the King James Version was "completely not a
nonsectarian book." Rabbi Irving Schnipper, in answer to a
question whether the teachings of the New Testament are in conflict
with his teaching of the children of the plaintiff Bernard Tudor,
testified:

> "Definitely, the New Testament itself is in direct opposition
> to the teachings of Judaism."

Nor is there any doubt that the King James version of the Bible
is as unacceptable to Catholics as the Douay version is to Protestants. According to the testimony in this case the canon law of the
Catholic Church provides that "Editions of the original test of the
sacred scriptures published by non-Catholics are forbidden *ipso jure.*"

The defendant refers us to various statements by legal scholars
and others to show that the Bible is not sectarian, but rather is
the universal book of the Christian world, but in many of these
statements the question of the New Testament was not discussed.
In *Doremus v. Board of Education of Borough of Hawthorne,* 5
N.J. 435 (1950), appeal dismissed 342 *U.S.* 429, 72 *S. Ct.* 394, 96
L. Ed. 475 (1952), relied on by the defendant, the issue was
whether *R. S.* 18:14-77 and 78, providing for compulsory reading
in the public schools of five verses of the Old Testament and
permissive reading of the Lord's Prayer violated the Federal
Constitution. In upholding the constitutionality of the statutes we
specifically stated 5 *N. J.,* at *page* 453:

"We consider that the Old Testament and the Lord's Prayer, pronounced without comment, are not sectarian, and that the short exercise provided by the statute does not constitute sectarian instruction or sectarian worship * * *."

We adhere to the *Doremus* case, but its holding does not apply here, where clearly the issue of sectarianism is present. Here the issue is the distribution of the New Testament. The uncontradicted evidence presented by the plaintiff reveals that as far as the Jewish faith is concerned, the Gideon Bible is a sectarian book, the teachings of which are in conflict with the doctrines of his religion as well as that of his child, who is a pupil in the Rutherford public school. The full force of the violation of both the State and Federal Constitutions is revealed when we perceive what might happen if a single school board were besieged by three separate applications for the distribution of Bibles—one from Protestants as here, another from Catholics for the distribution of the Douay Bible, and a third from Jews for the same privilege for their Bible.

[3, 4] We find from the evidence presented in this case that the Gideon Bible is a sectarian book, and that the resolution of the defendant board of education to permit its distribution through the public school system of the Borough of Rutherford was in violation of the First Amendment of the United States Constitution, as incorporated into the Fourteenth Amendment, and of Article I, paragraph 4, of the New Jersey Constitution. It therefore must be set aside.

V.

The defendant contends that the distribution of the Gideon Bible in no way injects any issue of the "free exercise" of religion, that "no one is forced to take a New Testament and no religious exercise or instrument is brought to the classrooms of the public schools." In other words, it asserts the arguments of *Zorach v. Clauson, supra,* 343 *U. S.* 306, 315, 72 *S. Ct.* 679, 96 *L. Ed.* 954, that the "accommodation" of religion is permissible. This argument, however, ignores the realities of life. In his concurring opinion joined in by three other members of the Court, Mr. Justice Frankfurter stated in *People of State of Illinois ex rel. McCollum v.*

Board of *Education, supra,* 333 *U. S.* 203, 227, 68 *S. Ct.* 461, 473, 92 *L. Ed.* 648:

"Religious education so conducted on school time and property is patently woven into the working scheme of the school. The Champaign arrangement thus presents powerful elements of inherent pressure by the school system in the interests of religious sects. The fact that this power has not been used to discriminate is beside the point. Separation is a requirement to abstain from fusing functions of Government and of religious sects, not merely to treat them all equally. That a child is offered an alternative may reduce the constraint; it does not eliminate the operation of influence by the school in matters sacred to conscience and outside the school's domain. The law of imitation operates, and non-conformity is not an outstanding characteristic of children. The result is an obvious pressure upon children to attend. Again, while the Champaign school population represents only a fraction of the more than two hundred and fifty sects of the nation, not even all the practicing sects in Champaign are willing or able to provide religious instruction. The children belonging to these non-participating sects will thus have inculcated in them a feeling of separatism when the school should be the training ground for habits of community, or they will have religious instruction in a faith which is not that of their parents. As a result, the public school system of Champaign actively furthers inculcation in the religious tenets of some faiths, and in the process sharpens the consciousness of religious differences at least among some of the children committed to its care. These are consequences not amenable to statistics. But they are precisely the consequences against which the Constitution was directed when it prohibited the Government common to all from becoming embroiled, however innocently, in the destructive religious conflicts of which the history of even this country records some dark pages."

In *State ex rel. Weiss v. District Board,* 76 *Wis.* 177, 44 *N. W.* 967, 7 *L. R. A.* 330 (*Sup. Ct.* 1890), it was stated:

"When * * * a small minority of the pupils in the public school is excluded, for any cause, from a stated school exercise, particularly when such cause is apparent hostility to the Bible which a majority of the pupils have been taught to revere, from that moment the excluded pupil loses caste with his fellows, and is liable to be regarded with aversion, and subjected to reproach and insult. But it is a sufficient refutation of the argument that the practice in question tends to destroy the equality of the pupils which the constitution seeks to establish and protect, and puts a portion of them to serious disadvantage in many ways with respect to the others." (at 44 *N. W.* 975)

Professor Isidore Chein, Supervisor of Psychology and Acting Director of the Research Center for Mental Health at New York University, testified on behalf of the plaintiff:

"* * * I would expect that a slip of this kind, distributed under the authority of the school, would create a subtle pressure on the child which would leave him with a sense that he is not quite as free as the statement on that slip says; in other words, that he will be something of an outcast and a pariah if he does not go along with this procedure."

"* * * I think that they would be in a situation where they have to play along with this or else feel themselves to be putting themselves in a public position where they are different, where they are not the same as other people, and the whole pressure would exist on them to conform."

Dr. Dan Dodson, professor in the School of Education of New York University and director of curriculum and research in the Center for Human Relations Studies, when questioned as to the divisive effect of the distribution of the Gideon Bible stated:

"I would say that any instance of this kind in which the * * * a document that has the importance that this has to certain religious groups, including my own, would be distributed or used as a means of propaganda or indoctrination by official channels, such as the school system, would create tensions among the religious groups; there would be a controversial problem."

"I would say that it would raise questions among the children as to who is and who isn't, in terms of receiving the Bible. It would also create problems as to why some accepted it and others didn't. That would be divisive."

See also *People ex rel. Ring v. Board of Education,* 245 *Ill.* 334, 92 *N. E.* 251, 29 *L. R. A., N. S.* 442 (*Sup. Ct.* 1910), where the court maintained that the fact that pupils could request to be excused from religious exercises did not make the requirement of

sectarian Bible reading constitutional, and *Miller v. Cooper, 56 N.M.
355, 244 P. 2d 520 (Sup. Ct.* 1952), where the plaintiffs brought
an action seeking, among other things, an injunction against the
dissemination of allegedly sectarian literature among the public
school pupils in violation of the provisions of the Federal and State
Constitutions. The court there granted this relief, saying:

> "The charge [that] the defendants were using the school
> as a medium for the dissemination of religious pamphlets
> published by the Presbyterian Church presents a different
> situation. It is true that the teachers did not hand them
> to the pupils or instruct that they be taken or read. The
> pamphlets were, however, kept in plain sight in a school
> room and were available to the pupils and the supply was
> evidently replenished from time to time. We condemned
> such practice in *Zellers v. Huff, supra,* and condemn it here
> and hold [that] the trial court was in error when it failed
> to enjoin such acts * * *." (at 244 *P.* 2d 521)

[5] We cannot accept the argument that here, as in the *Zorach*
case, *supra,* the State is merely "accommodating" religion. It matters little whether the teachers themselves will distribute the Bibles
or whether that will be done by members of the Gideons International. The same vice exists, that of preference of one religion
over another. This is all the more obvious when we realize the
motive of the Gideons. Its purpose is "to win men and women for
the Lord Jesus Christ, through * * * (c) placing the Bible—God's
Holy Word * * * or portions thereof in hotels, hospitals, schools,
institutions, and also through distribution of same for personal use."
The society is engaged in missionary work, accomplished in part
by placing the King James version of the Bible in the hands of
public school children throughout the United States. To achieve
this end it employs the public school system as the medium of
distribution. It is at the school that the pupil receives the request
slip to take to his parents for signature. It is at the school that
the pupil actually receives his Gideon Bible. In other words, the
public school machinery is used to bring about the distribution of
these Bibles to the children of Rutherford. In the eyes of the
pupils and their parents the board of education has placed its
stamp of approval upon this distribution and, in fact, upon the
Gideon Bible itself. Dr. Dodson further testified:

"I would say it would leave a lefthanded implication that the school thought this was preferential in terms of what is the divine word, and that the backing of the State would inevitably be interpreted as being behind it."

Dr. William Heard Kilpatrick stated:

"The Protestants would feel that the school is getting behind this thing; the Catholic would feel that the school is getting behind a Protestant affair; the Jews would feel that the school is getting behind the Protestant religion as opposed to their religion; and the people who don't accept any religion would feel that the school is actually trying to teach the religion through this means."

This is more than mere "accommodation" of religion permitted in the *Zorach* case. The school's part in this distribution is an active one and cannot be sustained on the basis of a mere assistance to religion.

We are here concerned with a vital question involving the very foundation of our civilization. Centuries ago our forefathers fought and died for the principles new contained in the Bill of Rights of the Federal and New Jersey Constitutions. It is our solemn duty to preserve these rights and to prohibit any encroachment upon them. To permit the distribution of the King James version of the Bible in the public schools of this State would be to cast aside all the progress made in the United States and throughout New Jersey in the field of religious toleration and freedom. We would be renewing the ancient struggles among the various religious faiths to the detriment of all. This we must decline to do.

The judgment below is reversed and the resolution of the Board of Education of the Borough of Rutherford under review is stricken.

Comparative Law

The truth of Henry Adams' oft-quoted remark about a teacher affecting eternity is illustrated anew when we observe the origin of Vanderbilt's interest in and his contributions to the field of comparative law. While a student at Columbia Law School, Vanderbilt came under the influence of Professor Munroe Smith who taught a course dealing with the development and interrelationship of English and European law. The lectures made so profound an impression on Vanderbilt that he later reproduced them from his classroom notes and included them in his book, "Studying Law."

Vanderbilt's interest in the subject never waned and after World World II he established the Inter-American Law Institute at the New York University Law Center. The Institute has provided many young lawyers of South and Central America with a knowledge of our law and legal system and of our political, social, and economic institutions. Some of these students have since attained high political office or have represented their particular countries in important diplomatic posts. The success of the Inter-American Law Institute led to the formation of the Institute of Comparative Law at the Law Center for the purpose of giving comparative law training to lawyers from Europe and the Middle East.

In 1953, the Institute of Comparative Law sponsored a sesquicentennial celebration of the Code Napoleon which was attended by eminent lawyers, law professors, and judges, from the United States, England, France, Canada and other countries. The following selection is the paper presented by Vanderbilt on that occasion.

THE RECONCILIATION OF THE CIVIL LAW AND THE COMMON LAW *

I

It is singular how few common lawyers, both English and American, have realized that, in addition to customary law, there were three great bodies of law—feudal, canon, and merchant—that long held sway throughout Central and Western Europe and that these three great bodies of law were quite as much in force in England as on the Continent. Thus, William the Conqueror brought with him to England the feudal law that he had known in Normandy, but he took good care to avoid the disintegrating tendency of Continental feudalism, traceable to the doctrine that "the man's man is not the Lord's man," by compelling "the man's man" in England to take a direct oath of allegiance to him. He had seen how largely independent of the French crown the dukes of Normandy had been, and he had no intention of permitting his vassals in England any such power over their subordinates at his expense. Henry II continued the process. He established royal courts that promptly took jurisdiction of feudal cases, and as a result the lower feudal courts were gradually deprived of all real authority.[1] Aside from these matters the European feudal system prevailed in England, but, as Maitland points out, Lord Coke in presenting the English law of the later Middle Ages reveals no knowledge of the European feudal system.[2] It remained for Coke's contemporary, the antiquarian Spelman, to make the grand discovery that English feudal law was really European feudal law and for Sir Martin Wright to spread the new learning and for Blackstone to popularize it.

Likewise English canon law was of European rather than of English origin. Again it was William the Conqueror who imported this second body of European law into England. He had had the support of the Pope on his crusade to conquer England, and in gratitude he established in England the wide jurisdiction of ecclesiastical law, proclaiming: "Things which pertain to the

---

* Code Napoleon And The Common Law World 389-395 (Schwartz, ed. N.Y.U. Press 1956).

governance of souls ought not to be in the jurisdiction of secular men." [3] The famous quarrel of Henry II with Archbishop Thomas à Becket served to give the Church courts even more authority in the punishment of clerks than they had on the Continent. The ecclesiastical jurisdiction even survived the Reformation, though Maitland has shown that the theory that England was governed by a special "King's canon law" before the time of Henry VIII was a legal fiction.[4] The canon law was administered in separate courts by a specialized bar with its own quarters, and even to this day its European origin is attested by a special division of Probate, Divorce and Admiralty in the English High Court of Justice and in this country by special courts of first instance, such as orphans' or probate or surrogates' courts.

Until the Tudor period commercial cases were decided as on the Continent in special commercial courts. When commercial cases were drawn into the royal courts by Lord Chief Justice Mansfield the law merchant, except in admiralty cases, ceased to be a separate body of law, but its European origin was unquestioned. Under Lord Mansfield it not only became integrated into the common law, but it reached a new high point of development by reason of his broad knowledge as a student of Scottish civil law of the several systems of European law.

It does not mean much simply to say that England accepted three bodies of European law, but when we note the wide scope of each of these legal systems and their wide influence on the daily life of the people, we can better understand the similarities of the common law and the civil law. Feudalism was at one and the same time a system of government and so of law, a system of society and a system of land tenure at a time when land was the chief kind of wealth. Not only have we derived much of our land law from feudalism, but it long dominated social and family relations and still does to a considerable degree in England. The expanse of the canon law was equally extensive. It had jurisdiction over the person of the clergy in both criminal and civil suits against them and of suits by them when they could not get justice in the civil suits. Widows, orphans, and the helpless generally had the same privilege. It took jurisdiction over crimes that were mostly sins, such as heresy, witchcraft, and sacrilege. It claimed jurisdiction over marriage as a sacrament whether the marriage was performed in the Church or not, and decided when it might decree separation or annulment, never, however, granting a divorce. It controlled marriage settlements, though not exclusively. It passed on questions of legitimacy and so came to control in large part the jurisdiction over family relations. By reason of its jurisdiction over marriages it dealt with all sexual crimes. It even had jurisdiction over seemingly secular offenses such as the falsification of weights and measures and of coins, forgery of documents, bearing false witness, libel and slander, and usury. It had cognizance of testamentary instruments, especially those disposing of personal property, and of the administration of estates of intestates. For a considerable time it had jurisdiction over contracts involving oaths, pledges of faith, and usury. The law merchant covered not only admiralty and charter parties, but insurance and bills and notes. One has but to epitomize the jurisdiction of these three bodies of European law to see how much of our Anglo-American law owes its origin to the civil law of Europe.

The chief distinction between English law and European law springs from the fact that in England the customary law grew especially under strong kings like Henry II and Edward I, into a sturdy body of common law, whereas in Europe the maze of law and national customs did not. There was need on the Continent, however, for a body of customary law such as England had developed; failing to achieve it, the nations of Western Europe turned to the Roman law following its revival in the universities of Ravenna, Bologna, and Padua in the eleventh and twelfth century, to make up the deficiency. That there was no reception of the Roman law in England in the sixteenth century was due, as Maitland has pointed out in his Rede Lecture, to the thoroughness of his teaching of the common law in the Inns of Court;[5] well might Maitland say that "Taught law is tough law."[6] But even though the Roman law was not received in England as a system, much Roman law found its way into England, in some degree through the writers of the early legal classics, but especially through the development of the equitable jurisdiction of the Chancellor. Not only was it procedure drawn from the canon law and hence Roman in its origin, but its pervading spirit of equity and good conscience may also be credited to the churchly influence of the canon law. Its greatest contribution to our substantive law—the trust—presents in its concept of the obligation of a trustee to the beneficiary the highest standards of good faith and unselfish conduct recognized anywhere in the law or elsewhere. In developing the doctrine of unjust enrichment through the action of general assumpsit, Lord Mansfield carried over into the law courts concepts of equity and of the ecclesiastical law that have exercised an influence far beyond the particular cases in which they were made the basis of decision.

Nor did this process end here. In this country following the Revolution the Jeffersonians favored the reception in France of the civil law, and even among those who were opposed to any such course it was perceived that the civil law had much to contribute to the jurisprudence of a new nation, especially in the field of commercial law. Thus we find Chancellor Kent, a Federalist, writing of his work as Chief Justice of the New York Supreme Court:

> "I could generally put my Brethren to rout & carry my point by mysterious use of French and civil law. The Judges were republicans [*i.e.* Jeffersonian democrats] & very kindly disposed to everything that was French & this enabled me without exciting any alarm or jealousy, to make free use of such authority & thusly enrich our commercial law." [7]

The civil law has also had great influence on our modern procedure. The fundamental concept of equity procedure was discovery, through the process of scraping the conscience of the defendant. By depositions it sought to compel the defendant to tell the truth. Within the last few years this concept of the civil law has been adopted in the Federal Rules of Civil Procedure and in the procedure of the states following its example in suits at law as well as in equity (1) to eliminate surprise and technicalities, and (2) to permit complete discovery in the interest of the truth and justice.

Although there are these wide fields of common origin in the civil law and the common law with respect to the three great systems of European law that we have been discussing, as well as in the gradual development of equity on both the substantive and the procedural side, there are also vast differences between them—particularly in the realm of public law. Roman law as it was revived in the Italian universities was the law of an imperial dictatorship under which the underlying maxim of public law was *"Quod pris cipi placuit, legis habet vigorem; ut pote cum lege regia, que de imperio ejus lata est, populus ei et in cum omne suum imperium es potestatem conferat"*—"The will of the emperor has the force of law; for, by the royal law which has been made concerning his authority, the people have conferred upon him all its sovereignty and power." [8] And this concept has left a deep imprint on the civil law in marked contrast to the constitutional doctrine of England and the constitutional republic of America. Our notions of an independent judiciary, of personal liberty, and of due process of law were unknown to the Romans, and likewise our right to a trial by jury and the prohibition against self-incrimination.

We differ widely, too, in procedure; theirs is inquisitorial, ours accusatorial. In the accusatorial process we developed the law of evidence and trial methods that are unknown on the Continent. Nor does the civil law have anything comparable to our prerogative writs, which are so important a part of our judicial machinery for maintaining the rights of citizens to the orderly process of government. There are many differences, too, in the field of private substantive law, but from an over-all point of view it may fairly be said that the resemblances outweigh the differences. Our unfamiliarity with the resemblances and differences of the two systems is due in part to our provincialism and in part to our linguistic limitations, especially with respect to German law, rather than to juristic differences.

II.

The judicial process in France, in England, and in America is much more alike than many of us suspect. Indeed, in some ways the judicial process in this country is nearer to that of France than it is to that of England today.

Our fundamental misconception as to the civil law is in supposing that the French Code covers everything. The French Code, unlike some American codes, especially some of our codes of civil procedure, does not attempt to cover everything. It deals rather with principles and standards. It makes no effort to cover details.[9] Thus in the French Code what we call torts are disposed of in five brief sections.[10] These five brief sections mean little more than that negligent acts create liability. We all know that the subject matter of torts covers innumerable situations; the four sturdy volumes of the American Law Institute *Restatement of the Law of Torts* is a daily reminder of this fact. With all of the law of torts comprehended in five brief sections of the French Code, it necessarily follows that there is quite as much judge-made law in the field of torts in France as there is with us. The same situation in varying degrees exists in other phases of private law. In the field of public law there is no administrative code;[11] all of the public law of France is judge-made.

What tends to mislead us is our failure to understand that, to the French, legislation is deemed the source of all law and their opinions appear to be merely a construction of legislation and not in any wise the making of law by the judges. We have had until the present century similar ideas with respect to law-finding by judges, and some judges still adhere to it in public; it is only in the present century that lawmaking by our judges as distinguished from law-finding has been frankly discussed.

Seemingly the process in deciding cases in the civil law is merely statutory interpretation, but Professor Munroe Smith has aptly described what actually happens:

> "For more than two thousand years it has been an accepted legal principle that, in interpreting the written law, effect should be given, as far as possible, to the spirit and intent of the law. Here again the possibilities of law-finding under cover of interpretation are very great. A distinguished German jurist, Windscheid, has remarked that in interpreting legislation modern courts may and habitually do 'think over again the thought which the legislator was trying to express,' but that the Roman jurist went further and 'thought out the thought which the legislator was trying to think.' Of this freer mode of

interpretation Windscheid might have found modern examples. The president of the highest French court, M. Ballot-Beaupré', explained, a few years ago, that the provisions of the Napoleonic legislation had been adapted to modern conditions by a judicial interpretation in 'le sens évolutif.' 'We do not inquire,' he said, 'what the legislator willed a century ago, but what he would have willed if he had known what our present conditions would be.'

"In English-speaking countries this freer mode of interpretation has always been applied to the unwritten or common law, and it is usually applied to the written law with a degree of boldness which is very closely proportioned to the difficulty of securing formal amendment. Thus the rigidity of our federal constitution has constrained the Supreme Court of the United States to push the interpreting power to its furtherest limits. This tribunal not only thinks out the thoughts which the Fathers were trying to think one hundred and twenty years ago, but it undertakes to determine what they would have thought if they could have foreseen the changed conditions and the novel problems of the present day. It has construed and reconstrued the constitution in 'the evolutive sense,' until in some respects that instrument has been reconstructed." [12]

This evolutive interpretation of legislation would be impossible in a country that adhered to the doctrine of *stare decisis* in the strict form in which it has developed in England. The English doctrine of absolute authority is stated by Professor Arthur L. Goodhart in his Inaugural Lecture:

"Absolute authority exists only in the following cases:

1. Every Court is absolutely bound by the decisions of all Courts superior to itself.

2. The House of Lords is absolutely bound by its own decisions.

3. The Court of Appeal is probably bound by its own decisions, though on this point there is some doubt.

But, even so limited, the doctrine of the binding precedent is of such importance that it may be said to furnish the fundamental distinction between the English and the Continental legal method." [13]

It is conceded that the English version of *stare decisis* results in injustice in some cases and in far-fetched distinctions in others and, because of the difficulty—one might almost say the impossibility—of getting bills for the improvement of the law through Parliament, is placing justice in a strait-jacket. The subject is probably the most controversial in English law, and the number of articles on the subject is legion.[14]

The English view of the effect of a decision even of a court of last resort is repudiated by the French. Says Professor Lambert of the University of Lyons:

"In France, the judicial precedent does not, *ipso facto,* bind either the tribunals which established it nor the lower courts; and the Court of Cassation itself retains the right to go back on its own decisions. The courts of appeal may oppose a doctrine proclaimed by the Court of Cassation, and this opposition has sometimes led to a change of opinion on the part of the higher court. The practice of the courts does not become a source of the law until it is definitely fixed by the repetition of precedents which are in agreement on a single point." [15]

What is the American attitude toward *stare decisis?* Dean Wigmore took an extreme position, which rivals the French repudiation of the doctrine:

"Is the judge to be bound by his precedent? This part of the question ought not to trouble us overmuch. *Stare decisis,* as an absolute dogma, has seemed to me an unreal fetich. The French Civil Code expressly repudiates it; and, though French and other Continental judges do follow precedents to some extent, they do so presumably only to the extent that justice requires it for safety's sake. *Stare decisis* is said to be indispensable for securing certainty to the application of the law. But the sufficient answer is that it has not in fact secured it. Our judicial law is uncertain as any law could well be. We possess all the detriment of uncertainty, which *stare decisis* was supposed to avoid, and also all the detriment of ancient law-lumber, which *stare decisis* concededly involves— the government of the living by the dead, as Herbert Spencer has called it." [16]

It is believed, however, that Justice Cardozo more accurately presents the modern American point of view:

> "I think adherence to precedent should be the rule and not the exception. . . . But I am ready to concede that the rule of adherence to precedent, though it ought not to be abandoned, ought to be in some degree relaxed. . . . There should be greater readiness to abandon an untenable position when the rule to be discarded may not reasonably be supposed to have determined the conduct of the litigants, and particularly when in its origin it was the product of institutions or conditions which have gained a new significance or development with the progress of the years." [17]

Illustrative of the application of the American view of the doctrine of *stare decisis* is the opinion of Mr. Justice Sutherland in the famous case of *Funk v. United States*:

> "That this court and the other federal courts, in this situation and by right of their own powers, may decline to enforce the ancient rule of the common law under conditions as they now exist we think is not fairly open to doubt." [18]

Clearly the American doctrine is nearer to the French doctrine than it is to the English. Equally it must seem to be more suited to the needs of a time in which the tempo of social change is rapid, indeed revolutionary.

In fairness to the English rule, even though we cannot agree with it, we must recall with Holdsworth the flexibility, in the past at least, of its law, despite the language of its doctrine:

> "If we compare the medieval common law with the law of the sixteenth and seventeenth centuries, and the law of the sixteenth and seventeenth centuries with the law of the nineteenth and twentieth centuries, this flexibility is apparent; and it is not difficult to see that this result is the consequence both of the English system of case law and of the reservations with which that system is applied in practice. It is true that the application of that system makes the law bulky and technical, and it is true that it imposes upon the lawyers a high degree of technical skill. But is that too high a price to pay for the benefits

of a legal system, which combines the virtues of certainty and flexibility in such a way that it has been found capable of continuous adaptation to the needs of successive ages, of a legal system which has enabled the lawyers to construct a body of scientific doctrine which is matched only by that constructed by the classical jurists of Rome?" [19]

The grave question presented, however, is whether the process Holdsworth outlines is gaited to the needs of a society that is changing more rapidly than any previously known to our system of law. True, the legal systems of England, of France, and of the United States have a common objective: the betterment of the average citizen through providing him with a strong effective government and vouchsafing to him as much individual freedom as is consistent therewith and with similar rights in others. In all three countries the state and the government exist for the benefit of the individual and not, as in the Soviet regime, the individual for the benefit of the state. It would be remarkable if they, having a common goal, did not grow toward each other in the field of private law, but the juristic methods of France and America would seem to lend themselves to a closer and quicker correspondence between their private law than the English doctrine of *stare decisis* would permit.

MODERNIZATION OF THE LAW

Legislative Background of the Federal Administrative Procedure Act.

[1] Pub. L. No. 610, 79th Cong., 2d Sess. (1946) approved Aug. 2, 1946.
[2] *Ibid.* Title IV.
[3] Pub. L. No. 404, 79th Cong., 2d Sess. (1946) approved June 11, 1946.
[4] (1946) 32 A. B. A. J. 377.
[5] The Principles of the Administrative Law of the United States (1905) at 17.
[6] Maitland, Constitutional History of England (1908) at 505, 506.
[7] Bell v. Hood, 327 U.S. 678, 66 Sup. Ct. 773, 90 L. ed. 758 (1946).
[8] Final Report of the Attorney General's Committee on Administrative Procedure (Sen. Doc. No. 8, 77th Cong., 1st Sess. 1941) at 7.
[9] *Ibid.* at 7-11.
[10] *Ibid.* p. 8.
[11] See note 8 *supra.*
[12] 1942 Annual Surv. Am. L. pp. 211-212.
[13] *Ibid.* pp. 212-214.
[14] *Ibid.* pp. 214-221.
[15] *Ibid.* pp. 221-228.
[16] 1943 Annual Surv. Am. L. pp. 172-175.
[17] 1944 Annual Surv. Am. L. pp. 281-284.
[18] 1945 Annual Surv. Am. L. pp. 340-341.
[19] 1946 Annual Surv. Am. L., article on "War Powers and Their Administration."
[20] 1944 Annual Surv. Am. L. p. 265; 1945 Annual Surv. Am. L. p. 323.
[21] Robson, Justice and Administrative Law (1928); Port, Administrative Law (1929); Allen, Bureaucracy Triumphant (1931).
[22] Lord Hewart of Bury, The New Despotism (1929).
[23] *Ibid.* at 13.
[24] Allen, Bureaucracy Triumphant (1931).
[25] Port, Administrative Law (1929).
[26] See note 24 *supra,* at p. 105.
[27] Report of the Committee on Ministers' Powers, Cmd. 4060 (1932).
[28] *Ibid.* pp. 64-70.
[29] *Ibid.* pp. 115-118.
[30] *Ibid.* at 7 (italics ours).
[31] Carr, Concerning English Administrative Law (1941).
[32] *Ibid.* pp. 29, 55, 174-175.
[33] Goodnow, Comparative Administrative Law (1893), Politics and Administration (1900), Principles of the Administrative Law of the United States (1905), Selected Cases on Government and Administration (1906), Selected Cases on the Law of Officers (1906); Freund, Cases on Administrative Law (1911, 2d ed. 1928), Standards of American Legislation (1917), Administrative Powers Over Persons and Property (1928), Legislative Regulation (1932); Frankfurter and Davison, Cases and Other Material on Administrative Law (1932, 2d ed. 1935).
[34] "One Hundred Years of Administrative Law," Law: A Century of Progress, 1835-1935 (1937) p. 122.
[35] (1938) 8 Am. L. School Rev. 1036-1037.
[36] Final Report of the Attorney General's Committee on Administrative Procedure (Sen. Doc. No. 8, 77th Cong., 1st Sess. 1941) pp. 25-33.
[37] Report on Administrative Management in the Executive Branch of the Government (1937).
[38] (1938) 63 A. B. A. Rep. 623-656; (1939) 64 A. B. A. Rep. 407-442.
[39] See note 36 *supra,* pp. 191, 217.

[40] National Conference of Commissioners on Uniform State Laws Handbook for 1943, p. 226 et seq. contains a draft as revised to September, 1943. The 1943 draft has been again revised but the final revision is not available in printed form.

[41] Study of State Administrative Agencies in New Jersey (1941).

[42] Report on Administrative Adjudication in the State of New York (1942).

[43] Tenth Biennial Report to the Governor and Legislature of California (1944).

[44] S. 5154, 70th Cong., 2d Sess. (1929).

[45] Port, Administrative Law (1929) p. 358.

[46] S. 3787, 74th Cong., 2d Sess. (1936).

[47] S. 674, S. 675, S. 918, 77th Cong., 1st Sess. (1941).

[48] See note 8, *supra*, at 208.

[49] See note 37 *supra*, at 40.

[50] See note 8 *supra*, pp. 207-208.

[51] *Ibid.* p. 208.

[52] Hearings Before a Subcommittee of the Committee on the Judiciary, United States Senate, 77th Congress, 1st Sess. (1941) on S. 674, S. 675, S. 918 pp. 13-14.

[53] Maitland, 2 Collected Papers (1911) 496.

The Importance of Procedure in the Work of the Practicing Lawyer and in the Study of Law; The Place of the Federal Rules of Civil and Criminal Procedure in the Movement for Judicial Reform; The Major Problems of Procedure.

[1] Holmes, The Common Law 253 (1881).

[2] Two examples will suffice. Even under rules of court permitting the liberal amendment of pleadings, able trial judges frequently decline to allow amendments to plead such "unpopular" acts as the Statute of Frauds or the Statute of Usury or an act forbidding foreign corporations to transact business in a state without a certificate of authorization. Again, under 28 U.S.C. § 1870 each party is allowed three peremptory challenges in a civil action. This may be ample in those districts where the trial judge conducts a searching examination of prospective jurors, excusing on his own motion any that are shown to be unfit. But three challenges may be quite inadequate when the trial judge leaves the examination of jurors and the challenging entirely to counsel.

[3] Some may question whether there is any such general right as a right to a fair trial, just as lawyers of an earlier day questioned whether there was a law of contracts and not merely actions in debt, covenant and assumpsit or a law of torts rather than a variety of actions *ex delicto*: cf. *Law in Science—Science in Law* in Holmes, Collected Legal Papers 218-223 (1920). I venture to prophesy that the growing concept of the right to a fair trial will be one of the major developments of the law in the twentieth century; see, *e.g.*, the concurring opinion of Jackson, J. in Shepherd v. Florida, 341 U.S. 50, 95 L. Ed. 742, 71 S. Ct. 549 (1951).

[4] 2 Camb. L. J. 340 (1926).

[5] *Summary*, 18 Uniform Crime Reports 71 (1951).

[6] N. Y. Times, Sept. 22, 1949.

[7] See Kefauver, Crime in America (1951).

[8] Herein at p. 1352.

[9] Pollock, *The King's Peace in the Middle Ages,* 2 Select Essays in Anglo-American Legal History 403 (1908); Howard, *On the Development*

of the King's Peace and the English Local Peace Magistracy, 1 Nebraska
University Studies 235 (1890).
10 See Maitland, The Forms of Action at Common Law 48-50 (1936),
herein at p. 1298.
11 Burdeau v. McDowell, 256 U. S. 465, 477, 65 L. Ed. 1048, 41 S. Ct.
574 (1921).
12 Cole v. Maunder, 2 Roll. Abr. 548 (1635).
13 Mostyn v. Fabrigas, 1 Cowp. 161 (K. B. 1774).
14 Wallace, The Reporters 338 (4th ed., rev. 1882).
15 Sec. 534.
16 *The Law in 1847 and the Law in 1889,* 37 Contemporary Rev. 787, 799-
801 (June, 1890), herein at p. 16.
17 Collected Legal Papers 301 (1920).
18 The Forms of Action at Common Law 2 (1936), herein at p. 1266.
19 1st ed. 1790-1794, last ed. (9th) 1828.
20 1st ed. 1809, last ed. (16th) 1876.
21 1st ed. 1837-1841, last ed. (7th) 1901.
22 Clark, *The Federal Rules in State Procedure,* 23 Rocky Mt. L. Rev.
521 (1951).
23 See *e.g.,* Gibson, *Should Jury Instructions Precede the Argument,* 20
Utah B. Bull. 151 (1950) in which an eminent member of the Utah bar urges
the adoption of the federal rule rather than state practice, after experiencing
a trial in the federal court.
24 41 U. S. 1, 10 L. Ed. 865 (1842).
25 304 U. S. 64, 82 L. Ed. 1188, 58 S. Ct. 817 (1938). See Guaranty
Trust Co. v. York, 326 U. S. 99, 89 L. Ed. 2079, 65 S. Ct. 1464 (1945),
herein at p. 232.
26 Wendell, Relations Between the Federal and State Courts 230 (1949).
27 The Federal Rules of Criminal Procedure have been slower in finding
acceptance in the states, partly because of the absence of the competitive
situation that exists with respect to the civil rules, partly because lawyers
generally and law schools alike have been less interested in criminal procedure
than in civil procedure. The Federal Rules of Criminal Procedure have had
more influence in New Jersey than in any other state.
28 63 A.B.A. Rep. 517-656 (1938), reprinted in Vanderbilt, Minimum
Standards of Judicial Administration 601-628 (1949).
29 Vanderbilt (1949), hereafter cited as Minimum Standards of Judicial
Administration.
30 For an interesting account of the part played by Charles Dickens, the
novelist, see Holdsworth, Charles Dickens as a Legal Historian, especially c.
IV, *Pickwick and the Procedure of the Common Law* (1928).
31 Fifoot, Lord Mansfield, c. III *Reform in Procedure* (1936).
32 *Cf.* 4 Burr. 2579, 2583-2584; 98 Eng. Rep. 355, 358 (1770).
33 Herein at p. 1266.
34 See Holdsworth, Charles Dickens as a Legal Historian, c. III, *Bleak
House and the Procedure of the Court of Chancery* (1928).
35 2d ed. 1883, herein at p. 1331.
36 Sunderland, *The English Struggle for Procedural Reform,* 39 Harv.
L. Rev. 726 (1926); *Hundred Years War for Legal Reform in England,*
15 Consensus, No. 3 (March, 1931).
37 *Cf.* Warren. History of the American Bar 225-239, 508-590 (1911).
38 Pound, *The Rule-making Power of the Courts,* 12 A.B.A.J. 599 (1926).
39 "They remodelled the whole law of descent, sweeping away nearly
everything that had grown out of the aristocratic state of society in England.
They simplified the creation and division of estates, and by introducing
grants for all transfers of land, they got rid of a host of subtle distinctions
and useless proceedings, by which they rendered the acquisition of real
property more simple and the possession of it more certain. They remodelled

real actions, abolishing the fictitious suits in which those two venerable gentlemen, John Doe and Richard Roe, had so long been the parties, and changed the whole law of perpetuities and of limitations, of last wills and testaments, and reconstructed the entire law relating to executors and administrators, by introducing important changes that made it more methodical and easy of administration. The vast subject of uses and trusts underwent at their hands a thorough revision, by which this important branch of the law became more simple, equitable and practical; and to these great changes are to be added the simplifying of proceedings upon the writ of habeas corpus and in other legal remedies, the changes made in the law of divorce, and the general provisions respecting domestic relations." Daly, Common Law 57-58 (1894).

For a classic lament at the discarding by the revisors of the outworn learning of three centuries in the field of real property and for an explanation of one reason why law reform comes so hard, see 4 Kent's Commentaries 233(a) (1830): "The juridical scholar [*i.e.*, Kent himself] on whom his great master Coke has bestowed some portion of the gladsome light of jurisprudence will scarcely be able to withhold an involuntary sigh, as he casts a retrospective glance over the piles of learning devoted to destruction by an edict as sweeping and unrelenting as the torch of Omar. He must bid adieu forever to the renowned disussions in Shelley's case, which were so vehement and protracted as to arouse the haughty Elizabeth. He may equally take leave of the multiplied specimens of profound logic, skilful criticism and refined distinctions which pervade the varied cases in law and equity, from those of Shelley and Archer down to the direct collision between the courts of law and equity in the time of Lord Hardwicke. He will have no more concern with the powerful and animated discussions in Perrin v. Blake, which awakened all that was noble and illustrious in talent through every precinct of Westminster Hall. He will have occasion no longer, in pursuit of the learning of that case, to tread the clear and bright paths illuminated by Sir William Blackstone's illustrations, or to study and admire the spirited and ingenious dissertations of Hargrave, the comprehensive and profound disquisition of Fearne, the acute and analytical essay of Preston, the neat and orderly abridgement of Cruise, and the severe and piercing criticisms of Reeves. What I have, therefore, written on this subject may be considered, so far as my native State is concerned, as an humble monument to the memory of departed learning."

[40] *The Law in* 1847 *and the Law in* 1889, 37 Contemporary Rev. 787, 798-802 (June, 1890).

[41] Special pleading was abolished in New Jersey by the Practice Act and Rules of Court of 1912.

[42] Rogers, American Bar Leaders 53 (1932).

[43] Pound in David Dudley Field Centenary Essays 10 (1949); Hepburn, The Historical Development of Code Pleading in America and England (1897), reprinted in part in 2 Select Essays in Anglo-American Legal History 643-690 (1908).

[44] Pound in Field, *op. cit.* note 43 above, at p. 15.

[45] For this story see Hepburn, *op. cit.* note 43 above. Mallonee, "Revised Statutes and Codes," 48 Am. L. Rev. 37 (1914).

[46] N. Y. Code § 62 (1848); N.Y.C.P.A. § 8; Calif. C.C.P. § 307. *Cf.* Ill. C.P.A. § 31 (1).

[47] For a discussion of legal fictions and the part they played in the development of the law, see Hepburn, *op. cit.* note 43 above at secs. 24-28; Maitland, The Forms of Action at Common Law, Lec. 7 (1936), herein at p. 1315.

[48] N.Y.C.P.A. § 214 (1950).

[49] Pound in David Dudley Field Centenary Essays 15 (1949).

[50] J. Am. Jud. Soc'y 176 (1937).

[51] 37 A.B.A. Rep. 434-435 (1912). See Shelton, *The Reform of Judicial Procedure,* 1 Va. L. Rev. 89 (1913).

[52] *Cf.* annual reports to A.B.A. of Committee on Uniform Judicial Procedure, which was headed by Shelton from 1913 to 1930; Sunderland, *The Grant of Rule-Making Power to the Supreme Court of the United States,* 32 Mich. L. Rev. 1116 (1934).

[53] Section 5 of the Conformity Act of 1872 provided: "The practice, pleadings, and forms and modes of proceeding in civil causes, other than equity and admiralty causes, in the district courts, shall conform, as near as may be, to the practice, pleadings, and forms and modes of proceeding existing at the time in like causes in the courts of record of the State within which such district courts are held, any rule of court to the contrary notwithstanding."

[54] See Walsh, *Address,* 55 A.B.A. Rep. 525-537 (1930). See Clark, *The Influence of Federal Procedural Reform,* 13 Law & Contemp. Prob. 144 (1948).

[55] 55 A.B.A. Rep. at 90-91 (1930).

[56] 57 *id.* at 117-119 (1932); 58 *id.* at 108-110 (1933).

[57] Cummings, *Immediate Problems for the Bar,* 20 A.B.A.J. 212 (1934).

[58] 48 Stat. 1064 (1934), 28 U.S.C. §§ 723b and 723c (1940).

[59] *Appointment of Committee to Draft Unified System of Equity and Law Rules,* 295 U. S. 774 (1935).

[60] Herein at pp. 9-10.

[61] *Amendments to Federal Rules of Civil Procedure,* 329 U. S. 843 (1946).

[62] *Id.,* 335 U. S. 923 (1948).

[63] 54 Stat. 688 (1940), 18 U.S.C. § 687 (1940).

[64] *Preparation of Rules of Pleading, Practice and Procedure in Criminal Cases,* 312 U.S. 717 (1941).

[65] Dession, *The New Federal Rules of Criminal Procedure,* 55 Yale L.J. 694 (1946).

[66] At p. 21.

[67] *The Rule-making Power of the Courts,* 12 A.B.A.J. 599 (1926).

[68] *Id.* at p. 603. See recommendation 1(1) of the American Bar Association: *"Regulation of Practice by Rules of Court.* That practice and procedure in the courts should be regulated by rules of court; and that to this end the courts should be given full rule-making power." 63 A.B.A. Rep. 523, see also p. 530 (1938); Minimum Standards of Judicial Administration 91-145.

[69] Pollock, The Genius of the Common Law 27-34 (1912).

[70] See for a comparison of the Field Code and the federal rules, Clark, *Code Pleading and Practice Today* in David Dudley Field centenary Essays 55 (1949): "For there can be no question but that they [the federal rules] represent a present-day interpretation and execution of what are at the bottom the Field principles . . . these directions actually embody his principles: the complete coalescence of law and equity actions, the broad party-joinder rules of equity, and the simple informative pleadings directed to the particular case in issue," at p. 64.

[71] For such reports and commentaries see Notes to the Rules of Civil Procedure. As Prepared Under the Direction of the Advisory Committee on Rules for Civil Procedure, March, 1938, Sen. Doc. No. 101, 76th Cong., 1st Sess. (1939) (hereinafter designated as 1938 Committee Notes) in which there is discussion and explanation of the source and meaning of the various rules. The Advisory Committee Notes to the original rules, and to the rules as amended, may be found in 28 U.S.C.A. following the cited rule, and in III Barron and Holtzoff, Federal Practice and Procedue 659 *et seq.* (Rules ed. 1950). See also Proceedings on Federal Rules of Civil Pro-

cedure, Cleveland, 1938 (Dawson ed. A.B.A. 1938) and Proceedings on the Federal Rules of Civil Procedure, Institutes, Washington and New York, 1938 (Hammond ed. A.B.A. 1938) for contemporary comment of several members of the Advisory Committee on Federal Rules of Civil Procedure.

Likewise see Notes to the Rules of Criminal Procedure for the District Courts of the United States as prepared under the direction of the Advisory Committee on Rules of Criminal Procedure (U. S. Government Printing Office, 1945), which may be found in 18 U.S.C.A., following the cited rule, and N.Y.U. School of Law Institute Proceedings on Federal Rules of Criminal Procedure (1946) for comment of several members of the Advisory Committee on Federal Rules of Criminal Procedure.

[72] Civil Rule 71A, recently approved, governs proceedings for condemnation of property.

The New Federal Criminal Rules.

[1] Pretrial practice, for example, which originated in the law courts, is being adapted to use in the federal administrative tribunals; see *Final Rep. Attorney General's Committee on Administrative Procedure* (1941) 64-68.

[2] 53 Stat. 1223 (1939), 28 U. S. C. §§ 444-50 (1940).

[3] See (1937) 23 A. B. A. J. 385, 387. The proposal for a "Proctor" was favored by 39,990 lawyers, opposed by 23,841, whereas the proposal to enlarge the Supreme Court was favored by 18,533, opposed by 51,156.

[4] See *Supreme Court Adopts Rules for Civil Procedure in Federal District Courts* (1938) 24 A. B. A. J. 97.

[5] 54 Stat. 688, 18 U. S. C. § 687 (1940).

[6] 47 Stat. 904 (1933), as amended, 48 Stat. 399 (1934), 18 U. S. C. § 688 (1940).

[7] See Rules 46, 7(c).

[8] Rule 10 of the Circuit Court of Appeals for the Fourth Circuit; Address of Claude M. Dean before the North Carolina Bar Association at Blowing Rock, N. C. (privately printed).

[9] Order of the Supreme Court of the United States, Jan. 5, 1942, 86 L. Ed. (adv. op.) 364.

[10] Compare Orfield, Criminal Appeals in America (1939); Pound, Organization of Courts (1940); Pound, Appellate Procedure in Civil Cases (1941).

[11] Penal Reform in England (1940) 75-91 (c. 5, "The Right to a Fair Trial").

The Growth of Substantive Law.

[1] So called by Matthew Hale: *History of the Common Law of England* (1716), 157; see Jenks, *Edward Plantagenet, The English Justinian or the Making of the Common Law* (1904).

[2] *History of the Common Law* (1716), 162.

[3] *Ibid.* at 158.

[4] 2 Pollock and Maitland: *History of English Law* (1923), 673-4.

[5] 5 Holdsworth: *History of English Law* (1924), 450-3.

[6] 6 *ibid.* at 112.

[7] 9 *ibid.* at 113-18; Holdsworth: *Some Lessons from Our Legal History* (1928), 67.

[8] 5 Holdsworth: *History of English Law* (1924), 423-93; see Palmer: "Edward Coke, Champion of Liberty," 32 A.B.A.J. 135 (1946).

[9] 6 Holdsworth: *History of English Law* (1924), 230-43.

[10] "No name being in the title-page, nor any information concerning the author obtainable from the bookseller, conjecture set itself to work. More than one father was found for it; each of the very first class; no minor one: Lord Mansfield, Lord Camden, and Mr. Dunning. . . ." Historical Preface, intended for second edition of the *Fragment on Government*, in 1 Bentham: *Works* 240 (Bowring ed., 1843).

[11] Maine: *Ancient Law* (1864), 76.

[12] Carr: *Concerning English Administrative Law* (1941), 3-4.

[13] *Ibid.* at 2.

[14] R. M. Jackson: *The Machinery of Justice in England* (1940), 120.

[15] Schuster: "Problems of Legal Administration," 2 *Politica* 239, 242 (1937).

[16] Quoted in 1 *The Intimate Papers of Colonel House* 178, n. 1 (Seymour ed., 1926).

[17] (2nd ed., 1930) at 63-4, 184-210.

[18] "Nationalization," 5 *Labor and Industry in Britain* 202 (1947).

[19] 60 Stat. 237 (1946) as amended, 5 U.S.C.A. §§ 1001-11 (Supp. 1947).

[20] Book Review, 50 *Law Q. Rev.* 435 (1934).

[21] Grant: *Marriage, Separation and Divorce* (1946), 75; Latey: *Law and Practice in Divorce and Matrimonial Causes* (13th ed., 1945), iii, 59-60.

[22] Whipple: *Our Ancient Liberties* (1927), 37 ff.

[23] Garrison: "Characteristics of American Organized Religion," 256 *Annals* 14-16 (March 1948). Virginia had provided the right to freedom of worship in 1776, but not until 1786, was there disestablishment of the church. See Zollman: "Religious Liberty in the American Law," in 2 *Selected Essays in Constitutional Law* 1108-15 (1938).

[24] Herbert: *The Abolitionist Crusade* (1912), 40.

[25] Morris: Primogeniture and Entailed Estates in America," 27 *Col. L. Rev.* 24 (1927).

[26] Vt. Const. Part I, Article 8 (1777). See 1 Morison and Commager: *Growth of the American Republic* 251, 507 (1942).

[27] Callcott: *Principles of Social Education* (1932), 219.

[28] Henderson: *Thomas Jefferson's Views on Public Education* (1890), 114.

[29] Cf. Schouler: *Domestic Relations* (6th ed., 1921), §§ 287, 288. These statutes in New York and Pennsylvania were enacted following some piecemeal legislation in others of the states also aimed at according fuller rights to married women.

[30] 26 Stat. 209 (1890), 15 U.S.C. §§ 1-7, 15 (1940); see 2 Morison and Commager, op. cit., *supra* note 26, at 135-45.

[31] 24 Stat. 379 (1887), 49 U.S.C. §§ 1-22, 25-7 (1940); see 2 Morison and Commager, op. cit., *supra* note 26, at 118-19.

[32] *E.g.*, Tariff Acts of 1867, 1870, 1872, 1875, McKinley Tariff of 1890, Wilson-Garner Tariff of 1894; Massachusetts Ten-Hour Act of 1874. New York Act of 1882; Immigration Acts of 1882, 1890, 1902, 1917; 2 Morison and Commager, op. cit., *supra* note 26, at 67-8, 133, 166-73, 184-8, 230-4, 253.

[33] 2 Morison and Commager op. cit., *supra* note 26, at 397-400.

[34] Federal Reserve Act, 38 Stat. 251 (1913), 12 U.S.C. various sections (1940); Federal Trade Commission, 38 Stat. 717 (1914), 15 U.S.C. §§ 41-51 (1940) Clayton Act, 38 Stat. 730 (1914), 15 U.S.C. §§ 12-27, 44 (1940).

[35] Dewey: *The Public and Its Problems* (1927), 120.

[36] *The Federalist*, No. 62.

[37] As quoted in Carr: *Concerning English Administrative Law* (1941), 138.

[38] See reports of the Committee on Legislative Drafting of the American Bar Association, 38 *A.B.A. Report* 622 (1913); 39 *ibid.* at 629 (1914); 40 *ibid.* at 532. Appendix: "Tentative Test of Manual for Legislative Drafting" (1915). See also Freund: *Legislative Regulation* (1932), 192; Freund: *Standards of American Legislation* (1917), 289-91, 303-6. See *infra* n. 56.

[39] Cf. Blackstone: *A Discourse on the Study of the Law* (1758), 8; see also Conrad: "New Ways to Write Laws," 56 *Yale L. J.* 458 (1947).

[40] 7 *The Book of the States*, 1948-1949, at 118-19.

[41] Laurent: *Legislative Reference Work in the United States* (1939), 14 ff.

[42] In fact, in several of the states (e.g., Connecticut and Vermont) submission to the drafting agency of all bills likely to become law is compulsory. *Ibid.* at 19.

[43] Cal. Stat. c. 278 (1931), the constitutionality of which was upheld in Pep Boys v. Pyroil, 299 U.S. 198, 57 Sup. Ct. 147, 81 L. Ed. 122 (1936).

[44] "That the vendee or producer require in delivery to whom he may resell such commodity to agree that he will not, in turn, resell except at the price stipulated by such vendor or by such vendee." See Martin: "The Fair Trade Act," 5 *Fordham Law Review* 50, 52 (1936). Compare also the unfavorable newspaper reports of a typographical error in the Federal Act regulating lobbying, commented upon in Zeller: "The Federal Regulation of Lobbying Act," 43 *Am. Pol. Sci. Rev.* 229, 251 (1948).

[45] Cal. Stat. c. 260 (1933). See present statute Cal. Bus. and Pro. Code §§ 16900-5 (1944).

[46] Legis: "The Fair Trade Laws," 36 *Col. L. Rev.* 293, 296 n. 20 (1936).

[47] Cf. Johnson & Johnson v. Weissbard, 121 N. J. Eq. 585, 191 Atl. 873 (1937); Calvert Distillers Corp. v. Nussbaum Liquor Store, 166 Misc. 342, 2 N.Y.S. (2d) 320 (1938).

[48] Ill. Rev. Stat. c. 140 sec. 8 et seq. (State Bar Assn. 1935). Constitutionality upheld in Old Dearborn Distributing Co. v. Seagram Distillers Corp., 299 U. S. 183, 57 Sup. Ct. 139, 81 L. Ed. 109 (1936).

[49] Iowa Code sec. 550.1 subs. 2 (1946).

[50] Carr: "Revised statutes," 45 *Law Q. Rev.* 168, 169 (1929).

[51] Freund: *Legislative Regulation* (1932), 423-6. Cf. Willoughby: *Principles of Legislative Organization and Administration* (1934), 584-5.

[52] See N. Y. Laws, c. 820 (1947), Educ. Law, Part 1 and 2.

[53] Cf. Warren: *History of the American Bar* (1911), 524 ff. e.g., N. Y. Laws (51st Sess., first meeting, 1828) cc. 321, 343 § 21; N. Y. Laws (51st Sess., second meeting 1828-9) cc. 20; 21; 22, §§ 15, 18.

[54] See Elmer: *Reminiscence of New Jersey*, 8 *Collection of the New Jersey Historical Society* 88-9 (1872); 1 Lewis: *Great American Lawyers* 239-41 (1907). Cf. Appendix, Report of the Judges of the Supreme Court of Pennsylvania "of the English statutes which are in force in the said commonwealth, and of those of the said statutes which in their opinion ought to be incorporated into the statute law of the said Commonwealth." 3 Binn. 532 (Penn., 1807).

[55] See 2 Lewis, op. cit., supra note 54, at 140-1.

[56] Cullen: "The Advantages of a System of Continuous Statutory Revision," 10 *Missouri Law Review* 113, 123 (1945). As to the actual workings of continuous statute revision and consolidation, see Brossard: "Wisconsin's Continuous Statute Revision," 10 A.B.A.J. 305 (1924); Mosely:

"Continuous Statute Research and Revision in North Carolina, 22 *North Carolina Law Review* 280 (1944); Tribble: "Statutory Revision in Florida," 26 A.B.A.J. 498 (1940).

[57] Cf. "Papers Relative to Codification," 4 Bentham, op. cit. *supra* note 10, at 453 ff.

[58] Franklin: "Concerning the Historic Importance of Edward Livingston," 11 *Tulane L. Rev.* 163, 170 n. 23, 180, 210 (1937); Smith: "Edward Livingston and the Louisiana Codes," 2 *Col. L. Rev.* 24 (1902).

[59] Field, Kelley, Lawton, Bonney, Dillon: "Codification," 20 *Am. L. Rev.* 1 ff. (1886). See Dee Mallonee: "Revised Statutes and Codes," 48 *Am. L. Rev.* 37 (1914).

[60] See James C. Carter: "The Proposed Codification of Our Common Law," a pamphlet prepared for the N. Y. City Bar Assn. (1884); Field: "A Short Response to a Long Discourse: An Answer to Mr. James C. Carter's Pamphlet" (1884).

[61] Smith: "The First Codification of Substantive Common Law," 4 *Tulane L. Rev.* 178-89 (1930).

[62] 3 Stephen: *History of the Criminal Law of England* 33, especially 298 ff. (1883).

[63] Cf. Stephen: *A Digest of the Criminal Law* (1877); 3 Stephen: *History of the Criminal Law,* c. 34 (1883); Burrows: "Criminal Law and Procedure," 51 *Law Q. Rev.* 36-57 (1935).

[64] Pollock: *A Digest of the Law of Partnerships* (1877); cf. Pollock's Introduction to the second edition of this treatise in 1880, and the Appendix in the edition of 1884. Cf. 1 *Holmes-Pollock Letters* 12 (Howe ed., 1941).

[65] Cf. *Chalmer's Digest of the Law of Bills of Exchange,* Preface (Batt. ed., 1947).

[66] Cf. three instances of codification of the criminal law, the Perjury Act, 1911, the Forgery Act, 1913, and the Larceny Act, 1916. Burrows, supra note 63, at 38.

[67] Smith: "Elements of Law," in *Studying Law* (Vanderbilt ed., 1945), 365-76.

[68] Winfield: "Recent Reforms of English Private Law," in Sayre: *Interpretations of Modern Legal Philosophies, Essays in Honor of Roscoe Pound* (1947), 788 ff.

[69] Cardozo: "A Ministry of Justice," 35 *Harv. L. Rev.* 113 (1922).

[70] Cf. *Reports of the Law Revision Commission, State of New York,* 1935 to date, MacDonald: "The Law Revision Commission of the State of New York," 26 *Geo. L. J.* 60 (1937).

[71] Shawcross: "The State and the Law," 11 *Modern Law Review* 1, 3 (1948).

[72] Cf. 12 *Fed. Reg.* 6321 (1947); see many comments, 33 *A.B.A.J.* 1, 213, 421, 688, 861 (1947).

[73] See criticisms, Cohen: "On Teaching of 'Legislation,'" 47 *Col. L. Rev.* 1301, 1307-9 (1947).

[74] 217 N. Y. 382, 111 N. E. 1050 (1916).

[75] 290 U. S. 371 at 382, 54 Sup. Ct. 212 at 219, 78 L. Ed. 369 at 375 (1933).

[76] 3 Burr. 1663, 97 Eng. Rep. 1035 (1765).

[77] 4 Bro. P.C. 27, 2 Eng. Rep. 18; opinion by Skynner, C.B., in 7 T.R. 350 n. (a), 101 Eng. Rep. 1014.

[78] "There is a prevalent notion, traceable to an opinion given in the House of Lords in 1778, in the case of Rann v. Hughes, 7 T.R. 350, n., that only contracts under seal can be specialties, all other contracts, whether written or oral, being merely simple contracts. The fallacy of this notion . . ." Index and Summary, Vol. II at 872 (1894).

[79] Winfield, op. cit., supra note 68.

80 Noted, 2 Doug., 689, 99 Eng. Rep. 437 (1774).

81 1 H. Bl. 273 n., 126 Eng. Rep. 160 (1777).

82 For biographical material on Lord Mansfield see: Fifoot: *Lord Mansfield* (1936); Birkenhead: *Fourteen English Judges* (1926), 168-97; 2 Campbell: *Lives of the Chief Justices of England* 302 ff. (1849); 8 Foss: *Judges of England* 335-47 (1864).

83 As quoted in 2 Campbell, op. cit. supra note 82, at 574.

84 *Ibid.* at 376.

85 *Ibid.* at 407 n.

86 Noted, 2 Doug. 689, 99 Eng. Rep. 437 (1774).

87 4 Burr. 2579, 98 Eng. Rep. 355 (1770).

88 Cf. Van Grutten v. Foxwell, A.C. (1897), 658, 669-70.

89 15 Geo. V. c. 20, sec. 131.

90 Pollock: *The Genius of the Common Law* (1912), 123.

91 2 Campbell, op. cit., supra note 82, at 476-93.

92 *Ibid.* at 374.

Judicial Deference As a Grave Cause of Constitutional Imbalance.

107 Concurring opinion of Justice Brandeis in *Ashwander v. Tennessee Valley Authority,* 297 U. S. 288, 346-348 (1936).

108 1 Cranch 137 (U. S. 1803), *supra.*

109 U. S. Const. Art. VI, § 3.

110 *Marbury v. Madison, op. cit.,* 178

111 262 U. S. 447 (1923).

112 *Massachusetts v. Mellon and Frothingham v. Mellon,* 262 U.S. 447, 480 (1923).

113 *Id.,* 483.

114 *Id.,* 485.

115 *Massachusetts v. Mellon, op. cit.,* 488.

116 *Id.,* 488-489.

117 *Texas v. White,* 7 Wall. 700, 725 (U.S. 1868).

118 *Separation and Delegation of Powers,* 41 Am. Pol. Sci. Rev. 1161, 1168-1169 (1947), citing: "On moot case, see *St. Pierre v. United States,* 319 U.S. 41 (1943). On party without interest, see *Tileston v. Ullman,* 318 U.S. 44 (1943); *Ex parte Albert Levitt,* 302 U.S. 633 (1937). On error in passing on constitutional question when case could be disposed of without considering it, see *Alma Motor Company v. Timken-Detroit Axle Company and United States,* 91 L. Ed. 150 (1946)."

119 328 U.S. 549 (1946).

120 *Id.,* 556.

121 339 U.S. 276 (1950).

122 U.S. Const. Art. 1, § 8. "The Congress shall have Power to lay and collect Taxes, Duties, Imposts and Excises, to pay the Debts and provide for the common Defence and general Welfare of the United States; but all Duties, Imposts and Excises shall be uniform throughout the United States." *Mulford v. Smith,* 307 U.S. 38, 59 S. Ct. 648 (1949); *Alabama Power Co. v. Ickes,* 302 U.S. 464, 58 S. Ct. 300 (1938); *Helvering v. Davis,* 301 U.S. 619, 57 S. Ct. 904 (1937); *Steward Machine Co. v. Davis,* 301 U.S. 548, 57 S. Ct. 883 (1937); *United States v. Butler,* 297 U.S. 1, 56 S. Ct. 312 (1936).

123 See *Sunshine Coal Co. v. Adkins,* 310 U.S. 381, 60 S. Ct. 907 (1940); *Tennessee Power Co. v. T. V. A.,* 306 U.S. 118, 59 S. Ct. 366 (1939); *Alabama Power Co. v. Ickes, id.; Helvering v. Davis, id.; Cincinnati Soap Co. v. U. S.,* 301 U.S. 308, 57 S. Ct. 764 (1937); *Sonzinsky v. U. S.* 300 U.S.

506, 57 S. Ct. 554 (1937); Dodd *Cases and Materials on Constitutional Law* 505 (4th ed., St. Paul, 1949), where he says: "As the validity of a federal spending act can be attacked only by a state or by an individual, if both are disqualified, the legislation is substantially not subject to review. The position of the court leaves to congressional discretion the question of how money derived from taxes shall be expended;" Corwin, *Constitutional Revolution, Ltd.* 108 (Claremont, 1941), where he says: "The establishment of the New Deal upon an indefeasible constitutional basis has unquestionably crowded judicial review of acts of Congress into narrow quarters, and for a reason which is easily comprehended once it is pointed out. This is, that in *choosing from among the formulas, rules, or devices of constitutional law which I set forth in my opening lecture those formulas, rules, devices which favored the New Deal legislation, the Court then and there eliminated, and probably for an indefinite future, the competing and antagonistic formulas, rules, devices.* Not again for a long time will the Court hold void an act of Congress against which nothing can be said by way of constitutional objection except that it invades the accustomed field of state power and tends to upset the Federal Equilibrium. Not again for a long time will it set aside an act of Congress— any act that Congress is likely to pass—on the ground solely that it deprives persons of liberty 'unreasonably,' and so without 'due process of law.' In a word, those doctrines of constitutional law which have been hitherto the chief sources of its broadly supervisory powers over congressional legislation have simply dried up, at least for the time being. If they still retain the spark of life, it is at least dormant."

124 "While entitled to entertain his personal views of political questions, and while not required to surrender his rights or opinions as a citizen, it is inevitable that suspicion of being warped by political bias will attach to a judge who becomes the active promoter of the interests of one political party as against another. He should avoid making political speeches, making or soliciting payment of assessments or contributions to party funds, the public endorsement of candidates for political office and participation in party conventions.

"He should neither accept nor retain a place on any party committee nor act as party leader, nor engage generally in partisan activities." Judicial Canon 28 of the Canons of Judicial Ethics of the American Bar Association (1947).

125 Baldwin, *The American Judiciary, op. cit.*, 44.

The Reconciliation of the Civil Law And the Common Law.

1 Munroe Smith, *A General View of European Legal History* 15, 23 (1927).

2 Maitland, *The Constitutional History of England* 142 (1931); cf. Scrutton, *The Influence of the Roman Law on the Law of England* 129-33 (1885).

3 Stubb's *Select Charters* 99 (1913).

4 Maitland, *Roman Canon Law in [the Church of] England* (1898).

5 Maitland, *English Law and the Renaissance* (1901).

6 *Id.* at 18.

7 Kent, "An American Law Student of a Hundred Years Ago," in *Select Essays in Anglo-American Law* 843 (1907).

8 Dig. 1. 4. 1; Inst. 1, 2. 1; Fleta, 1. 1, c. 17, §7; Brac. 107; Selden, *Diss. ad. Flet.* c. 3, §2.

[9] Deák, The Place of the Case in the Common and the Civil Law, 8 *Tulane L. Rev.* 337 at 345 (1934).

[10] Cod. Civ. Articles 1382-86.

[11] Schwartz, French Administrative Law and the Common Law World 1 (1954).

[12] Munroe Smith, "Jurisprudence" in *op. cit. supra* note 7, at 352.

[13] Goodhart, Precedent in English and Continental Law, *50 L. Q. Rev.* 40, 42 (1934).

[14] *Id. passim* and Holdsworth, *50 L. Q. Rev.* 180 (1934) and Goodhart, Case Law, a Short Replication, *50 L. Q. Rev.* 196 (1934).

[15] Lambert and Wasserman, The Case Method in Canada and the Possibilities of Its Adaptation to the Civil Law, *39 Yale L. J.* 1, 14 (1929).

[16] Wigmore, *Problems of Law* 79 (1920).

[17] Cardozo, *The Nature of the Judicial Process,* 149-51 (1921).

[18] 290 U.S. 371 at 382 (1933).

[19] Holdsworth, *50 L. Q. Rev.* 180 at 193 (1934).

Citizenship, Politics And Public Service

Training For Public Service

Vanderbilt exemplied the ideal politician. He had been active for almost thirty years in the politics of his county in New Jersey. As head of the Republican Clean Government movement which successfully campaigned against corrupt office holders, and as titular leader of the Republican Party in Essex County, he was the antithesis of the self-serving politician described by James Bryce in The American Commonwealth.

Dr. Thomas H. Reed, Professor of political science and author of Twenty Years of Government in Essex County describes Vanderbilt's activities as follows:—

"No one familiar with the affairs of Essex County will deny that Vanderbilt has exercised a pervasive influence in them or that any other man is so largely responsible for the quality of the results achieved. His influence, however, has been not so much directly upon measures as in the selection of candidates. Most of the members of the Board elected since 1919 have been of the sort who would not voluntarily become candidates for County office. They have had to be dragooned into running and Vanderbilt has done the dragooning. All his powers of persuasion, and they are considerable, have been employed in getting men and women of outstanding ability to let their names go on the ballot. One of his friends has dubbed him, very justly, a political impresario. Having filled the stage with able actors, he leaves them to play their parts without interference. Incidentally, he has never had to urge a member of the Board to run for re-election. They like their parts so well that they want to stick with the show."

To attract idealistic young people to participate in what they had been taught by their elders was the "dirty game of politics" was a problem difficult of solution. Vanderbilt began his effort to solve it while he was president of the American Bar Association. He inspired a nation-wide speaking campaign on the duties and privileges of citizenship, the theme of which was "old men for counsel, young men for action." In 1947, while Dean of the New York University School of Law, he called a national conference of political scientists, journalists, civil leaders, lawyers and educators from colleges and universities to the Citizenship Clearing House which he had established at New York University.

The Citizenship Clearing House, now called the National Center for Education in Politics, has since its inception gone a long way toward the achievement of Vanderbilt's objective. There are few campuses which have not felt its influence. By developing contacts between academicians and practical politicians, the National Center has served to remove the study of government and politics from the realm of the abstract and to give teachers and students alike a more realistic insight into political problems. It has also sponsored such widely used publications as Evaluation of Citizenship Training and Incentive in Colleges and Universities, and its continuing research projects develop data which equip the student with a foundation more solid than mere speculation when investigating the aspects of a political situation. In addition, the Center provides fellowships to young people for practical service with the official staffs of governors and mayors and with political parties.

BETTER MINDS FOR BETTER POLITICS *

In a country given to striking contrasts, the strangest of all, in view of our national history, is that disclosed by our tremendous capacity for patriotism in time of war and our general indifference to public affairs in peace. In an emergency we do not hesitate to sacrifice our greatest treasure—the younger generation—and to mortgage our financial future for decades to come in almost prodigal expenditures for our national defense. Even in wartime, however, we are not really concerned with public affairs at home. We are

---

* New York Times Magazine 10, 54. (March 9, 1947).

too busy or too careless to attend to the first duty of a citizen in a democracy—voting.

In 1938, 38 million people cast their ballots for members of Congress. Four years later, in 1942, eleven months after Pearl Harbor, at a time when we knew we were in for the fight of our lives, only 28 million people voted for members of the war Congress. A bare 54 per cent of the eligible voters were concerned as to who was to represent them in the body which would play a large part in the prosecution of a world-wide war and perhaps in the making of the peace. In four years there had been a sheer drop of 10 million votes.

Complete statistics on the election of 1946 are not yet available, although estimates reflect an increase of about 6½ million over 1942. The vote was, nevertheless, about 3½ million short of 1938, notwithstanding the fact that the American people were obviously indulging in one of their favorite political pastimes—"kicking the rascals out." In primary elections, devoted to the vital task of choosing candidates for the political parties, it is notorious that a mere fraction of the vote cast at general elections comes out to the polls.

Most of our citizens do not even know the names of many of the officials they have elected to office. I make this assertion rather confidently from personal experience in a test made in ideal circumstances. One night during a campaign I was impressed into service to hold an audience in Montclair pending the arrival of a distinguished candidate. I suggested to an audience of two or three hundred, made up largely of county committee men and women, election board members, officers of political clubs and public officeholders generally—all interested rather actively in politics—that we play a little game. Everyone would raise his hand and then drop it when a question was asked that he couldn't answer.

To insure fair play I announced at the end of the game I would quiz the winners. I then called for the names of the President, the Vice President (a few hands fell), the two United States Senators (more hands went down), their Congressman (not any Congressman from the county, but the Congressman (for their district—many more hands fell down), the State Senator, the

Assemblymen, the Sheriff, the County Clerk, the Surrogate, the County Register, the County Supervisor, the Chosen Freeholders (hands were falling like leaves in a hurricane) and the town commissioners.

I didn't have the heart to inquire as to the coroners and the justices of the peace. In this city of Montclair, "the Athens of America," rated by Professor Edward L. Thorndike in his "Your City" as the second best city in America in which to live, only 2 per cent of these practical politicians had survived the ordeal: What would be the rating of an ordinary audience in such a test?

I should not advise any reader of Dale Carnegie to play this game, but to any earnest seeker of the truth as to the political age of the American public in any particular community the test is sure to be illuminating. If we don't know even the names of our elected public officers, how slight must be our knowledge of their character and associations, their ability and policies? And if we don't know about our officials, both election and appointed, how can we be said to know our Government, or be good citizens?

In a national poll conducted recently there was submitted the question, "Would you be willing to have your son enter politics?" Sixty-seven per cent of the people responded that they would not. To a second question, "Do you believe a man can go into politics and remain honest?", 50 per cent responded that they did not believe it was possible. Now, I do not believe that 50 per cent of our politicians are dishonest, but I do submit that the fact that 50 per cent of our people think so and that 67 per cent of them are unwilling to have their sons enter politics, is cause for grave concern.

Lest we smugly think that our educated classes have higher civic standards than the average citizen, let me refer to a study made by Fortune a few years ago of the alumni of twelve of our most distinguished preparatory schools. Out of their 67,000 graduates these schools have produced but 27 United States Senators, one Associate Justice of the United States Supreme Court and one President.

Shortly after this study appeared the head of a prominent New England college in a speech at one of the very schools in question attempted to justify this deporable lack of interest in public life by saying that politics in the United States was such a dirty game that no gentleman could afford to become mired in it. He neglected to mention the only alternative to what he called a "dirty game"—a world-wide cataclysm every quarter-century involving the sacrifices of our best blood and the undermining of our civilization.

The result of this neglect of responsibility for government by our educated citizens strikingly reflected in a study made by Dean William E. Mosher of Syracuse University not so long ago of the membership of the county committees of the two great political parties in eighteen of the larger cities of New York State, New York City being excluded by reason of its peculiar problems.

In these eighteen cities 55 per cent of the district leaders had not gone beyond grammar school. Only 12 per cent were college men and women—and college men and women were defined for the purposes of this survey as including anyone who ever went to college, whether he was graduated or not and whether the institution was a college of liberal arts or a veterinary school. Of the collegians two-fifths were lawyers. I am not disparaging the leaders who never went beyond grammar school. Many of them, I am sure, are honest and capable. I am simply pointing out that our college graduates as a class have not been sustaining the burden of public leadership, either at the top or at the bottom of the political ladder.

Such evidence of lack of interest in public affairs and of ignorance of our political leaders must make us consider how long our increasingly complicated system of government, which depends so largely on wise public opinion and active citizen participation, can retain its traditional character of encouraging the maximum of personal freedom and individual initiative consistent with the general welfare. Surely nobody doubts that a democratic representative form of government is superior to any brand of totalitarianism. Surely everyone knows that no government, especially own our, is automatic.

True, in times of crisis we are willing to give all, but why must patriotism be exclusively a wartime virtue? Why should we be willing to die or send our own to death to preserve our nation and yet still be unwilling to give a very small fraction of our time and thought to preventing war by wise and effective government dominated by sound public opinion? Has history no meaning for us?

The causes of our lack of interest as citizens in our Government and for our failure to participate actively in politics are many. We live in an age of automatic machinery and we thoughtlessly liken government to a machine, which we fondly hope will work automatically, though we know when we stop to think about it that every liberty we enjoy has had to be fought for on the field of battle, in the legislative halls or in the courts.

We know, or should know, that the fight for freedom is not completely won; eternal vigilance and a willingness to fight again and yet again are, indeed, the price of liberty. Freedom is our birthright, but only because our forebears were prepared to fight for it in peace as in war. Nor can we hand it on to succeeding generations, if we lack their proud spirit.

Vast numbers of citizens are preoccupied with personal affairs. Many of them contemplate public service—at some more convenient season. If they ever get around to it they are likely to find themselves out of touch with the spirit of the times, eager to be helpful but unable to adjust themselves to the differences between things they thought they knew and things as they actually are.

Politics is an art as well as a science, and it takes time as well as practice to acquire an art. Many natural leaders of public affairs, too, are engaged in industries where participation in politics is taboo. As the field of government expands and more institutions are subjected to public regulation, the number of men of ability who will be deemed ineligible for public service will unfortunately multiply greatly. The percentage of natural leaders of public affairs thus withdrawn from the arena of politics is much greater than one may at first imagine.

Another deterrent to political activity is the fact that government today is so complicated that participation in politics is not only time-consuming, but calls for a high degree of intellectual ability. There are relatvely few men who can even pretend to be acquainted with the government of their city or county or State, not to mention the national government.

Indeed, it may be doubted that the Government even knows itself. There is one Federal agency, the Office of Dependency Benefits, that a year ago aided 11,500,000 dependents of 6,000,000 soldiers by issuing 59,000,000 checks of the face value of $3,380,-000,000, but it was not listed in the United States Government Manual or the Congressional directory for at least three years.

Truly ours is a "government nobody knows." The very magnitude of the task of becoming acquainted with government is not only staggering, it is likely to create a sense of the futility of individual efforts.

The greatest obstacle to active participation in politics, however, is the attitude of people generally toward their government and the men who run it. "Politics is a dirty game," said the college president. "I don't want my son to enter politics," say 67 per cent of the fathers and mothers. Anyone who enters politics is suspect.

Even though experts, such as Luther Gulick, president of the Institute of Public Administration, assure us that there is less direct dishonesty in politics than in business, the average citizen is still more suspicious of politicians and inclined to look down his nose at them. Certain it is that the politician may expect to be misrepresented in partisan attacks, to be misquoted, to be libeled and slandered. He will often recall with a sigh Shakespeare's words, "The greatest treasure mortal times afford is spotless reputation."

The ordinary man flinches at the thought of having his actions, his motives, his character misunderstood in the family circle, by his friends or the public, but the genuine citizen will wisely conclude that the pin-pricks of partisanship are a small price to pay compared with what the citizen-soldier has been called upon to endure in war—especially with war still being waged in various parts of the world, and with the thought of war never far from the public mind these days.

What can be done to encourage men to be good citizens, to enter politics? The Navy is planning to take approximately

5 per cent of the boys entering college and train them in science for the Navy. The Army is planning to take four times that number for the same purpose. The threat to civilian research is the subject of grave concern today in educational and college circles. Nobody seems at all troubled, however, as to where our political leads are to come from or where they are to be trained. Yet who can doubt that there is a greater premium today on political intelligence than on any other type of brains?

True, everyone who can read his daily newspaper must see that we are obviously living in an age of politics (much as we dislike the thought) in which accurate information and wise interpretation of it and still in its use both in respect to foreign countries and our own are essential to the preservation of the peace and to the safeguarding of the highways of progress. But what do we know of Russia? Of China? Of South America? Of the national government? Of our State government? Our our county? Or town or city? Or ward? Or even our own selection district?

Everyone knows, too, that our knowledge and use of the physical sciences have outstripped our progress in the social sciences. The same genius which has remade American civilization, through science and technology, has also given us the atomic bomb, the rocket and the undisclosed terrors of bacterial and chemical warfare with which to destroy our civilization.

These statements have become commonplace, but what is not commonplace is that our vast educational system—on which the American people have pinned their faith—is again falling down on its primary job of training citizens for their duties of leading public opinion and of developing wise, efficient poltical leaders.

I say again, because there can be no doubt in the light of the history of the twentieth century, that the warning of World War I was lost on the educational world. I say again, because there is no evidence of any conviction reflected in the many addresses, reports and books on higher education which have flooded the country in the past five years that the colleges are aware that it is their primary responsibility to train citizens and that in the world emergency of today that primary responsibilty transcends all other obligations.

To be specific, the obligation rests on college presidents, faculties and boards of trustees, on superintendents of schools, teachers and curriculum makers generally. The colleges and universities in particular owe the country the obligation of undertaking the work of simplifying and streamlining our complex system of government and of bringing it in line with the needs of the times.

The law schools, too, must play their part in the gigantic task of molding the law to meet new conditions. The gap between theory and practice—or, to be specific, between the academician and the man of public affairs—must be bridged. This will not be done, I fear, until an aroused public makes itself felt in the ivory towers through the press, the radio and by direct assault.

The most constructive force in this field is the great and ever increasing interest of students in the social sciences. Their instinct is sound. Unfortunately, much of the force of this constructive impulse is lost in part in some colleges through uninformed and uninspired teaching, in part for the reasons we have been discussing, but chiefly because there is no readily accessible road to political activity.

If a young college graduate is seeking a place for religious worship, church, doors by the dozen are open to him. If his aim is further education or entertainment, there are scores of opportunities in every city. But if he is seeking to do his duty as a citizen by participating actively in politics, it will be a matter of sheer good luck if he finds his way about.

The need of an agency to guide young men and women in the ways of active citizenship has long been felt by educators and by members of the legal profession. To meet this need a Citizenship Clearing House has been proposed. It would be manned by college instructors in government and would endeavor to introduce young graduates to honest and intelligent leaders of their own party, each in his or her own town. If no such leaders were available, it would try to bring groups of young people of each party together.

Next, it would aid these young people in organizing local discussion groups to debate—regardless of party—local, State, national and international problems of current interest.   It would also publish a small, informal magazine recording their successes and failures, and without taking sides on any issue would endeavor to point out sound and honest methods of citizenship organization. It would emphasize what the individual can do to improve government.   Finally, when technical advice in local or State government is desired, it would put them in touch with outstanding experts.

Such a Citizenship Clearing House is being planned by New York University School of Law, through its Legal Research Bureau. Committees from the American Political Science Association are studying the project with a view to cooperating and a committee from the Junior Bar Conference of the American Bar Association has been appointed to lend its aid.   It is hoped that the Citizenship Clearing House may be the spark to fire the native political aspirations of our best young college graduates.

BIBLIOGRAPHY OF THE WRITINGS OF
ARTHUR T. VANDERBILT

ADMINISTRATION OF JUSTICE, COURTS, JUDGES, JURORS AND LAW REFORM

Books

The challenge of law reform. Princeton, Princeton U. Press, 1955, 194 p. Chap. III reprinted in 41 Va. L. Rev. 1 (1955) as *The need for procedural reform and simplification of judicial structure.*

Improving the administration of justice—two decades of development. Cincinnati, College of Law, U. of Cin. 1957. 123 p.; 26 Cin. L. Rev. 155 (1957).

Judges and jurors: their functions, qualifications and selection. Boston, Bost. U. Press, 1956. 76 p.; 36 Bost. U. L. Rev. 1 (1956).

Minimum standards of judicial administration. New York, Nat. Conf. Jud. Coun., 1949. 752 p.

Speeches and Other Writings

Address. [Administration of justice] 1948 Wis. S.B.A. Proc. 120.

Address. [Judicial administration and the American Bar Association] before Judicial Section of the New York State Bar Association. 61 N.Y.S.B.A. Rep. 494 (1938).

Administration of justice, courts and law reform. In *Annual survey of American law,* New York, N.Y.U. School of Law. 1942 at 953, 1943 at 908, 1944 at 1191.

The administration of justice. 10 Ohio Op. Ann. 259 (1938).

Brief for a better court system. N.Y. Times (Magazine) May 5, 1957, p. 67-9. Reprinted by Committee for Modern Courts, New York, 1957.

Campaign to modernize judicial administration. 22 J. Am. Jud. Soc'y 5 (1938).

Changing attitude of the courts in construction of standard fire insurance policy. 5 N.Y.U. L. Rev. 121 (1928).

Clearing congested calendars 14 N.A.C.C.A.L.J. 326 (1954); 39 Mass. L.Q. 9 (1954); 22 J.B.A.D.C. 618 (1955).

Comments on: Dixon, Judicial administration in Maryland—the administrative office of the courts. 16 Md. L. Rev. 95. 185, 219 (1956).

The courts, the public and the bar. New York, N.Y. County Lawyers Assn., 1954. 15 p.

The efficiency of the higher courts in Connecticut. 21 J. Am. Jud. Soc'y 201 (1938).

213

The essentials of a sound judicial system. 48 Nw. U. L. Rev. (1953).

For better administration of justice. 30 State Govt. 28 (1957).

For business management of federal courts. 21 J. Am. Jud. Soc'y 195 (1938).

Foreword: Aumann, Instrumentalities of justice: their forms, functions, and limitations. Columbus, Ohio St. U. Press (1956).

Foreword: Reports of Section of Judicial Administration. 63 A.B.A. Rep. 517 (1938).

Foreword: Virtue, The basic structure of children's services in Michigan. Chicago, American Judicature Society, 1955.

The idea of a ministry of justice considered and its functions distributed. 78 N.Y.S.B.A. Rep. 152 (1955). 22 J.B.A.D.C. 346, 419, 473, 531 (Jul.-Oct. 1955).

Impasses in justice. 1956 Wash. U.L.Q. 267 (1956).

Juvenile conference committees, a unique and indispensable instrumentality for dealing with juvenile delinquency. 11 Rutgers L. Rev. 669 (1957).

Judicial councils as a means to a great end. 20 J. Am. Jud. Soc'y 6 (1936).

Judicial councils, the key to the solution of the paramount problems confronting the bar. 54 W.Va.B.A. Rep. 40 (1938); reprinted as *Judicial councils and administrative justice.* 19 J. Am. Jud. Soc'y 137 (1936).

Law and government in the development of the American way of life. Madison, U. of Wis., 1951. 23 p.

The law and human values. Pittsburgh, U. Pitt. Press, 1951. 32 p.

The modernization of the law. 36 Corn. L.Q. 433 (1951).

Need for procedural reform and simplification of judicial structure. 41 Va. L. Rev. 1 (1955).

New member of the Supreme Court of United States, Mr. Justice Brennan, 43 A.B.A.J. 526 (1957).

Our main order of business; the administration of justice. 24 A.B.A.J. 187 (1938).

[Random thoughts on improving the administration of justice] 28 Wis. B.A. Rep. 120 (1938).

The reconciliation of the civil law and the common law. Ch. 18 in *The Code Napoleon and the common law world.* New York, N.Y.U. Press, 1956.

Section of Judicial Administration launches program on wide front. 24 A.B.A.J. 5 (1938).

Some principles of judicial administration. 23 Calif. S.B. Proc. 49 (1950); 12 U. Pitt. L. Rev. 333 (1951); 22 Okla. B.A.J. 996 (1951).

United court system. Conference of Chief Justices and an integrated court system. 9 F.R.D. 635 (1949).

Use and abuse of dissenting opinions. Chicago Conference of Chief Justices, Council of State Govt., August, 1950, 2 p.

ADMINISTRATIVE LAW AND PROCEDURE

Books

Cases and materials on administrative law (with Carl McFarland). Albany, Matthew Bender, 1947. 2d ed., 1952. 1048 p.

One hundred years of administrative law. In I *Law, A Century of progress, 1835-1935,* 117. New York, N.Y.U. Press, 1937.

Other Writings

Administrative law. In *Annual survey of American law.* New York, N.Y.U. School of Law. 1942 at 89; 1943 at 101; 1944 at 169; 1945 at 184; 1946 at 187.

Administrative law. In 1946-1947 *Survey of New York Law.* 22 N.Y.U. L.Q. Rev. 565 (1947).

Administrative procedure: shall rules before agencies be uniform? 34 A.B.A.J. 896, 974 (1948); 16 I.C.C. Prac. J. 159 (1948).

Comments. Symposium on administrative law. 27 A.B.A.J. 207 (1941).

Introduction. Symposium. Hoover Commission and task force reports on legal services and procedures. 30 N.Y.U. L. Rev. 1267 (1955).

The place of administrative tribunals in our legal system. 24 A.B.A.J. 267 (1938).

Some fundamentals of administrative law. 1938 Proc. Ia. S.B.A. 57.

Techniques of proof before administrative bodies. 24 Ia. L. Rev. 464 (1939).

CITIZENSHIP AND GOVERNMENT

American freedoms. 8 J.B.A.D.C. 249 (1941).

Association aid enlisted in improving army courts-martial. 32 A.B.A.J. 255 (1946).

Better minds for better politics. N. Y. Times (Magazine) 10, 54 (March 9, 1947).

The citizen's participation in public affairs. In *Public affairs* 159. New York, Citizenship Clearing House [now National Center for Education in Politics] New York University, 1948.

Committee on American citizenship plans nationwide speaking campaign. 23 A.B.A.J. 920 (1937).

Foreword: The national economy in time of crisis. Baltimore, Lord Baltimore Press, 1951; reprinted 37 A.B.A.J. 663 (1951).

Internal aspects of national defense: the special responsibility of the lawyer. 27 A.B.A.J. 221 (1941).

Remarks, Section of Municipal Law, American Bar Association. 4 Legal Notes on Local Government 87 (September 1938).

Statement by Arthur T. Vanderbilt before a meeting of Headquarter's Committee of the Clean Government Republican Committee on April 11, 1947. 6 p. (Mimeographed. On file in the office of the Institute of Judicial Administration).

War powers and their administration. *Annual survey of American law,* N.Y.U. School of Law. 1942 at 106; 1943 at 115; 1944 at 214; 1945 at 254; 1946 at 259.

CONSTITUTIONAL LAW, STATE-FEDERAL RELATIONS

Book

Doctrine of the separation of powers and its present day significance. Lincoln, U. of Nebr. Press, 1953. 144 p. Reissued with introduction 1963. First lecture reprinted as *Separation of powers . . . the French interpretation.* 6 Va. L. Weekly (Dicta comp) 14 (1954-1955).

Speeches and Other Writings

Dominance of the federal government over the states. 51 Pub. Util. Fort. 399 (March 26, 1953).

Present day significance of the federal constitution. On the celebration of the 150th anniversary of the ratification of the United States Constitution by New Hampshire. 7 N.H.B.A. Proc. (n.s.) 53 (1938-1939); 24 A.B.A.J. 516 (1938).

CRIMINAL LAW AND PROCEDURE, CRIMINAL LAW ADMINISTRATION
See also *Procedure*

Speeches and Other Writings

An experiment in the trial of criminal indigent cases. 32 A.B.A.J. 434 (1946).

Foreword: The new federal criminal rules. 51 Yale L.J. 719 (1942).

Foreword: Organized crime and law enforcement. II A.B.A. Commission on Organized Crime xv (1953).

Introduction: Administration of criminal justice. 1 Va. L. Weekly (Dicta comp) iii (1948-1949).

New rules of federal criminal procedure. 29 A.B.A.J. 376 (1943); 6 Tex. B.J. 300 (1943).

Study of the work of the English Court of Criminal Appeal with special reference to the adaptability of its essential features to New Jersey. N.J. Jud. Conf. Rep. 112 (1935); 20 J. Am. Jud. Soc'y 95 (1936); 12 Wash. L. Rev. 52 (1937).

U.S. Supreme Court. Advisory Committee on Rules of Criminal Procedure. Federal rules of criminal procedure . . . Report of Advisory

Committee. Wash., D.C., U.S.G.P.O., 1944. 99 p. Arthur T. Vanderbilt, Chairman. See also First and Second preliminary reports published in 1943 and 1944 by G.P.O., also Federal rules of criminal procedure for the district courts of the United States . . . including notes prepared under the direction of the Advisory Committee, Arthur T. Vanderbilt, Chairman. St. Paul, West, 1946.

LAW SCHOOLS, LEGAL EDUCATION

Books

Men and measures in the law. N.Y., Knopf, 1949. 156 p.

Studying law. Selected writings of Albert J. Beveridge and others, ed. by Arthur T. Vanderbilt. New York, Wash. Sq. Pub. Corp., 1945. 2d ed, N.Y.U. Press, 1955. 753 p.

Speeches and Other Writings

Chief problems confronting the bar and the responsibilities of our law schools with respect thereto. 8 Amer. L. S. Rev. 1031 (1938).

Dedication of Ernest I. White Hall [Syracuse University College of Law] 6 Syr. L. Rev. 225 (1955).

Education for professional responsibility. Remarks as chairman of session on social and humanistic aspects of professional education held April 12-14, 1948. New York, Carnegie Press, 1948.

From where I sit. 25 Bar. Exam. 3 (1956).

The future of legal education: we must face the realities of modern life. 43 A.B.A.J. 207 (1957).

The idea of a law center. 23 N.Y.U.L.Q. Rev. 1 (1948).

Inter-American legal education as a factor in hemispheric trade. In report of the proceedings at the thirty-second National Foreign Trade Convention, New York, Nov. 13, 1945 at p. 28. N.Y., National Foreign Trade Council, Inc. 1945.

The law school in a changing society: a law center. 32 A.B.A.J. 525 (1946).

Law school study after the war. 20 N.Y.U.L.Q. Rev. 146 (1944); 22 Can. B. Rev. 68 (1944); reprinted in part as *Judicial administration in the law school curriculum*, 27 J. Am. Jud. Soc'y 179 (1944).

The law schools and government. 25 Bost. U. L. Rev. 133 (1945).

Law schools and the study of public law and government: the obligation of the bar. 29 Can. B.A. Proc. 99 (1938).

Legal aid in the law schools. 1 Record (Assn. Bar City of N.Y.) 296 (1946).

Legal education, bar organization and economics. *Annual survey of American law.* N.Y.U. School of Law. 1942 at 964; 1943 at 925; 1944 at 1205; 1945 at 1317; 1946 at 1272; 1947 at 1141.

The mission of a law center. 27 N.Y.U. L. Rev. 20 (1952).

[New York University School of Law.] Address. The function of the law school. 52d annual dinner. N.Y.U. L. Alumni Assn. 1938. 16 p.

[New York University School of Law.] Address. Leadership and the law school. 57th annual dinner. N.Y.U.L. Alumni Assn. 1944. 28 p.

[New York University School of Law.] Address. Opening dinner of the new building fund campaign of the N.Y.U. School of Law. June 6, 1946. 16 p.

[New York University School of Law.] Address. Inauguration of the Inter-American Law Institute of the N.Y.U. School of Law, at the Fifth Conference of the Inter-American Bar Association at Lima, Peru, April, 1947. New York, Institute of Judicial Administration. 12 p. Mimeographed.

[New York University School of Law.] Address. 60th annual dinner. N.Y.U. L. Alumni Assn. 1948. 15 p.

Reports of the Dean, New York University School of Law 1943-44, 1944-45, 1945-46, 1946-47, 1947-48.

Responsibilities of our law schools to the public and the profession. 3 J. Leg. Ed. 207 (1950) ; 2. S.C.L.Q. 399 (1950).

The significance of the legal center. Lawyers Week (Southwestern Legal Center) 59 (April 1951).

Some convictions as to legal education. 24 A.B.A.J. 717 (1938).

Trends in prelegal and legal education. 15 Tenn. L. Rev. 187 (1938).

University legal education and the American bar. 24 A.B.A.J. 105 (1938) ; 12 Tul. L. Rev. 167 (1938).

What constitutes a good legal education? 7 Amer. L.S. Rev. 902 (1933).

LAWYERS, LEGAL PROFESSION, BAR ASSOCIATIONS

Book

Men and measures in the law. New York, Knopf, 1949. 156 p.

Speeches and Other Writings

Address. [Judges] 63 N.Y.S.B.A. Proc. 578 (1939).

American Bar Association medal is presented to John J. Parker. 29 A.B.A.J. 558 (1943).

Bar and the public. 62 A.B.A. Rep. 464 (1937) ; 16 Nebr. L. Bull. 389 (December 1937) ; 28 Nebr. S.B. Proc. 389 (1937).

Chief Justice Maltbie as a judicial leader. 24 Conn. B.J. 1 (1950).

Five functions of the lawyer. 40 A.B.A.J. 31 (1954) ; 27 Ohio S.B.A. Rep. 131 (1954) ; 23 Utah B. Bull. 173 (1953) ; Gerhart, *The Lawyer's Treasury* at 211.

Forensic persuasion. Vol. I 1950 John Randolph Tucker Memorial Lectures 39. Published as pamphlet by Washington and Lee University

1952. 58 p. *Six factors in the work of an advocate* appears in 7 Wash. & Lee L. Rev. 123 (1950).

Function of bar organizations in the improvement of judicial administration. 22 J. Am. Jud. Soc'y 117 (1938).

General introduction: Social meaning of legal concepts. N.Y.U. School of Law, 1948, at v.

Integration of the bar. 3 N.J.S.B.A.Q. 320 (1936).

Judges and lawyers, English and American. 1938 Ia. S.B.A. Rep. 45.

Legal education, bar organization and economics. *Annual survey of American law.* N.Y.U. School of Law. 1942 at 964; 1943 at 925; 1944 at 1205; 1945 at 1317; 1946 at 1272; 1947 at 1141.

Major business of a bar association: judicial reform. 61 N.Y.S.B.A. Rep. 468 (1938); entitled *Administration of justice* in 10 Ohio Op. Ann. 259 (1938).

On being president of the American Bar Association. 1938 N.J.S.B.A. Yrbk. 208 (1938).

Past, present and future of the legal profession. 20 J. Am. Jud. Soc'y 208 (1937); 22 Mass. L.Q. 12 (January 1937).

Prelegal requirements for admission to practice law. 16 Bar. exam. 41 (1947).

Progress by the bar. In *The legal profession: 50 years stocktaking,* 5 J. Pub. L. 283 (1956).

Public opinion and the professions. 25 A.B.A.J. 999 (1939).

The role of the lawyer in the post-war era. 51 Md. S.B.A. 312 (1946).

Some obligations of the bench and bar in the task of preserving democracy. 46 Ia. S.B.A. Proc. 17 (1940).

Survey of the legal profession. 72 A.B.A. Rep. 349 (1947); 31 J. Am. Jud. Soc'y 75 (1947); 31 Can. B.A. Proc. 104 (1949); condensed in 53 Case and Com. 8 (March-April 1948).

The task of young men in a changing world. 24 A.B.A.J. 716 (1938).

United we stand. 63 A.B.A. Rep. 698 (1938); 24 A.B.A.J. 597 (1938); 8 Law. Soc. J. 218 (1938).

What is bar integration? 60 N.J.L.J. 397 (December 16, 1937).

Whither the bar? 16 Nebr. L. Bull. 389 (1937); 28 Nebr. S.B. Proc. 389 (1937).

NEW JERSEY COURTS

Court administration rules. 71 N.J.L.J. 329, 333-7 (September 16, 1948).

Famous firsts in New Jersey jurisprudence. Newark, Harvard Law School Assn. of N.J., 1956. 31 p.; 79 N.J.L.J. 249, 265 (July 12, 19, 1956).

Judicial administration in New Jersey steps ahead. 30 Mich. S.B.J. 24 (1951).

Manual of pretrial practice. Newark, N.J. Supreme Court. 1953. 35 p.

New Jersey courts under the new constitution. 56 Pa. B.A. Rep. 510 (1950).

New Jersey Judicial Council reports, 1930-1947. Arthur T. Vanderbilt, Chairman.

The New Jersey Municipal Court—the most important court in New Jersey: its remarkable progress and its unsolved problems. 10 Rutgers L. Rev. 647 (1956).

New judicial system in New Jersey. 72 N.Y.S.B.A. Rep. 277 (1949).

New rules of the Supreme Court on appellate procedure. 2 Rutgers L. Rev. 1 (1948); published as *New rules of the Supreme Court on argument and deciding of appeals.* 1949 N.J.S.B.A. Yrbk. 23; 71 N.J.L.J. 97 (March 18, 1948).

On overcoming the law's delay. 73 N.J.L.J. 153 (May 18, 1950).

Open letter from the Chief Justice to the Superior Court judges, the county judges and the county prosecutors. 72 N.J.L.J. 285, 287, 289. (September 1, 1949).

Our new judicial establishment: the record of the first year. 4 Rutgers L. Rev. 353 (1949); Record of the New Jersey courts in the second year under the new constitution. 5 Rutgers L. Rev. 335 (1951); Record of the New Jersey courts in the third year under the new Constitution. 6 Rutgers L. Rev. 367 (1952); Record of the New Jersey courts in the fourth year under the new constitution. 7 Rutgers L. Rev. 317 (1953); The first five years of New Jersey courts under the constitution of 1947. 8 Rutgers L. Rev. 289 (1954); Record of the New Jersey courts in the sixth year of the constitution of 1947. 9 Rutgers L. Rev. 489 (1955); Record of the New Jersey courts in the seventh year under the constitution. 10 Rutgers L. Rev. 397 (1956).

Price of greater court efficiency. 8 Bar. Bull. (N.Y. Co. L.A.) 21 (January 1951).

Proceedings of the first judicial conference. Rutgers L. Rev. (Spec. No.) 1 (November 1948).

The reorganization of the New Jersey courts. 34 Chi. B. Rec. 161 (1953).

Report of committee on pretrial and calendar control. Arthur T. Vanderbilt, chairman. Trenton, N.J. Supreme Court. 1957. 12 p.

Statement of Chief Justice Designate Vanderbilt with reference to the assignment of judges. Rutgers L. Rev. (Spec. No.) 55 (November 1948).

Work of the judicial council of New Jersey. 1 N.J.S.B.A.Q. 30 (April 1934).

PRELEGAL AND GENERAL EDUCATION

Address at the inauguration of Lawrence Lee Pelletier as sixteenth president of Allegheny College. Friday, May 11, 1956. Supplement to the Allegheny College Bulletin, June, 1956.

Address: An example to emulate. Delivered at the anniversary dinner for the Phi Beta Kappa Association of Philadelphia. December 5, 1951. 15 p. Reprinted from 52 South Atlantic Quarterly (No. 1, 1953). 16 p.

Centennial address on the occasion of the one hundredth anniversary of the founding of the Mystical Seven Society of Wesleyan University, Middletown, Conn. June 18, 1937. 11 p.

Commencement address, Colgate University. June 1, 1956. 16 p.

Commencement address, Ohio Wesleyan University. June 12, 1950. 10 p.

Commencement address, University of Toledo. June 11, 1954. 10 p. Typewritten ms. on file in office of the Institute of Judicial Administration.

General education and the law. 27 N.Y.U. L. Rev. 39 (1952).

Prelegal education. 17 Bar. Exam. 85, 107 (1948).

The primary responsibility of the colleges of today. 32 Assn. of Amer. Coll. Bull. 370 (October 1946); condensed from the Deke Q. (December 1946) in 52 Case and Com. 24 (May-June 1947).

Report on adult education. Ford Foundation, 1955. (Confidential report, not released).

Report on prelegal education: to Section on Legal Education and Admissions to the Bar, A.B.A. September 12, 1944 and to Assn. of American Colleges January 11, 1945. Reprinted in part in 17 Bar Exam 85 (1948); in *Studying Law*, 2d ed., at 627; expanded and updated 25 N.Y.U. L. Rev. 199 (1950).

The responsibility of colleges for government. New York, National Foundation for Education in American Citizenship [1948] 7 p.

Trends in prelegal and legal education. 15 Tenn. L. Rev. 187 (1938).

Welcome to ninth president of Wesleyan University by A. T. Vanderbilt, president of student body. November 12, 1909. Middletown, Conn. Wesleyan University.

Wesleyan University creed. Address as president of the Board of Trustees. 1938. Middletown, Conn. Wesleyan University.

PROCEDURE

Book

Cases and materials on modern procedure and judicial administration. New York, Wash. Sq. Publ. Corp., 1952. 1390 p.

Other Writings

Foreword. [The history of procedural reform.] Barron and Holtzoff, *Federal practice and procedure with forms*; rules ed. St. Paul, West (1956).

Procedure as the core of undergraduate study. 1943 Handbook of the Association of American Law Schools at p. 42.

Statements as chairman at open forum discussion and suggestions as to the draft of the proposed rules of civil procedure for federal courts. 61 A.B.A. Rep. 86 (1936); 22 A.B.A.J. (1936).

TRAFFIC

Need for a traffic court study. 23 J. Am. Jud. Soc'y 144 (1939).

No-fix ticket systems. 12 Watch (No. 4, 1956). Published by Amer. Mut. Liab. Ins. Co.

Report to the National Conference of Judicial Councils, Section of Judicial Administration, Criminal Law Section, Junior Bar Conference, Arthur T. Vanderbilt, Chairman. Baltimore, Lord Baltimore Press, 1940, 65 p.; also in Vanderbilt, *Minimum Standards* at 639; recommendations in 31 J. Crim. L. and Crim. 324 (1940).

Traffic—A problem in human relations. November 29, 1956. (Mimeographed. On file in the office of the Institute of Judicial Administration, N.Y.)

Traffic law enforcement and the sixteen resolutions of the chief justices and the governors. New York, Institute of Judicial Administration, 1953. 23 p.

Traffic law enforcement from the standpoint of the courts. 4 Rutgers L. Rev. 555 (1949).

BOOK REVIEWS

Bowen, Lion and the throne: the life and times of Sir Edward Coke (1552-1634). 42 Mass. L.Q. 72 (March, 1957); N. Y. Times (Sunday Book Review Section) March 10, 1957, p. 1. *That the law shall be supreme.*

Carr, Concerning English administrative law. 16 Temp. U. L.Q. 101 (1941).

Cushman, Independent regulatory commissions. 28 Va. L. Rev. 716 (1942).

Denning, Road to justice. 72 L. Q. Rev. 282 (1956).

French, The automobile compensation plan. 19 Corn. L. Q. 510 (1934).

Gellhorn, Administrative law; cases and comments. 89 U. Pa. L. Rev. 1113 (1941).

Goble, Cases and materials on the law of insurance. 9 N.Y.U.L.Q. Rev. 251 (1931).

Harno, Legal education in the United States. 39 A.B.A.J. 997 (1953).

Interpretation of modern legal philosophies: essays in honor of Roscoe Pound. 33 A.B.A.J. 256 (1947).

Jackson, F. H., Simeon E. Baldwin: lawyer, social scientist, statesman. 56 Col. L. Rev. 1248 (1956).

Jackson, R. M., The machinery of justice in England. 2d ed. 40 A.B.A.J. 224 (1953).

Konefsky, Legacy of Holmes and Brandeis. N. Y. Times (Sunday Book Review Section), December 2, 1956. *Two great voices of dissent.*

Lord Macmillan, A man of law's tale. 39 A.B.A.J. 310 (1953).

Mason, Harlan Fiske Stone: pillar of the law. N. Y. Tribune (Book Review Section), November 11, 1956. *Chief Justice Stone: His progress and achievement.*

Mayers, The American legal system: the administration of justice in the United States by judicial, administrative, military and arbitral tribunals. 41 A.B.A.J. 448 (1955).

Nims, Pretrial. 56 Case. and Com. 18 (January-February 1951).

Perkins, Charles Evans Hughes and American democratic statesmanship, N. Y. Times (Book Review Section), July 15, 1956. *Titan on the bench.*

Puttkammer, Administration of criminal law. 63 Yale L.J. 756 (1954).

Reuschlein, Jurisprudence—its American prophets. 38 A.B.A.J. 1024 (1952).

Schwartz, American administrative law. 36 A.B.A.J. 836 (1950).

Schwartz, American constitutional law. 42 A.B.A.J. 61 (1956).

Seagle, Law, the science of inefficiency. 27 N.Y.U. L. Rev. 732 (1952).

Scott, Select cases and other authorities on the law of trusts. 1 Mercer Beasley L. Rev. 81 (1932).

Vance, Cases on insurance, 2d ed. 9 N.Y.U.L.Q. Rev. 251 (1931).

Virtue, Survey of metropolitan trial courts: Detroit area. 37 A.B.A.J. 47 (1951).

Vom Bauer, Federal administrative law. 91 U. Pa. L. Rev. 772 (1943).

Wiener, Effective appellate advocacy. 25 N.Y.U. L. Rev. 933 (1950).

Williams, Proof of guilt: a study of English criminal trials. 6 J. Pub. L. 231 (1957).

MEMORIALS AND OTHER BIOGRAPHICAL MATERIALS

Arthur T. Vanderbilt, Chief Justice of the New Jersey Supreme Court. 35 A.B.A.J. 740 (1949).

Bernstein, J. L, Chief Justice Vanderbilt; Profile and Commentary. Parts 1-5. The Reporter (Passaic County Bar Assn.) (Jan.-Apr. 1955).

——————————— The Crowded Years. Notes for a Biography of Arthur T. Vanderbilt. 6 N.J. State Bar J. 899, 920 (1963).

Chief Justice Arthur T. Vanderbilt. 26 U. Cin. L. Rev. 491 (1957).

Clapp, A. C., In Memoriam: Arthur T. Vanderbilt. 12 Rutgers L. Rev. 1 (1957).

Death comes to the C.C.H. Founder. 5 Citizenship Clearing House Bull. 1 (Aug. 1957)

Elliott, S. D., Arthur T. Vanderbilt: Administrator of Justice. 31 State Govt. 224 (1958).

Gerhart, E. C., Chief Justice Vanderbilt and Teaching Procedure. 4 Syracuse L. Rev. 205 (1953).

——————————— Arthur T. Vanderbilt Biography in process.

In Honor of Arthur T. Vanderbilt. W. J. Brennan, Jr., Arthur T. Vanderbilt; R. D. Niles, Arthur T. Vanderbilt: His Institutional Sense. 32 N.Y.U. L. Rev. 1167 (1957).

Johnson, E. J., The Legal Statesmanship of Arthur T. Vanderbilt. Address, delivered at Annual Meeting of the National Conference of Judicial Councils in Washington, May 22nd, 1958. Washington, D. C.

Maxwell, D. F., Hon. Arthur T. Vanderbilt. 1 Am. J. Leg. Hist. 270 (1957).

Memorial to Arthur T. Vanderbilt, Member of the Board of Governors 1934-1937. 82 Rep. A.B.A. 203 (1957) by Judge John J. Parker.

Memorial to the Hon. Arthur T. Vanderbilt, Late Chief Justice of the Supreme Court of New Jersey, 1948-1957 before the Supreme Court of New Jersey. Proceedings. Supreme Court, Newark, N. J. Sept. 4, 1957.

Niles, R. D., Arthur T. Vanderbilt. 13 Tax L. Rev. 1 (1957).

——————————— Arthur T. Vanderbilt and Legal History. 1 Am. J. Leg. Hist. 275 (1957).

Pirsig, M. E. Chief Justice Arthur T. Vanderbilt in Retrospect. 12 Rutgers L. Rev. 427 (1958).

The President of the American Bar Association—Arthur T. Vanderbilt. 23 A.B.A.J. 869 (1937).

Reid, J. P., Chief Justice Doe and Chief Justice Vanderbilt, A Comparison in the Techniques of Reform. 46 A.B.A.J. 278, 325 (1960).

Reuschlein, H. G., Vanderbilt and Jurisprudence in *Jurisprudence—Its American Prophets,* 161-167 (1951).

Rix, C. B., Chief Justice Arthur T. Vanderbilt, 1888-1957. 43 A.B.A.J. 631 (1957).

Schwartz, B., Chief Justice Vanderbilt, and Administrative Law. 34 N.Y.U. L. Rev. 691 (1959).

Stason, E. B., The Cook Lectures; Men and Measures in the Law—Arthur T. Vanderbilt. 24 N.Y.U. L.Q. Rev. 22 (1949).

Vanderbilt Memorial. Convocation. R. Pound, The Legal Educator; C. S. Rhyne, The Bar Association President; T. E. Dewey, The Political Leader; W. A. Wachenfeld, The Chief Justice; W. J. Brennan, Jr., The Judicial Administrator. 6 N.Y.U. L. Center Bull. 2 (Fall, 1957).

The Vanderbilt Portrait. Remarks of M. H. Diverty, E. R. McGlynn, W. A. Wachenfeld, 2 N.J.S.B.J. 224 (1959).

Williams, G. H., Arthur T. Vanderbilt and Legal Education. 24 N.Y.U. L.Q. Rev. 1 (1949); Lawyer and Law Notes 3:5 (Spring 1949).

Letters to New York Times and Herald Tribune. Editorial pages June 21, 1957.

HONORARY DEGREES AND AWARDS

Degrees

D.C.L.

Boston University	1945
New York University	1948
McGill University	1948
Princeton University	1954
Colgate University	1956

LL.D.

Tulane University	1938
Wesleyan University (Conn.)	1938
Western Reserve University	1938
University of British Columbia	1938
Tusculum College (Tennessee)	1939
American University	1941
University of Michigan	1942
Northwestern University	1944
Marietta College	1945
University of Pennsylvania	1945
Rutgers University	1948
Lafayette College	1948
Washington and Lee University	1949
Bowdoin College	1950
Ohio Wesleyan University	1950

Pennsylvania Military College	1950
St. Peter's College (New Jersey)	1952
Seton Hall University	1953
University of Chicago	1953
Temple University	1954
Southern Methodist University	1954
University of Toledo	1954
Syracuse University	1954
Washington University	1956
Allegheny College	1956
Fairleigh Dickinson University	1956

L.H.D.

Rutgers University	1956

Awards

American Bar Association Gold Medal Award	1948
Columbia University Lion Award	1954
New York State Bar Association Gold Medal	1955
American Bar Foundation Award	1957
American Judicature Society Golden Anniversary Award	1964

INDEX

Adams, Henry, 178
Administrative law, 53
Administrative Office of the United States Courts, 88, 98
Advocacy, 5, 7
Allen, C. K., *Bureaucracy Triumphant,* 58;
Law and *Orders,* 60
American Bar Association, 60, 61, 62, 79, 87, 88, 90, 97, 104, 203, 212
American Civil Liberties Union, 152
American Law Institute, 110;
Model Code of Criminal Procedure, 102
American Law Student Association, 3
American Municipal Association, 104
American Political Science Association, 212
Ames, James Barr, *Cases on Bills and Notes,* 133;
Cases on Pleading, 72, 73;
Lectures on Legal History and Miscellaneous Legal Essays, 73
Amos, Maurice Sheldon, 70
Appellate argument, 25, 44
Appellate procedure, English, 26
Aristotle, 45
Armstrong, Walter, P., Jr., 110
Ashwander v. *Tennessee Valley Authority,* 153, 157
Association of American Law Schools, 60
Assumptions of the age, 11
Attorney General's Conference on Organized Crime, 104

Bacon, Francis, 47, 116
Baker v. *Carr,* 153
Baldwin, Roger, N., 34, 152
Benjamin report, 61
Bentham, Jeremy, 116, 119, 125, 129, 132
Bill of Rights, 124
Bills of Exchange Act, 130
Bolingbroke, Lord, 71

Boone v. *Eyre,* 134
Boswell, James, *Life of Samuel Johnson,* 126
Bracton, Henry, 116
Brandeis, Justice, 71
Briefs, appellate, 26, 31
British Marine Insurance Act of 1906, 136
Bryan, William Jennings, 122
Bryce, James, *The American Commonwealth,* 203
Butler, Benjamin, F, 128
Butler, Nicholas Murray, 28

Camden, Lord, 119
Campbell, Lord, 85, 135, 136
Canons of Professional and Judicial Ethics, 88, 94, 158
Cardozo, Justice, 14, 42, 114, 131, 187
Carnegie, Dale, 206
Carr, Cecil Thomas, 119;
Concerning English Administrative Law, 59
Carter, James C., 129
Celler, Representative, 62
Chadwick, Edwin, 120
Chalmers, Mackenzie, *Digest of Law of Negotiable Instruments,* 130
Chitty's *Pleading,* 76, 81
Choate, Joseph H., 5
Cicero, 45
Citizenship Clearing House, 204, 211, 212
Civil law and common law, 179
Clayton Act, 125
Cleveland Crime Survey, 102
Codification, 129
Coke, Chief Justice, 116, 138, 179
Colegrove v. *Green,* 156, 157
Coleridge, Lord Chief Justice, 73, 74, 83
Columbia University, 28
Columbia University Law School, 3, 60, 112, 178

Commission on Organized Crime, 104, 106, 108, 110
Common law, 138
Conant, Michael, 153
Constitutional law, 152
Comparative law, 178
Council of State Governments, 109
Counseling, 4
Court of Chancery, 81, 92
Criminal law enforcement, 70
Crane, Chief Justice, 40
Cummings, Homer S., 88

Daniell, *Equity Pleading and Practice,* 76
Davis, John W., 43
Demosthenes, 45
Denman, Lord, 36
Dewey, John, 125
Dicey, Albert Venn, 11;
    Law and Public Opinion in England, 122
Dickens, *Bleak House,* 82
Dillon, John F., 116
Donoughmore, Lord, 59
Duer, John, 128

Ecclesiastical law, 179
Edward I, 116, 117, 181
Eldon, Lord Chancellor, 14, 116
Erie Railroad v. *Tompkins,* 78
Erle, William, 85
Evaluation of Citizenship Training and Incentive in Colleges and Universities, 204

Fair-Trade Acts, 127
Fair trial, right to, 69
Facts of a case, 8, 16
Fearne, Charles, *Contingent Remainders,* 137
Federal Administrative Procedure Act, 53, 54, 88, 123
Federal rules of civil procedure, 66, 77, 78, 79, 80, 88, 89, 92, 94, 97, 99, 182
Federal rules of criminal procedure, 66, 77, 78, 80, 88, 90, 91, 92, 97, 98
Federal Tort Claims Act, 54
Federalist papers, 126
Field, David Dudley, 66, 86, 129

Field, Justice, 129
Field, Oliver, P., 156
Field Centenary Essays, 66
Field Code of Procedure, 86, 87
Finch, Elizabeth, 135
Fitzwilliam, Lord, 122
Fordham University Law School, 112
Fortescue, John, 116
Fox v. *Snow,* 115, 138
Frankfurter, Justice, 28, 60
French Civil Code, 186
French Code, 184
Freund, Ernst, 60
Funk v. *United States,* 132, 187

Gellhorn, Walter, 53
Glanvil, Ranulf de, 116
Goodhart, Arthur L., 185
Goodnow, Frank J., 55, 60
Gossett, William T., 12
Graves, Frank P., 128
Gulick, Luther, 209
Gummere, Chief Justice, 34

Habeas Corpus Act, 118
Hale, Matthew, 117
Hall, Marshall, 24
Hardwicke, Lord, 116, 122, 136
Hartshorne, Judge, 112
Harvard University Law School, 60
Henry, Patrick, 48
Henry II, 179, 180, 181
Henry VIII, 180
Herbert, A. P., *Holy Deadlock,* 123
Hewart, Lord Chief Justice, *The New Despotism,* 58
Hilary Rules, 92
Holdsworth, William, 187, 188
Holmes, Justice, 5, 22, 74, 114, 115
Hoover, J. Edgar, 104
Hughes, Chief Justice, 34, 42
Human nature, 10

Indebitatus assumpsit, 137
Indigent criminal cases, 111
Inns of Court, 181
Institute of Comparative Law, 178
Institute of Public Administration, 209
Institutes of Justinian, 134
Inter-American Law Institute, 178
Interstate Commerce Act, 124

Jackson, Justice, 89
Jackson, R. M., 122
Jacobs-Vogel Report, 61
Jarndyce v. *Jarndyce*, 82
Jefferson, Thomas, 124, 125
John Marshall Law School, 112
Johnson, Edward F., 12
Johnson, Samuel, 134
Jones, Samuel, 128
Jowitt, Lord Chancellor, 26, 27
Judicial activists, 152
Judicial administration, 95
Judicial deference, 152, 153
Judicial process, 138, 183
Judicial rule-making, 91, 98
Junior Bar Conference, 212
Junius, 138
Jury, 17

Keener, William A., *Cases on Quasi-Contract,* 134
Kefauver Committee, 70, 104, 105
Kent, Chancellor, 116, 182;
    Commentaries on American Law, 74
King's Canon law, 180
Kingston v. *Preston,* 134, 137

Langdell, *A Summary of Equity Pleading,* 73, 82
Law merchant, 180, 181
Law of Property Act of 1925, 137
Leach, John, 47
Leach, W. Barton, 3, 115
Leadership, 6
Legal reasoning, 12
Legislative reapportionment, 153, 156
Legislative Reorganization Act, 54
Lewis, J. Hamilton, 41
Lindbergh, Charles, 6
Littleton, 116;
    Tenures, 72
Livingston, Edward, *Codes,* 129
Logan, Senator, 61
Logan-Celler Bill, 62
Logicians, 3, 9

McCarran-Sumners Bill, 63
McCulloch v. *Maryland,* 27
McFarland, Carl J., 53
McKelvey, John J., *Common Law Pleading,* 73

MacPherson v. *Buick Motor Co.,* 131
Macauley, Thomas B., 9;
    Indian Penal Code, 129
Macmillan, Lord, 40
Magna Carta, 117
Maitland, F. W., 74, 179, 180;
    The Constitutional History of England, 55;
    English Law and the Renaissance, 181;
    The Forms of Action at Common Law, 81
Mansfield, Lord Chief Justice, 33, 81, 116, 119, 132, 133, 134, 180, 182
Marbury v. *Madison,* 153
Marshall, Chief Justice, 28, 118, 132
Mason, George, 124
Massachusetts v. *Mellon,* 153, 157
Matrimonial Laws Act of 1937, 123
Maule, William, 85
Medalie, George Z., 103
Medina, Judge, 66
Meeson & Welsby's *Reports,* 85
Middleton, Justice, 22
Miller, Judge, 103
Mitchell, William D., 89
Model Department of Justice Act, 106
Model Police Council Act, 107
Model Witness Immunity Act, 108
Model Youth Correction Act, 110
Mosher, William E., 207

National Center for Education in Politics, 204
National Conference of Commissioners on Uniform State Laws, 102, 108, 127
New Jersey Constitution of 1947, 109
New York Law Revision Commission, 131
New York University Law Center, 178
New York University Law School, 54, 112, 203, 212
Newark University Law School, 112
Nottingham, Lord Chancellor, 116, 135

O'Conor, Senator, 104, 105
Office of Dependency Benefits, 209
"One-judge opinions," 29

Opening a case, 14
Oral argument, 26, 30, 49
Ordinance de la Marine, 134
Organized crime and law enforcement, 102
Oxford University, 88, 123, 134

Palmer, George Herbert, *Self-Cultivation in English*, 36, 48
Parke, Baron, 84, 85, 86
Parker, Judge, 103
Parry, Judge, *Seven Lamps of Advocacy*, 47
Partnership Act, 130
Paterson, Chancellor, 128
Pateshull, Justice, 118
Patterson, Judge, 110
Perrin v. *Blake*, 137
Petition of right, 118
Phillips, Wendell, 46
Pillans v. *Van Mierop*, 133
Ploscowe, Judge, 111
Pollock, Frederick, 137; *Digest of Law of Partnership*, 130
Pollock and Maitland, *History of English Law*, 117
Pope, Alexander, 11, 134
Port, F. J., *Administrative Law*, 59, 61
Pound, Roscoe, 87, 88, 91, 102, 103, 104, 111, 114
Pitt, William, 134
Precedent, 138
President's Committee on Administrative Management, 61, 64
Privilege against self-incrimination, 107
Procedure, 66, 68
Prosecutors, 106, 107
Public opinion, 6
Public service, 6

Questioning from the bench, 26, 40
Quintilian, 45

Radcliffe, Jacob, 128
Raleigh, Justice, 118
Raleigh, Sir Walter, 138
Rann v. *Hughes*, 133
Reed, Thomas, H., *Twenty Years of Government in Essex County*, 203

Reform Act of 1832, 119
Report of Attorney General's Committee on Administrative Procedure, 53, 56, 57, 62, 63, 64, 65
Report of the Committee on Ministers' Powers, 59, 60, 61
Report of Judicial Council of California on Administrative Agencies Survey, 61
Restatement of the law, 35, 184
Reuschlein, Harold G., *Jurisprudence —Its American Prophets*, 66
Revised Statutes of 1828 (*N. Y.*), 83
Right to fair trial, 101
Roman law, 181
Roosevelt, Franklin D., 6, 53, 88, 116, 125
Roosevelt, Theodore, 5, 88, 116, 125
Rosenberry, Chief Justice, 28
Rule in *Shelley's case*, 137
Rules of law, 10
Ryder, Dudley, 135

Sankey, Lord Chancellor, 59, 130
Shakespeare, William, 11, 209
Shattuck, George, 22
Shelton, Thomas W., 88
Sherman Act, 124
Shawcross, Hartley, 131
Skynner, Chief Baron, 133
Smith, Munroe, 30, 178, 184
Smuts, Jan C., 88
Socrates, 28
Social sciences, 11, 211
South v. *Peters*, 157
Spelman, Henry, 179
Spencer, John C., 128
Star chamber, 118
Stare decisis, 185
Stephen, James 130
Steuer, Max D., 17, 18
Story, Justice, 116
Stowell, Lord, 116, 132
Substantive law, 114
Summary of oral argument, 43
Summation, 18
Sutherland, Justice, 132, 187
Swift, Chief Justice, 128
Swift v. *Tyson*, 78
Syracuse University, 207

Taft, Chief Justice, 28
Taney, Chief Justice, 28
Thorndike, Edward L., *Your City,*
  206
Throop, Montgomery, 87
Tidd's *Practice,* 76, 81
Training for public service, 203
Tudor v. *Board of Education,* 153,
  158

Uniform rules of criminal procedure,
  102
University of Chicago Law School,
  60
University of Lyon, 186
University of Michigan Law School,
  114

Vanderbilt, Commodore, 3
Varick, Richard, 128
Vidal v. *Girard's Executor,* 27

Walsh, Thomas A., 88
Wambaugh, Eugene, *Cases on Insur-
  ance,* 134
Washington and Lee University, 3
Webster, Daniel, 5, 28, 72
Wesleyan University, 3
Westbury, Lord, 47
Wheaton, Henry, 128
White, Andrew D., *Autobiography,* 47
White, Chief Justice, 39, 45
Wickersham Commission, 102
Wigmore, John H., 87, 186
Willes, James, 85
William the Conqueror, 179
Williams, *Notes to Saunders Reports,*
  72, 81
Williams, Montague, 23
Wilson, Woodrow, 25, 116, 125
Winchelsea, Earl of, 135
Words, use of, 13
Wright, Martin, 179

Year books, 55